MAROON & GOLD FOREVER
Celebrating 125 Years of Gopher Football

by
Ross Bernstein

MAROON & GOLD FOREVER

Celebrating 125 Years of Gopher Football

by
Ross Bernstein

Proudly sponsored by TCF Bank

ISBN: 0-9787809-5-7

Printed by Printing Enterprises, New Brighton, MN

Photos courtesy of the University of Minnesota

All proceeds from the sale of this book proudly benefit the University of Minnesota's Golden Gopher Fund, which supports scholarships for student athletes.
Thank you for your support!

COVER ART BY
TERRENCE FOGARTY

The painting on the cover is by nationally recognized Minnesota artist Terrence Fogarty.

Immediately after the Golden Gophers and The Air Force Academy Falcons christen TCF Bank Stadium on September 12, 2009, artist Terrence Fogarty will begin work on a commemorative painting that will capture this historic opening game in all it's dramatic detail. A signed, limited edition print of the original oil painting will be available in December 2009. Please call **952-443-0028** for more information and to reserve this piece of Golden Gopher football history as depicted by one of the country's most acclaimed and collectible artists.

For more information on the artist and to see other paintings from the Fogarty collection, please log on to **www.terrencefogarty.com**. Thank you!

A FEW WORDS FROM TCF BANK'S WILLIAM COOPER & MARK JETER

Gopher Fans,

TCF Bank is a Minnesota company with roots that have run deep since 1923. We share many common attributes with the University of Minnesota, including a tradition of excellence, a proud history, a strong Midwest work ethic, and a value system based on honesty, trust and determination. We are firmly committed to supporting the University of Minnesota community, which is such a critical economic engine for the vitality of the entire state. TCF Bank takes its commitment to giving back to the state of Minnesota very seriously. Our employees arc active in many communities throughout the state and give graciously of their time, talents and financial resources. TCF Bank Stadium will serve as a testament to our involvement in the community.

We could not be more proud and honored to share our name with the University's premier athletic venue. TCF Bank Stadium will help the University of Minnesota continue to attract the nation's best and brightest students and future leaders. The University of Minnesota has a special place in the hearts of TCF Bank. Many of our employees are proud alumni, some of us even met our spouses at the U of M, and all of us are true Golden Gophers fans.

TCF Bank Stadium is a treasure that the whole state of Minnesota will cherish for decades to come. Commonly referred to as the finest on-campus stadium in America, we are truly honored to have been the catalyst that made the dream of bringing Gopher Football back to campus a reality. What started with a vision by the leadership of both the University and TCF Bank, has grown to a tremendous relationship rooted in respect and admiration. We celebrated each milestone along the way from the Stadium bill passing through the legislative process, to the unveiling of the logo, to the groundbreaking, and finally to the inaugural season.

Thank you to our many customers, friends and neighbors for helping make TCF Bank Stadium a reality. We look forward to sharing many Saturday's with the state of Minnesota cheering our mighty Gophers on to victory.

Very Sincerely,

William Cooper, Chairman and CEO, TCF Financial Corporation
Mark Jeter, President, TCF Bank Minnesota

William Cooper

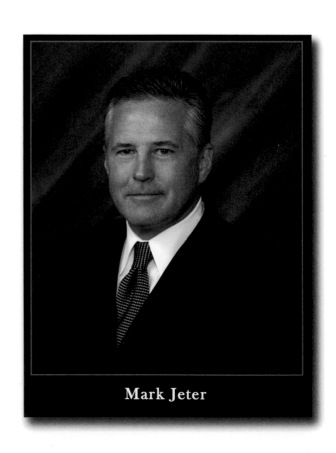

Mark Jeter

A FEW WORDS FROM UNIVERSITY ATHLETICS DIRECTOR JOEL MATURI

Gopher Fans,

The opening of TCF Bank Stadium means many things to those of us who love the Gophers. There is the obvious: we return football to campus where it rightfully belongs. The stadium will also be the home for the "Pride of Minnesota," our outstanding Marching Band. The Athletics Department will realize additional income that will assist in the needed support of our successful 25 sport program. TCF Bank Stadium will be utilized on an almost daily basis by students in kinesiology classes, intramural and recreational sports and the University and Minnesota community will have access to the stadium for meetings, banquets, receptions and other appropriate gatherings. Soon we may host commencement, outdoor hockey, summer concerts and even Olympic Soccer.

TCF Bank Stadium honors the Native American Communities of Minnesota, our Minnesota Veterans and all of Minnesota with the recognition of each of our 87 counties. Importantly we recognize and thank the many individuals, corporations, foundations, University students and Minnesota Legislature for their gifts/sponsorships/appropriation that made this remarkable facility possible. I would be remiss if I did not single out President Robert Bruininks. If not for his vision, courage and leadership this day would never have come. John and Nancy Lindahl have led our fund raising efforts from the very beginning and are our unsung heroes.

Personally, I look at this historic day as one that will change the culture of campus life forever. We are celebrating a facility that will help enhance the visibility, value and mission of this great institution. All Minnesotans should feel a sense of pride today and appreciate the accomplishment we achieved together. Thank you to Ross Bernstein for his continued support of the Gophers and for allowing me the opportunity to share my message in his book.

Go Gophers!

We Arc...Minnesota!

Joel Maturi
Director of Athletics

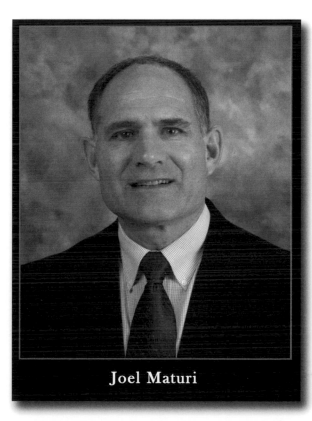

Joel Maturi

INTRODUCTION BY ROSS BERNSTEIN

Welcome to "Maroon & Gold Forever" and thank you for supporting Golden Gopher football. History will be made on September 12, 2009, when the Gophers take the field for the very first time at TCF Bank Stadium to do battle against Air Force. It is a day many die-hards such as myself have longed for in Gold Country, a day in which we can watch our beloved rodents play the game as it was originally intended — outside in the elements. That's right, "old school."

I say rodents, by the way, with not only a deep sense of love and admiration, but also with some authority. That's right. You see, I used to be a rodent. In fact, I was THE rodent... as in *Goldy the Gopher.* It's kind of a crazy story, but back in the late '80s I was a walk-on to Coach Woog's Gopher Hockey team and wound up getting cut. I had always dreamt of wearing the Maroon and Gold, so I was really crushed when I got the news. It turned out, however, that there was another job opening on the team — one not quite as sexy as "first line center," but pretty darn close: team mascot.

Now, there were two basic criteria for the job: first, you had to be a decent hockey player (because in years past the mascot had always been a member of the marching band and I think the powers-that-be were just tired of Bucky the Badger coming to town and beating the snot out of Goldy); and secondly, you had to be a complete idiot. I apparently fit on both accounts and got the gig. From there I began dressing up as a giant rodent and making a fool out of myself in front of thousands of people at old Mariucci Arena. Go figure.

My love for the Gophers has always been there though, ever since I was a kid. I grew up in a Gopher household for sure. My mom and dad met at the U back in the early 60s and my two big brothers are Gopher grads as well. I have great memories of walking down University Avenue with my dad and brothers on homecoming morning, watching in amazement as the floats drove by in the parade and looking up in awe at the fraternity houses all decorated with pomp and chicken wire. Then, to head over to old Memorial Stadium, the Brick House, to watch our beloved Gophers — it didn't get any better than that. What a place. It just wreaked of history and tradition in there. I, like so many other fans, was pretty bummed out when they finally tore it down. I was actually living in a frat house across the street during those days when it sat empty. I even remember playing intramural football in there. How surreal is that, me playing on the same field as Bruce Smith and Paul Giel? It was so sad to see the old gal all dilapidated at that point, just a shell of her former self.

I gotta be honest, I was never a big fan of the Dome — which is why I am so excited about the new stadium. To see Gopher football leave campus was tough. I even lived in Middlebrook Hall my freshman year, which was only a 10 minute walk through the West Bank to get there. My buddies and I all had season tickets and we lived for Saturday afternoons in the Fall. We would walk over to tailgate in the parking lots before heading in to watch our guy tear it up, Darrell Thompson. He was the best. Darrell and I became friends way back then and I am proud to still call him my friend today. Thank you, DT, for letting me honor you with the foreword to this book — I couldn't think of anybody more deserving. I will never forget those life size posters that the Gopher Athletics Department had made of him as promotional giveaways when they were hyping him for the Heisman back in 1989. Funny story... I met my wonderful wife Sara while I was at the U and she later informed me that prior to meeting me, she had actually *"slept"* with Darrell every single night during her entire freshman year. Turned out she had one of those posters on her wall! Darrell still razzes me about that to this day.

As for the genesis of this book, it has been a two year odyssey of sorts that I am thrilled to finally see come to fruition. I wanted to do something to give back to the University that has given me so much, so I approached them with the idea of doing a book to be given away on opening day — as a gesture of thanks to the season ticket holders and boosters. They loved the idea. Then, once TCF Bank got on board, the project just took on a life of its own. I am proud to say that 100% of the proceeds from the sale of the book will benefit the Golden Gopher Fund, which supports scholarships for student athletes at the U of M. In addition to TCF Bank Vice President Ryan Wilder, I would like to thank University President Dr. Robert Bruininks, University Athletics Director Joel Maturi and University Senior Associate Athletics Director Tom Wistrcill for all their support. Thanks too to Jeff Keiser, in Media Relations, for all your help with regards to photo research. I couldn't have done it without you.

Needless to say, I am thrilled with the final product. I have written several other books which have chronicled Gopher football, but nothing like this. This was intense. I was able to meet and interview dozens and dozens of current and former players along the way, which was really quite a thrill. Your memories and stories are priceless, so thanks to all of you who contributed. I have to issue a few caveats of sorts, however, to better explain the who, what, why, when and where of the book. For starters, I only had so much real estate to work with. As such, I couldn't get every former player's name or photo in the book. That would be an encyclopedia, not a coffee table book. This book is not a list of the best players of all-time either, it is a fun sampling of many great players who have all contributed in making Gopher football one of the top programs in the country. For those players who I left out, I sincerely apologize. After writing more than 40 books, I know that people can get bent out of shape sometimes over this stuff, so I wanted to throw that out there.

As for content, I chose to go pretty vanilla. I really wanted to give a broad overview of the 125 year history of the program, so I focused on the big names and the big events. There are also many more bios of the older players, versus the newer ones, and that was just about me paying respect to the old school guys — nothing more, nothing less. I was able to scan in several hundred photos too, and they really help to tell the story. Sadly, they don't necessarily align with the text though, due to the fact that I chose to get as many photos in the book as humanly possible. This book isn't intended to be read in one sitting, it is the kind you can pick up or put down at any time to enjoy a quick bio or even a *"Cliff Claven"* tid-bit. Go ahead, put it on the coffee table or even in the bathroom — I don't care — as long as you read it and enjoy it. I didn't interject too many opinions or funny quips either, I just tried to stick with the facts. I wanted it to be "timeless" in the historical sense, and hopefully I accomplished my goal. Going year by year in chronological order can tend to be monotonous, but I think it all worked out in the end.

It was truly a thrill to be able to honor the legacies of so many amazing individuals by bringing this project to life. Again, thanks for your support. See you at the stadium. *Go Gophers!*

ABOUT TCF BANK STADIUM

TCF Bank Stadium isn't just a football venue. It's a monumental contribution to University of Minnesota heritage — as well as a living, breathing icon for the whole community to enjoy. First it was a dream, now it's a reality. But along the way was an intensive planning process that brought stakeholders together and made sure success was the only option. The University began actively exploring a new on-campus football stadium in 2003. The process began with a feasibility study that determined the appropriate size and type of stadium, preliminary construction and operating costs, revenue potential, and uses beyond football. A set of guiding principles for development of a Minneapolis campus stadium was then drafted. Including usage for both the Gopher football team and related athletic and academic purposes of the University, the principles were soon endorsed by the Board of Regents of the University. An environmental review of the stadium project then examined the impact the development of the proposed stadium facility would have on the environment. It included consideration of traffic and air quality and identified needed environmental remediation for the site.

On March 24, 2005, TCF Financial Corporation and University of Minnesota officials announced a $35 million, 25-year corporate sponsorship for a new stadium. Infrastructure work at the site began in late June 2006, capped by a ceremonial groundbreaking on September 30, 2006. The beginning of construction on the stadium itself, along with the unveiling of the stadium's logo, took place on July 11, 2007. The stadium's impressive skeleton consists of more than 8,800 tons of steel, 97% of it recycled, that took six months to put into place — from January to July 2008. Installation of the brick and cast stone portion of the building began in the summer of 2008 with the first brick being laid by Hilding Mortenson, 100 years old, who was a bricklayer working on Memorial Stadium back in 1924.

Designing TCF Bank Stadium was a singularly focused effort: to create the best on-campus stadium in college football. HOK Architects is the primary architect and designer of TCF Bank Stadium. The facility is a traditional horseshoe-style college stadium that retains many of the design elements of Memorial Stadium. Seating capacity of TCF Bank Stadium is approximately 50,000. Flexibility is also a key component of the design, with expansion up to 80,000 seats. All those seats are housed in a collegiate look and feel that will complement the campus environment, create two landscaped plazas, and accommodate other uses. There are 39 suites, 59 loge boxes, and 300 indoor club seats.

The playing field will consist of FieldTurf, which is also the artificial playing surface also used by Illinois, Indiana, Iowa, Michigan, Northwestern, Ohio State and Wisconsin. The stadium's field is oriented in an east-west configuration, the only football stadium in the Big Ten to be laid out in such a way. Fans will understand this orientation come game day, with the sweeping views of both campus as well as the glimmering Minneapolis skyline through the structure's magnificently open west end. TCF Bank Stadium will also feature the second largest video board in all of college football. Designed and built by Daktronics, the video board is 48 feet high by 108 feet wide and includes Daktronics' HD-X LED video display technology.

A football stadium of nation-leading caliber requires commitment, broad community support, and major financial partners. Fortunately, TCF Bank Stadium benefited from all three. Total construction costs for TCF Bank Stadium are $288.5 million, including site preparation and infrastructure improvements. The improvements are particularly notable. The stadium is part of a 75 acre expansion of the Twin Cities campus—the largest since the West Bank was built in the 1960s. Current plans for the area call for the construction of as many as 10 new academic buildings by 2015. The proposed Central Corridor light rail transit line is expected to run near the stadium, with a station in Stadium Village serving the facility.

The University is funding 52 percent of the cost with non-state dollars from a variety of sources, including private funds, parking revenues, student fees, and athletics department funds. The state of Minnesota will fund the remaining 48 percent of the cost, or $137.2 million. Of course, the most significant financing event occurred on March 24, 2005, when TCF Financial Corporation (TCF) and University of Minnesota officials announced a $35 million, 25-year corporate sponsorship for a new stadium. The deal provides TCF with exclusive naming rights for the stadium, to be called "TCF Bank Stadium™." In addition to the naming rights portion of the sponsorship, other agreements provide the University with benefits that will extend far beyond football. Together with the University's existing business arrangements with TCF, which total $18 million, the University's expanded relationship with the bank could produce more than $96 million in revenue for the U's academic and athletic priorities over the life of the agreements. Other major corporate sponsors and donors include a $10 million gift from the Shakopee Mdewakanton Sioux Community (SMSC), a $2.5 million sponsorship agreement with Dairy Queen, $2.5 million in support from Best Buy, and a $2 million gift from Target.

FOREWORD BY DARRELL THOMPSON

Minnesota has long been known for its "three yards and a cloud of dust" style of play in the Big Ten and has seemingly always had a solid running game. There have been so many outstanding running backs to wear the "M" over the years, including the likes of Bronko Nagurski, Bruce Smith, Paul Giel, Pug Lund, Bill Daley, Bob McNamara, Marion Barber, Rick Upchurch, Chris Darkins, and Marion Barber III and Laurence Maroney, as of late. All were great in their own right, but none of them could run like Darrell Thompson, who rewrote the record books during his tenure in Gold Country from 1986-89. When it was all said and done he owned nearly every rushing record on campus, including Total Rushing Yards (4,654), Rushing Touchdowns (40), and All Purpose Yards (5,109), while ranking second in Career Points Scored (262). A first round draft pick in 1990, Darrell would go on to play professionally in the NFL with the Green Bay Packers for five seasons. Darrell currently lives in the Twin Cities with his wife and three children, where he serves as the director of Bolder Options — a Minneapolis-based early intervention youth mentoring program. In addition, he also does color analysis for Gopher football games alongside Dave Mona and Dave Lee on WCCO Radio. So, who better to talk about the next 125 years of Gopher football than the pride of Rochester, Darrell Thompson...

"Being a Gopher means the world to me," said Thompson. "It was a dream come true for me to get the opportunity to play football at the University of Minnesota. I took a lot of pride in wearing that maroon and gold jersey and that big 'M' on my helmet. John Gutekunst was the head coach when I got here in 1986, but I was originally recruited by Lou Holtz. Lou had just led the team to the Independence Bowl the year before and I was in awe of the guy."

"When I was being recruited I went to schools like Nebraska, Wisconsin, and Iowa, but I didn't think that I would want to live in those towns after my football career was over. They are all great football towns, but the Twin Cities is a great place to live and build your career. As a high school senior I didn't think that playing in the NFL was a very real-istic expectation. Because of that, I figured it would be a smart decision to stay close to home. Looking back, I definitely made the right choice. In fact, I see a lot of Big Ten football players from all over the country living here now because it's just a great place to work and raise a family. Athletes can carve out a real nice niche in the community here and I'd like to see more kids from Minnesota experiencing the same pleasure that I had. I am sure that our beautiful new stadium is going to go a long way in making that happen.

"Once I learned about the University's rich history and storied tradition, I wanted in. I will never forget the day I got that letter in the mail from the Athletics Department, letting me know that I had been accepted. It was such an honor to be recruited and to get a scholarship to play football for the Gophers. I was so excited about the opportunity to showcase what I could do out on the field. I just wanted to dive in and help out the team any way that I could.

"There was a lot of momentum going for Gopher Football back when I came in as a freshman. It was a pretty exciting time. The Metrodome was only four years old at that point and still pretty new; Coach Gutekunst had just taken over from Coach Holtz; and the team was led by a young quarterback by the name of Rickey Foggie — one of the most dynamic players ever to play at Minnesota. We were coming off of a big bowl victory the year before and expectations were running high.

"I remember my first day of practice, talk about intimidation. I learned pretty quickly that I was going to have to work harder than I had ever worked before in order to be able to compete at that level. It was pretty humbling. I ended up as the third string tailback in our season opener against Bowling Green behind Terry Stewart and Ed Penn. Needless to say, I had no aspirations of getting a lot of touches. I had prepared myself mentally to serve as a backup that season and to be ready to make the most of my opportunities when they presented themselves.

"We were running the wishbone in those days, however, so the coaches threw me in there a few times to get my feet wet. I think I had three measly yards rushing in the first half. I had gotten a little bit of confidence from being in there though, and wound up rushing for more than 200 yards and four touchdowns in the second half. Rickey would pitch me the ball and for whatever the reason, I just had it that day. We wound up winning the game 31-7, it was pretty amazing.

"Well, I got the start the next week but was brought back to earth pretty quickly when I rushed for just 35 yards in an embarrassing 63-0 loss to the University of Oklahoma. That one still hurts. They had like nine guys who went pro that next year, they crushed us. I learned a lot about humility that afternoon, that was for sure. We lost again that next week, but then got on a roll by beating Purdue, Northwestern and Indiana.

"After losing to Ohio State and Michigan State in Weeks Seven and Eight, we rebounded by beating Wisconsin, 27-20, to retain Paul Bunyan's Axe. In that game, I wound up rushing for 117 yards to become the first Gopher freshman to run for 1,000 yards in a single season. It was pretty special. From there, we carried that momentum straight into Ann Arbor, where we pulled off one of the biggest upsets in Minnesota football history by beating the No. 2 ranked Wolverines.

"This was just an incredible game, back and forth all afternoon. Down 17-16 with just over two minutes to go in the game, Michigan Coach Bo Schembechler went for the tie instead of a two-pointer to win. They scored, which gave us the ball back along with a chance to win. We drove downfield and just rode Rickey's back all of the way. With 47 seconds left, he took off from the Michigan 48 yard line and ran for 31 yards to the 17. We were all so nervous, it was intense. Then, as time ran out, Chip Lohmiller came out and kicked the game-winning 30-yard field goal to give us the 20-17 victory. We went nuts. We couldn't believe what we had done.

"I will never forget the speech that (assistant coach) Butch Nash gave us before the game about 'personal dedication and commitment.' Guys were tearing up listening to him speak, it was very emotional. We went out and played really disciplined football and just like we had planned, we were in the game at the end. We all left everything we had on the field that day. It was one of the greatest wins in Gopher football history, without a doubt. I will never forget coming back into the locker room after the game and seeing all of the older players crying. I had hurt my shoulder so

badly that I couldn't even get my shoulder pads off. I didn't care though, I was so happy. We all just sat there, passing around the Little Brown Jug, laughing and celebrating. It was a wonderful moment and something I will never forget.

"We wound up losing to Iowa at home that next week, 30-27, to finish up the regular season. That was a really tough loss. I think that we were just all so jacked up from beating Michigan that we let our guards down. In the end it didn't matter, because we still got an invitation to play the University of Tennessee in the Liberty Bowl down in Memphis. Hey, it wasn't the Rose Bowl, but we didn't care. We were all so excited to be playing football in December. I had grown up watching bowl games on TV, so to finally get to play in one was pretty neat.

"I remember the Vols jumping out to a 14-0 lead and we just tried to play catch-up from there. I remember fumbling on a critical play early on deep in their end and feeling just awful about it. We came out strong in the second half though and rallied behind Rickey. He scored midway through the third quarter and I wound up going in on a two-point conversion to make the score 14-11. We had another big drive shortly thereafter but had to settle for a game-tying field goal. They scored again to make it 21-14 and that was as close as we could get. We drove down in the final minutes but came up short in the end. We were all pretty bummed out. I wound up earning All-Big Ten honors following the season, which was a huge honor, but would have gladly traded it for a Liberty Bowl win.

"My sophomore year was a 'tale of two seasons.' We started out on fire, winning our first five games, but then lost a tough game against Indiana, 18-17, and it was like the wheels came off. We wound up losing five in a row, including a brutal loss at home to Michigan. Despite losing the game, which was so tough, I got into the history books with a 98-yard touchdown run. I put up 200 yards that day, which was apparently the most ever surrendered by a Wolverine team. That was pretty cool, something I can for sure tell my grandchildren one day.

"We got it together that next week to beat Wisconsin on the road, 14-7, and reclaimed Paul Bunyan's Axe. We knew that if we could beat Iowa in the season finale that we would be in a good position to get another bowl game bid, but we wound up losing at the Dome, 31-22, to end the season on a real downer. We were all so devastated after that one, words can't even describe how we all felt. We wanted to get to a bowl game so badly, not just for us, but for our fans. We all know how cold it is during the Winter up here, and we wanted to reward our fans with a trip somewhere warm. That was so disappointing.

"Let's just say that my junior year was 'difficult' to say the least. Rickey turned pro that off-season and Scott Schaffner took over under center. The offense seemed totally different without Rickey in there and we struggled as a team. I injured my knee midway through the season and things just started to spiral out of control for us from there. We ended up going 0-6-2, good for just ninth in the Big 10. I wanted to get out there and help my teammates so badly, but could only watch from the sidelines. I learned a lot about adversity that season, that was for sure.

"We came out strong in 1989, my senior year, with a solid 5-1 record. My knee was healthy and I was able to cut back on that hard Metrodome turf like I had been able to prior to my injury. I felt confident and I was having fun. One of the lowlights form that season that I remember was losing a heart-breaker to Ohio State, 41-37. We had a 30-point lead at halftime and then let them off the hook. Believe it or not, that one still haunts me to this day. We beat the Badgers the next week, which was awesome, but then lost to Michigan State and Michigan, back to back down the stretch. That was how it was that year, 'one step forward and two steps back.'

"The highlight of the season came at the end, when we beat Iowa on the road to reclaim Floyd of Rosedale. That was my last game as a Gopher and it was special. My sister and future wife were both Hawkeyes, so that made the win even that much sweeter for me. We finished with a 6-5 record but wound up not getting an invitation to go to a bowl game. That was tough. We thought that by beating Iowa we would make it to the post-season, but it never panned out for us. There were a lot less bowl games in those days as compared to now, and I guess it just wasn't in the cards for us that year.

"When it was all said and done, when I took off that maroon and gold jersey for the last time, it was sad. Really sad. I found some redemption that season though. I had come back from my knee injury, which was very gratifying, and I was really proud of the way my teammates all played together. I was also proud of the fact that I finished what I had started. A lot of people don't know this, but I considered leaving school early the year before to play in the NFL. I came to my senses though and in retrospect, it was a great decision. I didn't want to quit on my teammates. No way.

"All in all, I was really proud to have been a Gopher, what an amazing experience it was. I made so many great friends and have so many wonderful memories. I miss those days, absolutely. Looking forward though, I am thrilled about the direction that the program is headed in. Words can not even describe how happy I am that the team will finally be playing outside in a stadium of their own. This is huge for Gopher football fans, huge.

"While I enjoyed playing in the Dome, nothing compares to playing football outside in the elements – the way it is supposed to be played, especially back on campus. Being back on campus is huge for the kids, huge for the community, and huge for the state of Minnesota. In reality, playing in the Dome was sort of like playing an 'away' game. I mean we would take a bus downtown, stay in a hotel, and then leave right afterwards. I remember going to basketball games at Williams Arena and hockey games at Mariucci Arena, and always feeling so jealous. The students are right on top of the action in there and that is how it is going to be at the new stadium.

"Yes, TCF Bank Stadium is such an amazing

place. TCF, thank you. You really stepped up. You got behind this project early on and stuck by it. You did the right thing. It is a challenging time right now and you recognized the need for this in our community. I think we should all be really appreciative of the people who went out on a limb to see to it that this project came to fruition. So many people worked tirelessly on this project for so many years and if I could thank them all I would.

"Together, the University and TCF really rolled out the red carpet. They just took care of everybody. Even the band has a room now. Those guys used to have to get dressed in the hallways. Now they will have a place to call their own. That is awesome. The former players will also have a place in the new stadium as well, a club room, which is wonderful. We are really excited about that and sincerely feel so appreciative. What a respectful thing to do. Again, thank you.

"They then went around the country and took all of the little things from each of the top stadiums and incorporated them into this one. It is a wonderful mix of old and new. I think they did a great job of respecting the history and tradition of the past, while creating some new and exciting things for the future. The field is fantastic and the locker room is unlike anything I have ever seen before. The fans are going to love it because there aren't any bad seats in there. The fans are really close to the action and they will finally be able to see football like it was intended to be seen. The players will feed off of that energy, from having the students so close to them on the field, and that will make for a great home field advantage. Finally!

"Being on the radio for Gopher games still allows me to be around the players, which is something I really enjoy. When the younger guys come up to me and ask me for advice, wow, what a rush. To be able to share a little bit of wisdom about life, both on and off the field, I feel very blessed to be a part of that. You know, I have been doing color analysis on WCCO for 12 years now and all I can say is, what a thrill. The older I get, the more I appreciate being up in the press box with Dave Mona and Dave Lee. Being able to work with a legend like Ray Christenson was so wonderful too. Those guys are amazing people and just phenomenal journalists. They have mentored me through the years and I think the world of those guys. I have learned so much from them and appreciate everything that they do for me. They push me to do my homework and to always strive to get better. It is hard work calling games, but I would like to think I have improved a little bit every year I have been up there and hopefully there will be many, many more in the years to come.

"Overall, I am extremely optimistic about the future of Gopher football. Sure, there are challenges that lie ahead, but the program is in great hands. You know what they say? The No. 1 issue is recruiting, the No. 2 issue is recruiting and, yes, the No. 3 issue is... recruiting. Well, the bottom line is that new recruits, especially Minnesotans, are going to fall in love with this place. It is going to put us on par with all of the other Big Ten schools and finally prevent them from recruiting against us. Coach Brewster is an outstanding recruiter and I like his style a lot. He really cares about the kids and he is determined to make this a winning program.

There are going to be a lot of great memories created in our new TCF Bank Stadium over the ensuing years and I can't wait to be a part of all the action. Minnesota fans, you are the best of the best and I can't thank you enough for all your support and encouragement over the years. Go Gophers!

— Darrell Thompson —

IN THE BEGINNING...

With roots which can be traced back for nearly 125 years, the University of Minnesota Golden Gopher football program has a long and epic history dotted with peaks and valleys. While the Gophers of today are an up and coming force to be reckoned with in the Big Ten, many don't realize what a powerhouse program this used to be. Did you know that in the first half of the 20th century alone, the Gophers won five national championships, 16 conference titles and posted 11 undefeated seasons? In those days the Gophers were referred to by the rest of the football world as the "Giants of the North." There wasn't a young boy in the state who didn't dream about one day playing football at Memorial Stadium. For the lucky few who could actually get down to University Avenue to see them, they were truly the "Legends of the Fall." For everyone else, which included a loyal following of fans throughout the Midwest, sitting around and listening to the action on the radio was pure heaven. Back in the day, the Minneapolis Tribune Newspaper had a section called the "Peach," which was delivered all the way to the Dakotas and even into Montana, where Gopher fans anxiously awaited to read all about their beloved team. The Gopher football program wreaks of a tradition that has become woven into the very fabric of our state's rich history. So let's go back, way back to the beginning, and see how far these Golden Gophers have come — and just how far they can go in the future.

The Early Years

The University of Minnesota was founded along the banks of the Mississippi River in Minneapolis back in 1851, fully seven years before the "Minnesota Territory" had even achieved statehood. The first official intercollegiate football game, meanwhile, occurred out on the east coast in 1869 between Rutgers and Princeton. By the latter part of the 1870s the gridiron game had started its migration west and it didn't take long for the new sport to find its way to Gold Country. It first popped up on campus at the intramural level.

The student newspaper, the Ariel, first made mention of this new college fad in October of 1878, referring to it as an "all-absorbing amusement." The article went on to describe the new rugby-like sport as a "barbaric charade which featured 15 men on a side engaged in a jaw-to-jaw, man-to-man style of combat on the line of scrimmage, while a ball carrier tried to run around or go over the battle area." Back then, when the ball carrier started to run, the linemen squared off in man-to-man brawls. When the runner attempted to cross the line of scrimmage, he could be picked up and carried back toward his own goal until his teammates halted the effort by whichever means possible. Defenders could simply hold on to the ball carriers legs and pull, while the offense pushed, sometimes getting leverage while grasping arms, or even hair. "We are anxiously waiting for some one to get his head knocked off," the Ariel stated. It even went on to describe an "inter-class" freshman vs. sophomore scrimmage having to be canceled due to the "non-arrival of the ball," which was apparently a hard item to come by back then.

With the increasing popularity and interest in sports during that time, the University formed an Ath-

letic Association, for the purpose of fostering all athletic endeavors, but especially football. It didn't catch on right away though. Just a year later, an editorial in the Ariel reported that while football had reached a high standing among eastern universities, "our University seems perfectly dead in this respect."

History was finally made on September 30th, 1882 when the U of M, Carleton and Hamline were to take part in a "Field Day," which included a number of track events, that been scheduled at the Colonel King State Fairgrounds (near Riverside and Franklin in South Minneapolis). While the Gophers were supposed to play Carleton in a friendly game of football, they wound up playing against Hamline instead, due to the fact that Carleton insisted upon playing by the rules of rugby. With Carleton respectfully declining, Hamline thus agreed to play in what would become the first intercollegiate football game in Minnesota history. That historic first game saw the Gophers win 4-0 in "55 minutes of hard play," thanks to the efforts of team captain A.J. Baldwin, who scored all four Gopher points. (Touchdowns counted for two points in those days.) Spectators came out to watch the game, with "many ladies from both institutions so thoughtful as to bring elegant floral offerings to the victors." Hamline then issued a challenge for a rematch, later getting revenge when they beat the Gophers 2-0 just a few

Alf Pillsbury

weeks later on a controversial last-minute score.

In the fall of 1883 Professor Thomas Peebles, an Irish immigrant who played football at Princeton, came to the U of M to teach philosophy. Knowing that he was well versed in the school of American football, the Gopher players asked him to be their coach for an upcoming game against Carleton. Peebles got the team organized, and even got them practicing on their own practice field — a sandy burr which is the ground now occupied by Folwell Hall, in the heart of campus. The boys then hopped the train for Northfield, and once there, realized that Carleton, in addition to allowing their faculty to play, also insisted upon using a big old fashioned round, inflated, rugby ball — instead of an oval football which was the standard for American football. Despite the U's protest, the game was played with Carleton winning by the final score of 4-2. They later went on to beat Hamline again that season, 5-0, only to later lose to a group of ex-collegians by the final of 4-2.

In addition to Hamline, Carleton and Shattuck Military Academy, the Gophers also began to play against some of the other local teams, including Macalester, the Minneapolis Football Club, the Eastern College Alumni Team (former stars from Yale, Harvard, Dartmouth and Princeton — all native sons of the state of Minnesota), Minneapolis High School,

St. Paul Central High School, and the Northfield-Carleton Farmers Alliance Football Association.

In the fall of 1885, Frederick Jones, a former star football player at Yale, arrived on campus via a brief teaching and coaching stint at the Shattuck Military Academy in Faribault. Jones, who would later go on to serve as the Dean of the University's Law School, was asked to help coach the Gopher's squad. It would be the beginning of a lifelong relationship with the school that would ultimately earn him the nickname as the "Father of Minnesota Football." Jones had been schooled in the rugby style of football played at Yale, while Peebles was a student of the soccer-style system — which created somewhat of a rivalry between the two.

This rivalry, however, was quickly ended when Alf Pillsbury, or "Pilly" as he was known (son of John Pillsbury, the former governor of the state, and heir

Pudge Heffelfinger

to the famous flour company bearing his name), arrived on campus with his brand new shiny rugby ball. Because balls were in such short supply in those days, it was just understood that the Gophers would pursue the rugby style of play to make things a whole lot easier. Pilly became the team's first star, an honor he would hold for an amazing eight years (due to attending law school after his undergraduate studies). One might say that there were advantages to having your own ball back in the day!

Because Jones spent some time at Shattuck prior to coming to the U of M, it was only natural that a rivalry would emerge between the two schools over the ensuing years. One day, as the Gopher team was about to board the train to Faribault to play the Shads, Pilly observed that his squad was one man short. As he looked up into the crowd of anxious on-lookers and fans who had come to see the team off at the train

SIG HARRIS

Sigmund Harris, a Minneapolis Central High School grad, was one of the Golden Gopher's first stars from 1901-04. Harris was an All-American quarterback for the powerful U of M teams under Dr. Henry Williams from 1902-04. Although small in stature, at just 145 pounds, Harris threw his weight around out on the gridiron and also saw time as a blocking back, punter, punt returner and safety. In 1902 Harris guided the team to a 9-2-1 record and in 1903 he led the team to a share of the Western Conference title with a 14-0-1 mark as they out-scored their opponents 618-12 that season. Minnesota's 6-6 tie with Michigan on Oct. 31, 1903, was one of the biggest games in the history of both programs, and served as the contest that inaugurated the famed Little Brown Jug rivalry that continues to this day. Harris, who called all of the team's plays on offense, was also a great defender and equalized Michigan's All-American running back Willie Heston en route to preserving the tie. As a senior, Harris led his Gophers to a 13-0 season and a second consecutive co-Western Conference championship — out-scoring their opponents that year by the insane margin of 725-12. Upon graduating, Harris went on to serve as a Gopher assistant coach from 1905-20, and again from 1929-41 — a position he would hold for 28 years in all. He later founded a machinery business in Minneapolis, but always found time to support his beloved Gophers. Harris would later be inducted into the International Jewish Sports Hall of Fame, and was also selected as the quarterback on Knute Rockne's All-Time Jewish Team. Harris died in 1964 at the age of 81. "He was a dynamic little man who literally breathed Minnesota spirit, and was known and admired by thousands of alumni," said George Barton of Harris, the former sports editor of the Minneapolis Tribune. A real Golden Gopher legend, Sig Harris was one of the program's best all-around players and played a big part in its future successes both on and off the field.

depot, he noticed a big, six-foot-three, 200-pound kid standing in the distance. Pilly had a light bulb go off above his head and went over to talk to him. The kid's name was Walter "Pudge" Heffelfinger, a Minneapolis Central High School student who had come down to root on the Gophers for their road trip.

Pilly asked him if he wanted to suit up and join them on their trip. He gladly agreed and the rest they say, is history. (Back then there were no eligibility rules about things like this.) Heffelfinger, who ran and got a change of clothes, played so well that he even wound up playing his entire senior year of high school with the Gophers. (After Pudge played for Minnesota for one year, he then went out east to Yale, where he became a three-time All-American guard and was re-

garded by most sports writers of that era as the nation's best college football player. He would later become America's first-ever professional football player when, on November 12, 1892, he was paid a whopping $500 by the Allegheny Athletic Association to play in a game against the rival Pittsburgh Athletic Club.)

In 1888, the Gophers hosted a return visit by the Shads in one of their biggest games of the year, beating them 14-0. That next day the Ariel stated: "Everybody turned out, and faculty, students, and small boys united to encourage the home team with mighty yelling. The unusual noise, together with the surprisingly mountainous contour of the campus, disconcerted the visitors, and gave the victory to the home team." The game was followed by a bus ride

GILMORE DOBIE

Gil Dobie played for the Gophers from 1899-1901. From there, he would go on to become a college football coaching legend. Dobie started out at North Dakota State, where he posted two consecutive undefeated seasons. He then went to the University of Washington, where, incredibly, he kept that unbeaten streak in tact for the next nine seasons. In Dobie's nine years with the Huskies, his teams outscored their opponents 1,930 to 118, and recorded 26 shutouts. He had compiled a astounding record of 58-0-3, which transpired into a streak of 61 consecutive games without a defeat when he left Washington for the University of Maryland that next year — an NCAA record which still stands to this day. Dobie coached through 1935, moving from Navy to Cornell, where he won a pair of National Championships in 1921 and 1922. Ironically, his only two losing seasons in coaching would come at Cornell, where, upon his firing he made the legendary quip "You can't win with Phi Beta Kappas." Dobie rounded out his 33-year career at Boston College, where he retired with an amazing 180-45-15 career record. Dobie was inducted into the College Football Hall of Fame in 1951.

around the city, as the University and Shattuck Yells (or cheers) combined to make the day "hideous till supper time."

The Gophers' were heralded as "Champions of the Northwest" in 1890 when they commenced their first out-of-state competition. After first beating Iowa's Grinnell College, 18-13, Minnesota then went on to beat the University of Wisconsin, 63-0, starting a tradition that has become the longest running rivalry in major college football history. The game was not without its share of controversy though, as Pillsbury, who was not only the quarterback but also the team's top runner, devised a play where he handed the ball off to a running back and then got it right back on a lateral. This razzle-dazzle play was extremely controversial at the time, and led to the changing of many of the rules which involved carrying the ball — which had

now started to replace the exclusively "kicking game." (Back then there was no forward or lateral passing, only backwards passes, and always through the hands of the quarterback to a halfback, for a running play, or to the fullback, for a punt or a drop kick.)

Minnesota's program got serious in the early 1890s, as the team's management began a fund-raising drive to improve itself. Among the items on its agenda were to build a new ball-field (which would eventually become Northrop Field), employ a trainer, and start a daily training table — which was established at nearby Johnson's Restaurant. There, the men ate together and were quizzed on strategy and signal drills. The team also got new uniforms, those being of the wool turtleneck sweater variety. In addition, the basement of the campus YMCA served as the team's new locker room, where one bathtub was shared by the entire

tcam. The new tactics and amenities paid instant dividends though, as the team's first undefeated, untied record came in 1892, when they beat Michigan, 14-6, Northwestern, 16-12, and Iowa, 42-4. For their efforts, the team was officially named as the winners of their first-ever conference title, the newly-formed Intercollegiate Athletic Association of the Northwest. They were

Arthur Erdall

of control, Purdue University President James H. Smart, along with the presidents of six other universities (Minnesota, University of Chicago, Illinois, Michigan, Northwestern and Wisconsin), met on January 11, 1895, to create the new Western Conference. (Minnesota was considered a Far West team by the East back in the day, since anything west of the Hud-

hailed in the newspapers as "Champions of the Northwest." (Incidentally, from 1892 to 1898, a touchdown was worth four points and from 1898 to 1911, it was worth five points.)

The Gophers went undefeated again that next year, but received no accolades because the Athletic Association was disbanded due to financial problems, as well as pressures from the public regarding the increasing level of violence in the game. Seeing that something needed to be done about the game's lack

son River was still considered wild frontier land.) The Western Conference later became the Big Seven Conference. (Indiana and Iowa joined the conference in 1899, followed by Ohio State in 1912. The conference would gradually evolve into the Big Eight, Big Nine & Big Ten — which now of course has 11 teams.)

In 1895 Pudge Heffelfinger returned from an illustrious career at Yale University to take a one-year coaching stint at Minnesota. After posting a modest 7-3 record, which included a thrilling 10-6 come-from-

CLARK SHAUGHNESSY

Clark Shaughnessy grew up in St. Cloud and went on to earn All-American honors as a Gopher fullback and tackle in 1913. From there, Shaughnessy would go on to become one of the most prolific coaches in Minnesota sports history. Shaughnessy coached college football at Tulane University from 1915-20 and again from 1922-25. He then went on to coach at Loyola from 1926-32, and then at the University of Chicago from 1933-39. In 1940, Shaughnessy went to Stanford where, as head coach, he created his version of the T-formation. During his first year at Stanford, Shaughnessy's team went undefeated and won the national championship, defeating Nebraska by a score of 21 to 13 in the Rose Bowl. Shaughnessy then went on to coach football at the University of Maryland in 1942 and 1946, while also coaching basketball at Pittsburgh from 1943 to 1945 as well. From there, Shaughnessy got into the pro game. After serving as an assistant coach with the NFL's Washington Redskins in 1947, Shaughnessy became head coach of the Los Angeles Rams in 1948. There, his Rams won the Western Division title in 1949, before losing to Philadelphia, 14-0, in the NFL Championship game. Shaugh-

nessy would post a 14-7-3 record with the Rams before moving on to become a consultant for the Chicago Bears from 1950-62. Shaughnessy gave college coaching one more try from there, and he ended his career as coach of the University of Hawaii in 1965. Shaughnessy would retire with a career college coaching record of 149-106-14. Shaughnessy, who studied military tactics to learn new strategies, was truly a student of the game. He is also credited with inventing the "Man in Motion T–Formation," a version of the T-formation used today by almost all high school, college, and professional football teams. A true innovator of the game, Clark Shaughnessy died in 1970 at the age of 78.

behind victory over Chicago, he decided to turn pro full time. From then until the turn of the century, the Gophers went through a dismal stretch. One of the more memorable games during this era though, was an 11-10 loss to Illinois on Thanksgiving Day, 1898, which was played in 12 below zero conditions at Northrop Field. Despite a blizzard dumping several feet of deep snow on the field, John Pillsbury (then the student manager), hired a crew that worked through the night to clear the field with horse-drawn plows. The game was even delayed several times while the officials searched inside the snow-banks for the often-buried football.

Twelve days earlier, on Nov. 12th, 1898, the Gophers beat Northwestern, 17-6, in Minneapolis. It was the team's only conference win of the year and what is significant about it is the fact that one of the students, Johnny Campbell, led an organized group of "yell leaders" throughout the game to root on the squad. As a result, the sport of cheerleading was officially born in college football. The star of this era was John Harrison, a left end from Minneapolis Central who became the first Gopher to earn All-Western Conference honors.

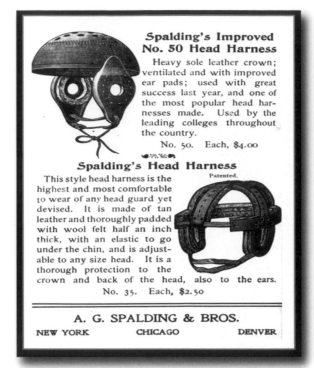

Spalding's Improved
No. 50 Head Harness
Heavy sole leather crown; ventilated and with improved ear pads; used with great success last year, and one of the most popular head harnesses made. Used by the leading colleges throughout the country.
No. 50. Each, $4.00

Spalding's Head Harness
This style head harness is the highest and most comfortable to wear of any head guard yet devised. It is made of tan leather and thoroughly padded with wool felt half an inch thick, with an elastic to go under the chin, and is adjustable to any size head. It is a thorough protection to the crown and back of the head, also to the ears.
No. 35. Each, $2.50

A. G. SPALDING & BROS.
NEW YORK   CHICAGO   DENVER

Enter the Good Doctor

Something, or rather someone, big happened to Minnesota in 1900. That was the year that University officials, after a string of one-year coaching stints from a variety of former players, hired Dr. Henry L. Williams on a part-time basis to serve as its football and track coach. Williams, a former star player and teammate of Heffelfinger at Yale University, who then attended medical school at the University of Pennsylvania, accepted a three-year, $2,500 contract, with the understanding that he also be able to carry on his medical practice. Williams, whose three-year commitment ultimately turned into the University's first full-time coaching job, which would last for more than 22 years, marked the beginning of a new football era in Minnesota during which the Gophers would win or share eight conference titles over the next 16-seasons.

Williams was the innovator of several football innovations that would place him among the immortals of the game. Among his contributions to the sport included: the advent of the Forward Pass (which became legal in 1905); Criss-Cross Plays, which halfbacks and ends passed the ball back and forth to each other while going in opposite directions; Revolving Wedges; Tackle-Back formations, On-Side Quarterback Kicks; and perhaps most importantly was the

JOHN MCGOVERN

John McGovern was an All-American quarterback for Minnesota in 1909 and a first-team All Big-Ten selection in both 1909 and 1910. McGovern, who was inducted into the College Football Hall of Fame in 1966, was a durable player on both sides of the ball, missing just one game in his three seasons in Gold Country. It was McGovern's kicking toe that stunned coach Amos Alonzo Stagg's powerful Chicago team in 1909, however, as the five-foot-nine, 155-pounder kicked three field goals to give the Gophers a 20-6 upset victory. McGovern was also extremely intelligent and wound up becoming the master strategist in running coach Henry Williams' offense, one of the first in the game to use sophisticated shifts. A well rounded athlete, McGovern was also a champion wrestler for the Gophers as well. In fact, he helped lead the team to a Big Ten title in its first year of existence in 1910. After graduation, McGovern worked as sports editor for a Minneapolis newspaper before starting a successful law practice in Washington, D.C.

BERT BASTON

Bert Baston was a two-time All-American end in both 1915 and 1916, the first player in Gopher history to earn the honor in back-to-back seasons. Baston was one third of the Gopher triple-threat of this era, with quarterback Pudge Wyman throwing him the ball and running back Bernie Bierman carrying it into the end zone. The Gophers were tough during those days, and Baston played a big role in leading the team to a 12-1-1 record during his junior and senior campaigns while averaging nearly 50 points per contest. Among Baston's many honors and accolades, he was inducted into the College Football Hall of Fame in 1954. The St. Louis Park native later served as a Gopher assistant under head coach Bernie Bierman for nearly two decades as well.

now infamous "Minnesota Shift," which was the forerunner of all quick shifts since implemented in the game, and long considered as the most devastating offensive weapon introduced into modern football.

Under Williams' tutelage, Minnesota, which was led by Quarterback Gilmore Dobie, won the newly formed Big Nine Conference title in 1900, finishing with an undefeated 10-0-2 record. After beating the likes of Illinois, Northwestern, Wisconsin, Nebraska, North Dakota, Grinnell, Carleton, Ames College and St. Paul Central High School, they tied Chicago and Minneapolis Central High School. Minneapolis Central, who held the Gophers to a 0-0 stalemate, featured a couple of future Gopher stars in-waiting: Sig Harris and Bobby Marshall.

The good doctor had turned around the slumping program, and brought to it a new sense of

style. He even held the team's pre-season training camp at Lake Minnetonka, just to give the kids a fresh outlook each season. With each of the starters towering at least six-feet tall, this team was dubbed as the "Giants of the North." With the forward pass not yet legal, Williams' early teams featured a ground attack similar to that of a battering-ram. In this system, the runner had to just get behind his offensive linemen, who would simply lock arms and mow down any defender who got in their way.

Football was a barbaric game in those days and it ultimately started to come under fire. Due to the pressure that coaches were putting on their teams to "win at any price," gridiron injuries and even deaths were on the rise. The public was calling for the abolition of the sport, which soon caught the attention of then-President Theodore Roosevelt. Teddy called

Johnny goes through Wisconsin.

upon radical change for the game, and the coaches listened. New rule changes set by faculty representatives included: shortening the halves from 40 minutes to 30, requiring at least six players on the line of scrimmage, legalizing the forward pass, establishing a neutral zone, and forbidding certain types of hurdling and violent tackling.

The 1902 Gophers, after outscoring their opponents 299-23, generated a lot of enthusiasm on campus. Against Grinnell that year, Robert Liggett scored seven touchdowns! The only points they gave up that season were to Michigan, in a game that they lost 23-6. (Michigan would go on to slaughter Stanford, 49-0, in the first-ever Rose Bowl that year.) School spirit skyrocketed in 1903, when the U of M plowed over everybody, and even got to exact a little revenge on the national champion Michigan Wolverines, whom they battled to a historic 6-6 tie. That game, more so perhaps than any other at that time, would put Minnesota on the football map. It would also be the start of an amazing rivalry that would forever linked together by a small, brown piece of crockery — the Little Brown Jug, which has become one of college football's most enduring trophies.

On October 31, 1903, Halloween day, the undefeated Gophers hosted the undefeated Michigan Wolverines at the newly renovated and expanded Northrop Field. The game had all the hype of a modern day Super Bowl going in, and left the fans begging for more when the final whistle was blown. A huge

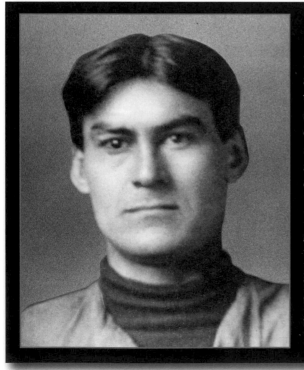

ED ROGERS

Born and raised in Walker, Minn., the son of a pioneer lumberman and a Chippewa Indian mother, Ed Rogers' free-spirited boyhood was reflected in his wild style of play on the gridiron. Rogers, who first started out playing football as an end at the Carlisle Institute, later came to the University of Minnesota in 1902. Rogers' playing career spanned seven seasons, four as a member of the Carlisle Redmen, and three with the Gophers. A true leader, Rogers served as the team captain at Carlisle in 1900 and then again in Minnesota in 1903. The 1903 Minnesota team had a 11-0-1 record and was highlighted by Rogers' kicking the tying field goal in the first ever Little Brown Jug game against Michigan. The two-time All-American then returned to Carlisle in 1904, where he led the team to a 9-2 record as their head coach. The following year he returned to Minneapolis and began practicing law. He would go on to work as a lawyer for 62 years before retiring at the age of 90. Rogers was inducted into the National Collegiate Football Hall of Fame in 1968 as well as the National Indian Athletic Hall of Fame in 1973.

bonfire was lit for thousands of fans the night before this classic showdown of titans, which featured a couple of would-be coaching legends: Fielding Yost and Dr. Henry Williams. Yost's "Point-a-Minute" Michigan juggernaut came in with a three year, 29-game unbeaten and untied winning streak. (The team literally averaged about 60 points per 60-minute game while yielding just a couple of touchdowns during the entire streak!) Williams' squad was no slouch either, having won 10 straight coming in, including a 75-0 rout of Iowa, an 85-0 pasting of Hamline and a 112-0 shellacking of Macalester.

Dr. Henry Williams

The pre-game build-up was tremendous and the fans got there early. Northrop's 20,000 wooden seats were filled beyond her capacity, while thousands of other die-hard fans scrambled onto neighboring roof-tops in hopes of catching a glimpse. One newspaper account read: "By nine in the morning the trees and telegraph poles overlooking Northrop Field began to fill and by ten not a point of vantage from which the field could be seen was left unoccupied."

The game got underway that Saturday afternoon with the Gophers outplaying the Wolverines in a scoreless first half — piling up 17 first downs to the Wolverines' three. A disallowed safety and a missed place-kick were all that Michigan could muster as Minnesota's defense played outstanding. Willie Heston, Michigan's All-American Running Back, was held in check during the first half by a venerable United Nations-like defense that included the likes of a 140-pound Jewish Quarterback/Cornerback named Sig Harris, a pair of Chippewa Native American and African American Defensive Ends in Ed Rogers and Bobby Marshall, respectively, along with an assortment of Germans, Italians and Swedes. (Incidentally, Marshall was the first African American to play in the conference.)

The second half was another story though, as Heston, who finished his collegiate career with 93 TDs, finally capped off a solid Michigan drive on a one yard touchdown plunge to make it 5-0. (Touchdowns were worth five points back then.) The extra point was good and the lead now stood at 6-0. The Gophers mounted a comeback, but by then nearly all of their starting running backs — Earl Current, James Irsfield and Otto Davies, had been sidelined with injuries. Even Harris' 43-yard kick-off return in the third quarter couldn't get the Maroon and Gold on

LORIN SOLON

Lorin Solon was a two-time All-Big Nine Conference and All-American selection as both a running back and defensive end for the Gophers in 1913 and 1914. The Chippewa Falls, Wis., native is one of the few players ever to be selected as an All-American at two different positions. Solon was an outstanding athlete and was called upon to perform place kicking, punting and occasionally even to play quarterback. Solon, who also starred as a catcher on the Gopher baseball team, was set to become the U of M's first three-time All-American on the gridiron, but had his college eligibility cut short after the first three games of his senior year when it was learned that he had played semi-pro baseball in Montana during the Summer prior to his senior year. So highly regarded was the Chippewa Falls, Wis., native that when he left the team midway through his senior year to play professional baseball, University President Vincent even held a farewell dinner in his honor. From there, in addition to playing professional baseball, Solon also played professional football, emerging as the highest paid professional football player in the country at one point. In addition, he also served as a Colonel in both WWI and WWII,

BOBBY MARSHALL

Bobby Marshall was one of Minnesota's first great athletes. The Minneapolis Central High School grad went on to become the first man of color to play in the Big Nine (later the Big Ten) as an end for the football Gophers. From 1904-06 he led the team to an amazing record of 27-2, as they outscored their opponents 1,238-63. In 1906 he even kicked a game-winning 60-yard field goal in the rain and mud to beat the University of Chicago, 4-2 (field goals counted 4 points back then). He received All-Western honors for all three of his years in Minnesota. In addition to football, he earned all-conference honors as a first baseman on the U of M baseball team and also lettered in track as a sprinter. As a professional, he was a star in football, baseball, boxing and even hockey, where, in 1908, he became the first African American to play professionally, when he suited up for the semi-pro Minneapolis Wanderers, and later with the Hillsdale Hockey Club in Pennsylvania. In baseball, he played for the Colored Gophers and the Chicago Leland Giants professional Negro-League teams; and on the gridiron he played professionally with the Minneapolis Deans (which were undefeated with Marshall playing), Minneapolis Marines, Duluth Eskimos and Rock Island Independents — all of the early NFL. In 1971, Marshall was inducted into the College Football Hall of Fame, and several years later he was named to the National Football Foundation's Hall of Fame.

the board. Since no one had been able to score a touchdown against Michigan up to that point in the season, things started to look bleak.

On defense, Harris was a one-man wrecking crew, making game-saving tackles all day on Heston. On one play, an end-around, he hit Heston so hard that both of them were knocked unconscious. They were both revived, however, and both continued to play. Coach Williams, ever the innovator, had shut down Heston by devising a seven-man defensive line (teams of this era had consisted of nine-man lines), with the other four players dispersed behind — like modern-day defensive backs. Even if Heston broke through the line, he would have four others there to deal with. It is something we take for granted today, but back in the day it was revolutionary.

After another series, Minnesota's Freddie Burgan returned a short punt to the Michigan 38-yard line. (Punting was the one area of Michigan's game that was rusty, after all, up until this game they had not punted all season long — they never needed to!) With the good field position, things started to look up. Fred "Germany" Schacht, a huge 210-pound lineman and All-American from Fergus Falls, who was now playing running back, along with Winona's James Kremer, alternated on carrying the ball deep into Wolverine territory. Then, on third and "last down," from the Michigan three, Egil Boeckmann, on a cross-buck, dove straight through the hole Tackle Dan Smith had opened for him into an area of the end zone nick-

named "coffin corner." (Back then teams had three downs to go five yards for a first down on a 110-yard field.) With the score 6-5, the drama began to unfold with regards to the matter of the extra point.

In those days, an extra point had to be attempted from behind the spot where the touchdown was scored, unless a team made successful "punt-out," in which case the extra point could then be attempted from a better angle. The Gophers did just that, thanks to the leg of Kremer, who punted it straight up in the air from his 15-yard line and straight down to the awaiting Burgan, who came down with the "jump-ball" in the end zone. Burgan then held on for dear life as he squeezed the cradled ball like a baby, despite the viscous beating he immediately took by the awaiting Michigan players in an attempt to make him drop it. Having now earned the right to try the extra point from a much better angle, team captain Ed Rogers, with Harris holding, calmly came out and kicked it through the uprights for the tie.

It was at that point, despite the fact that there were still a couple of minutes remaining on the clock, that the crowd went nuts and stormed the field. In the pandemonium both coaches reluctantly conceded the tie. From there, the festivities officially began and culminated in a downtown Minneapolis parade that lasted well into the evening. Streetcars lined up to take the mob of fans downtown to celebrate, as they yelled "Ski-U-Mah!" all the way there. Minnesota was now being heralded as the new "Champions of the West."

After the smoke had cleared that next day, the clean-up began. That's when Oscar Munson, a Norwegian immigrant who served as the team's equipment manager, made a discovery of sorts. It had appeared that in the mayhem, the Wolverines had left behind their big crockery water jug. Munson took the jug and, in his thick Scandinavian accent whereupon "j's" were pronounced as "y's," presented it to Louis Cooke (as in Cooke Hall), then the head of the athletic department, proclaiming: "Yost left his Yug..." (Michigan, fearing some sort of diabolical contamination from the rival Minnesotans, actually brought its own drinking water in a barrel from Ann Arbor. Then, on the morning of the game, Wolverine team manager Tommy Roberts went out to the Busy Bee Variety Store, on Hennepin Avenue, where he purchased the five gallon water jug for the sum of 30¢.)

Cooke then sent word to Yost back in Ann Arbor, telling him that he had left his water jug behind. "If you want your Jug, you'll have win it back," he said sarcastically. Yost accepted the challenge and thus the Little Brown Jug tradition was born. (Yost would have to wait six years, however, to reclaim the Jug. Due to scheduling problems, the Wolverines and Gophers did not play each other again until 1909. In 1910, Michigan, who had won the Jug back the year before, left the conference in protest against the abolishment of the team training table, among other things, and Minnesota didn't have a chance to win it back until 1919. That year the Gophers, led by their star Arnie Oss, stormed into Ann Arbor and spanked the Wolverines, 34-7, on their own Ferry Field. When Minnesota asked for the symbolic trophy at the end of the game, Michigan mysteriously couldn't find it. But the Gopher players persisted, until Wolverine equipment manager Henry Hatch came up with it after a short time, saying that he found it "overgrown behind a clump of shrubbery near the gym." (In reality it was found padlocked inside a trophy case inside the gymnasium!)

Cooke, who kept the jug on his desk for those first six years, even went ahead and painted the score of the game on it with a big "6" for Minnesota, dwarfing a little "6" for Michigan. Under that he painted the caption: "Michigan Jug — Captured by Oscar on October 31, 1903." (Scores of each game have since been added to the vessel, which was later repainted brown with both a maroon and blue "M" on each side, representing the colors of the two Universities.) Cooke once mused of the strange power within the stoneware crock, "I sometimes think that the jug has been filled with spirits, not alcoholic, but the disembodied spirits of the countless players who have fought for it on the gridiron..." It is without question the most famous of all college rivalry trophies, and no other inanimate object can come close to the aura of tradition like that of the Little Brown Jug.

Simply Dominant

After outscoring their opponents 618-12 in 1903, the Gophers once again went undefeated in 1904, even bettering their scoring margin of the year before to an amazing 725-12. (Those 725 points remain second all-time to only Harvard's record of 765 back in 1886.) One of the highlights of the season came against Grinnell, whom the Gophers thrashed, 146-0. At the time it broke what was referred to as the "World's Scoring

EARL MARTINEAU

Earl Martineau played football for the Gophers from 1921-24, earning Walter Camp All-American honors as a senior. Martineau was also an outstanding track & field athlete at Minnesota and was named the recipient of the Western Conference Medal for proficiency in athletics and scholarship prior to his graduation in 1924. Acclaimed for his offensive prowess, Martineau is most remembered for a remarkable defensive play versus Wisconsin in 1923. Badger halfback Rollie Williams had broken through the initial Gopher defense and was being led by a tandem of blockers. Martineau was all that stood between the Wisconsin players and the goal line. Noting that his opponents were in perfect position to block him, Martineau leaped over them, and tackled Williams to avert a sure touchdown. Among his many honors and accolades, Martineau received the Croix de Guerre and Distinguished Service Cross for gallantry as a Marine Corps lieutenant serving in France during World War I. After playing with the Gophers, he went on to become a successful assistant to head football coach Fritz Crisler at both Princeton and the University of Michigan.

DID YOU KNOW THAT TOUCH-FOOTBALL WAS ORIGINATED AT THE UNIVERSITY OF MINNESOTA?

That's right, in 1920 W. R. Smith, then-head of the University's intramural program, saw some frat boys playing the game without pads and with no tackling. Inspired, he thought that the idea might just fly as a school sanctioned sport. So, that Fall he added it to the intramural sports program and it took off from there. Soon, other schools from around the nation picked up on it and the rest, they say, is history.

Record," with the previous honor being held by Michigan, who had previously beaten West Virginia, 130-0. Against Wisconsin that year Minnesota racked up an amazing 1,183 yards of offense! The Gophers were led that season by All-American Center Moses Strathern, from Hastings.

In 1905 the forward pass was finally legalized, making the game much more exciting and much more tactical. The Gophers suffered their first loss in two years when they were beaten in by Wisconsin, 16-12. The heartbreaking contest featured long touchdown runs by Wisconsin's All-American Running Back Ralph Vanderboom, and Minnesota's star Halfback Joe Cutting. They did manage to go 10-1 that year, even outscoring their opponents 542-22. As far as

Doc Williams' first five-year report card, a not too shabby 52-3-3 overall record.

From there the team went on to win conference crowns in 1906, 1909, 1910, 1911 and 1915, while only once losing more than two of their seven games. (Under President Theodore Roosevelt's sports initiative recommendation, teams now only played seven-game schedules.) The 1906 conference title was won on Bobby Marshall's 60-yard kick at the buzzer to defeat Amos Alonzo Stagg's University of Chicago Maroons, 4-2. (A field goal counted four points at the time.) Their only loss that year, 17-0, came against Pop Warner's famous Carlisle Indians, who were led by future NFL Hall of Famer, Jim Thorpe. The Gophers came back to beat the Indi-

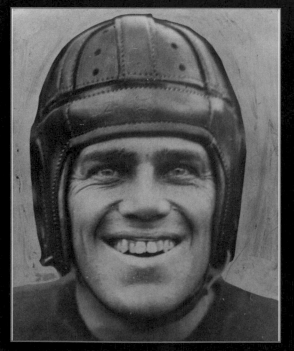

MALVIN NYDAHL

One of only a handful of three-sport stars to compete at Minnesota from 1926-28, Malvin Nydahl was one of the top athletes of his day. In fact, Nydahl was so well respected by his coaches and peers that he was named as the captain of both the baseball and basketball squads. On the gridiron, meanwhile, "Mally" was a star fullback and quarterback. For his efforts, he won the prestigious Big Ten Conference Medal of Honor in 1928, given annually to the league's top student-athlete on the basis of athletic and scholastic achievement. Nydahl later went on to play professional football in the NFL with both Minneapolis and Frankford from 1929-31.

ans that next year though, behind the legendary running of Minnesota's Left End, Ed Chestnut, who recovered an Indian fumble on the Gopher goal line and raced 100 yards for the game-winning touchdown.

Five-foot-five Gopher Quarterback Johnny McGovern, a native of Arlington, Minn., was the first to finally get a hang of this new forward passing thing, and for his efforts was named as the team's first consensus Walter Camp All-American in 1909. McGovern was also a terror on defense, a great passer and receiver, a talented punter and drop-kicker, and an overall excellent field general. McGovern, despite having a broken collarbone, played heroically against Michigan that year, only to come up short as the team was beaten, 15-6, for its only loss. In 1910 the game was divided into four equal quarters, instead of two halves. Leading the charge that year was Tackle James Walker, a Minneapolis native who became Minnesota's second consensus Walter Camp All-American.

In 1913 Clark Shaughnessy earned All-American honors as a fullback and tackle. (Shaughnessy would later become known for his coaching exploits, as he coached Tulane, Loyola, Chicago, Stanford,

Ken Haycraft

Maryland, Pittsburgh and finally the Los Angeles Rams. A student of the game, he studied military tactics for strategy and is also credited with inventing the "Man in Motion T–Formation.") Another interesting thing happened in 1914. That was the first year that the University featured a homecoming game, complete with a campus bon fire to evoke a plethora of school spirit.

The Gophers of 1915 featured perhaps one of the toughest offense backfields in college football prior to World War I: the trio of two-time All-American End Bert Baston of St. Louis Park, Half Back Arnold 'Pudge' Wyman, and ace Running Back and team captain, Bernie Bierman. All-American End Lorin Solon scored four touchdowns in the Gopher's win over Iowa State that season. After the game, however, he was ruled ineligible when it was found out that he had played pro baseball under an assumed name.

Bierman would replace him as team captain for the next game on the road against Illinois. There, due in large part to Bierman's untimely sprained ankle, the Illini managed to eke out a 6-6 tie. Minnesota drew first blood in the opening quarter of the game when Joe Sprafka scored on a 29-yard run

CLARENCE "BIGGIE" MUNN

Clarence "Biggie" Munn was a tough guard who earned Big Ten MVP and All-American honors for the Gophers in 1931. Munn, who also played fullback, was a ball carrying machine known for his great quickness. In fact, Munn was a sprinter on the Gopher track team as well from 1929-31. Also the team's punter, Munn weighed 215 pounds and stood just under six-feet tall — huge for those days. After graduation, the Minneapolis native got into coaching, where, over a period of 22 years, he coached at Albright, Syracuse and Michigan State. As head coach at MSU from 1947-53, Munn led the Spartans to an impressive 54-9-2 record. In fact, his 1951 and 1952 teams were unbeaten and even won back-to-back NCAA National Championships. For his efforts, he was named as the American Football Coaches Association's Coach of the Year in 1952. A year later, after leading his Spartans past UCLA in the Rose Bowl, Munn stepped down from coaching in order to become the school's athletic director. Among his many honors, including being inducted into the College Football Hall of Fame, the hockey arena at Michigan State was renamed after him in his honor after he died in 1975.

around the left end. Kicker Al Quist then failed to convert what could have been the winning point, as Illinois answered by scoring in the second quarter on a fourth down pass from Bart Macomber to Potsy Clark. When Macomber's extra point kick went wide, the score remained tied. The Gophers outplayed the Illini down in the sweltering heat of Champagne for the rest of the game, but just couldn't get into the end-zone.

Bierman's ankle would recover though, and thanks to his two touchdowns and four pass interceptions, Minnesota went on to defeat Wisconsin, 20-3, to finish the season unbeaten and tied for a share of the Big Nine crown. Wyman to Baston was the ultimate dynamic duo that year, as Baston, a tireless work-horse with tremendous leaping ability, had established himself as one of the game's premier receivers.

All-American Quarterback Clare (Shorty) Long, led the 1916 Gophers to what Walter Camp, the era's preeminent football expert, had called the "most perfect team of history." After blowing out nearly everyone that season — including a 67-0 thrashing of Iowa and an 81-0 spanking of South Dakota — Coach Bob Zuppke's Fighting Illini, led by the Papa Bear himself, George Halas, came to town. Despite being considered as three-touchdown underdogs, Illinois would catch the Gophers off guard. The Illini came out and did something unheard of — they passed on first down. In addition, Zuppke had scouted and capitalized on a bizarre Gopher superstition whereby he learned that they opened each game by giving the pigskin to Sprafka, Wyman and Long, always in succession and always in the same order. Zuppke then had his defense key in on those three and wound up stopping each one cold. On fourth down Minnesota was forced to punt, and so began what was considered at the time by many to be the greatest upset in college football history. To make matters worse, the game's greatest prognosticators of the time: Walter Camp, E. C. Patterson (of Colliers Magazine), and Grantland Rice, had each made the trek up to Minneapolis to see the squad first hand.

Down 7-0 early in the first, Wyman threw an interception into the hands of Illinois' Kraft, who ran 55 yards for a TD. Minnesota got on the board in the second half on a key fourth down play when Sprafka shot into the end-zone from the five. Wyman booted the extra point and the Gophers added a safety late but came up short, 14-9. With the loss, the embarrassed and dejected Gophers, who were 35-1 odds-on favorites going in, finished in a tie for second in the conference and out of the national championship running. It was even rumored that before the ugly upset that Camp was going to name as many as seven Gophers to his prestigious All-American team. The next day the Chicago Tribune's big front page headline read: "HOLD ON TIGHT WHEN YOU READ THIS!"

The Gophers rebounded that next week, crushing the University of Wisconsin, 54-0, followed by the University of Chicago, 49-0, thus giving legendary coach Amos Alonzo Stagg the worst defeat of his career. After the game a Chicago sports writer commented on the visiting Gophers: "It is impossible to single out one individual star, for every player on the team was a star."

In 1917 the Gophers went 5-1, losing only

ROBERT TANNER

Robert Tanner holds the distinction of being the first athlete in University of Minnesota history to earn a combined nine letters in the sports of football, baseball and basketball — from 1927-29. On the gridiron, Tanner earned All American and All Conference honors as an end in 1929. In addition, Tanner was a two-time recipient of the prestigious Conference Medal of Honor, recognizing his achievements as a student-athlete. Tanner even went on to serve as the captain of the East squad in the East-West All Star Game following his senior year as well. In addition to playing the forward position on the hardwood, Tanner served as the captain of the baseball team in 1929 as well. Upon graduating, the three-sport star went on to play in the NFL with the Frankford Yellow Jackets.

once to Wisconsin. Leading the way that year was All-American George Hauser, who allowed just one first down all season at the defensive tackle position. World War I soon came on though and Coach Williams lost most of his good prospects to military service. In 1918, despite the fact that several games were played under quarantine — because of an influenza epidemic, Minnesota had a good year, even beating up on Carleton so badly that they were forced to punt a whopping 50 times during the game. Another outstanding year was 1919, when the speedy Half Back Arnie Oss suited up for the Gophers. Oss single-handedly beat Indiana and then had the game of his life against Michigan, scoring on an amazing 67-yard zig-zag run en route to crushing the Wolverines by the final of 34-7. With the win, for the first time since 1903, the Little Brown Jug would come back to Minnesota.

After Williams posted just average teams in both 1920 and 1921, the University Athletic Board, which had a lot of power in those days, fired him as the team's head coach. Perhaps the final straw came in 1921 when Williams finally gave in to demands that he put numbers on his players' uniforms — like the other teams in college football had been doing. In-

The boys weren't the only ones getting dirty out on the gridiron back in the early 1920s...

stead of using the one and two digit variety, however, he instead put four digits on each player so that the fans were just as confused as the team's opposition. It was a bitter ending for one of Minnesota's greatest coaches. Many didn't realize it, but Williams never had more than one assistant through all his years behind the bench, and through it all he continued to practice medicine full-time as well. Sadly, he died only 10 years later, in 1931.

There was a great deal of speculation with regards to who was going to be the good doctor's successor as Minnesota's football coach. Rumors ran rampant with the front-runner appearing to be former quarterback and then current St. Thomas College head coach, Johnny McGovern. But, in a shocker, the University regents decided to go with William H. Spaulding, then coach of Kalamazoo Normal School in Michigan. Spaulding, who played his football at Wabash College, was an unknown, causing a lot of dissension amongst the Maroon and Gold faithful.

Spaulding got off to a respectable start and eventually settled in. One of the more emotional games of his tenure came on November 17, 1923, when the Gophers played their last game ever at

HERB JOESTING

Herb Joesting was a two-time All-American fullback for the University of Minnesota in both 1926 and 1927. Joesting was a triple threat at halfback for the Golden Gophers who could run, pass or catch. Gopher coach Clarence "Doc" Spears built his offense around the powerful runner and it paid off in spades as he gained 1,850 yards in 24 games for a career average of 4.2 yards a carry. Joesting led the Gophers to an undefeated 6-0-2 season in 1927, tops in the conference. The "Owatonna Thunderbolt," as he was affectionately known, later served as the player/coach of the 1929 Minneapolis Red Jackets, one of Minnesota's first NFL teams. He later played professionally with the NFL's Philadelphia Yellow Jackets and Chicago Bears. Among his many honors and accolades, Joesting was inducted into the College Football Hall of Fame in 1954.

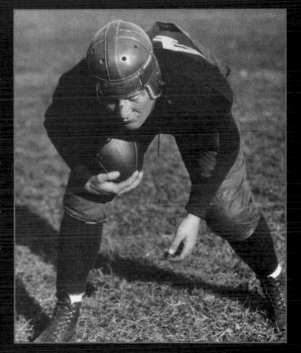

GLENN SEIDEL

Glenn Seidel was the starting quarterback for the Gophers during their amazing undefeated stretch between 1933-35, when they won two straight national championships. Seidel served as the captain of the 1935 title team and when he was done he passed the torch, literally, to the next team leader. That tradition is now called the Captain's Torch, which is passed down each season to the new captain. Seidel, who also played hockey for the Gophers from 1935-36, went on to play in the College Football All-Star Game after his senior season. Among his many honors and accolades, Seidel received the Western Conference Medal for scholarship and athletics, as well as the Sport's Illustrated Silver Anniversary All-American Award.

Northrop Field, defeating a much heavier Iowa squad, 20-7. All-American Running Back Earl "The Flying Frenchman" Martineau scored two of the three Gopher touchdowns while passing to All-American End Ray Eklund for the other.

Perhaps the highlight of Spaulding's three-year tenure came in 1924, when the Gophers upset a formidable Illinois team, 20-7, which featured three-time All-American Halfback Red Grange in its backfield. That game would forever go down in history, not only because of the victory, but because it marked the dedication of Minnesota's newly constructed 55,000-seat Memorial Stadium, or "Brick House" as it would become affectionately known — which paid tribute to the men and women who served in W.W.I. Grange, otherwise known as the "Galloping Ghost," had ironically just christened Illinois' new Memorial Stadium in Champaign just a few weeks earlier by scoring six touchdowns against a fearsome Michigan squad.

Grange opened the scoring in the game when he took the pigskin into the end-zone from around the right end for a touchdown. He then kicked the extra point to make it 7-0 for Illinois. Minnesota would get 20 unanswered points that day though, thanks in large part to the efforts of Running Back Clarence Schutte. After Malcolm Graham's 27-yard double pass reception, Schutte plunged over for a one-yard touchdown to tie it up. Schutte then scored again on a 31-yarder near the end of the first half, followed by yet another five-yard touchdown late in the third after a 34-yard scamper deep into enemy territory. Schutte showed up the great Grange on this day as he finished the afternoon with 282 yards on 32 carries for three TDs. While Minnesota, incredibly, had

played the game with just 12 men, Illinois responded by not scheduling the Gophers on their docket for the next 17 years.

Minnesota's hopes for a conference title were dashed on the final Saturday of that season when Michigan, despite being held to just 66 yards rushing, beat the Gophers, 10-0, in Ann Arbor. After three years and a modest 11-7-4 record, it had appeared that the nay-sayer's would get their wish. Spaulding was fired at the close of the 1924 season, only to be rehired that next season as UCLA's new head coach. Taking his place was Dr. Clarence W. Spears, a former All-American guard at Dartmouth who had coached at the University of Virginia. Spears had a reputation for being a tough, stern disciplinarian, who played to win. With just a handful of holdovers, Spears dove in with a bunch of youngsters and started the rebuilding process. The early star of the team during this era was a kid by the name of Herb Joesting, a sophomore fullback who would become known simply as the "Owatonna Thunderbolt."

The 1925 Gophers rolled over North Dakota University, Grinnell College and Wabash College, before getting beat by the defending national champs from Notre Dame, 19-7. Knute Rockne's Irish, even without the recently graduated legendary "Four Horsemen," waged a terrific battle against the Gophers. Minnesota, despite Herb Joesting's brilliant running and Harold Almquist's early touchdown, came up short before the capacity crowd at Memorial Stadium. Even in defeat, Minnesota's fans were pleased at the solid performance. That quickly changed the next week though, when Spears, despite being up 12-0 in the fourth quarter against Wisconsin, sent in an entire team of substitutes who let the Badgers back in the game to tie it at 12-12. (The rules at that time dictated that players leaving the game in any quarter could not return to the line-up during the same quarter, so Spears was unable to get his regulars back into the game.)

The Gophers came back to beat Butler College, 33-7, and Iowa, 33-0, before being blanked by Michigan, 35-0. (Incidentally, in 1926 the Gophers played Michigan twice, becoming just the first team to ever play a double-header against a conference foe. The Wolverines unfortunately won both games. So big was that Michigan away game, that back home in Minneapolis, reports of the game were telegraphed back and the scrubs who didn't travel, reenacted the plays, live, to the home fans who had gathered to root them on at Memorial Stadium.)

The 1927 season was a special one in Min-nesota history, as it marked the entry of International Falls' Fullback/Tackle, Bronko Nagurski into varsity competition. The "Bronk" would go on to become arguably the greatest all-around football player ever to play the game, at any level, eventually landing in the Pro Football Hall of Fame. Led by Nagurski, Quarterback Fred Hovde, All-America Guard Harold Hanson, and a trio of running backs in Herb Joesting, Mally Nydahl and Shorty Almquist, the 1927 Gophers had their most successful season under Dr. Spears. In their first undefeated campaign since 1915, Minnesota, despite a pair of ties with Notre Dame, 7-7, and Indiana, 14-14, went on to earn a share of the conference crown with Illinois by defeating Michigan, 13-7. More than 10,000 fans made the trip to Ann Arbor to watch the Gophers reclaim the Jug as Joesting and All-American End Kenneth Haycraft tallied for the Gophers in this one. They then beat Iowa, 38-0, Wis-

MEMORIAL STADIUM

Opened on Oct. 14, 1924, Memorial Stadium served as the home of the Golden Gophers for 57 years. The stadium was dedicated to the 3,527 university workers and graduates who served in World War I, 98 of whom died in service. Built on approximately 11 acres where the current University Recreation Center, Aquatic Center and McNamara Alumni Center stand today, Memorial Stadium had 52,736 permanent seats but could seat over 56,000. The horseshoe-shaped stadium also served as the home track and field facility. With the addition of temporary bleacher seating, more than 60,000 fans could fit into Memorial Stadium as a stadium-record 66,284 fans watched Minnesota face Purdue on Nov. 18, 1966. The stadium, which took seven months to construct, cost $572,000 to build. More than 475 workers were employed for the construction that required more than 1.4 million feet of lumber, one million bricks and 90,000 sacks of cement. Minnesota played its first game in Memorial Stadium on Oct. 14, 1924, defeating North Dakota 14-0. Tickets for the inaugural game were just one dollar. The Golden Gophers had a stellar record in Memorial Stadium, including 12 unbeaten seasons at home. They didn't suffer a losing season at home from the building's inception in 1924 until 1950, a span of 26 years. Memorial Stadium was changed to artificial turf in 1970 but then switched back to natural grass in 1977. The stadium was demolished in 1989 and 2,000 of the original bricks were used in the building of Mariucci Arena. University officials debated renovation of Memorial Stadium, but instead opted for a move to the Metrodome in 1982.

(Source: U of M)

BRONKO NAGURSKI

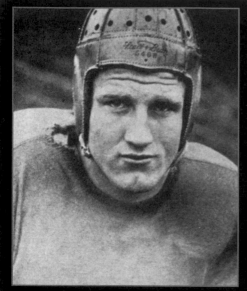

The legend of Bronko Nagurski began back in 1926, when then-Gopher Coach Clarence "Doc" Spears was on a recruiting trip up in northern Minnesota. As the story goes, one day while driving through International Falls, Spears saw a hulking young man plowing a field — without a horse. When the curious Spears stopped to ask for directions, instead of using his finger, the kid just lifted the enormous plow and pointed with it! No, it wasn't Paul Bunyan... it was just Bronko.

Bronislau Nagurski was born Nov. 3, 1908, on the Canadian side of Rainy Lake in Rainy River, Ontario. At the age of four, his family moved to International Falls, just a slap-shot away on the other side of the U.S. border. His nickname supposedly came about when his first-grade teacher, after not being able to understand his mother's thick Ukrainian accent, called the youngster "Bronko," and it stuck.

He grew up loving all sports, but, amazingly, in his two years of prep football at International Falls High School, his sophomore and junior years, he never played on a team that won a game. In fact, he even transferred to neighboring Bemidji High School for his senior year, because he was upset when his principal canceled the team's trip to a district tournament when a couple of other players required some disciplining. There, the transfer student was ruled ineligible to play football, but he did manage to play basketball and run track. It was hardly the kind of a prep career that would have attracted college recruiters, even in those days.

Following high school, the "Bronk" headed south, to wear the Maroon and Gold at the University of Minnesota. (In reality, he met Doc Spears while he was up north fishing, and convinced him to come to the University.) Once there, Spears' greatest dilemma quickly became deciding where to play his new star. Then he finally figured it out — he would play him everywhere. And that's exactly what he did. Bronko would go on to play tackle, fullback, defensive end, offensive end, linebacker and he even passed the ball as a quarterback from time to time as well.

He was a massive man for his time, measuring six-feet-two and weighing in at 235 pounds. He had giant hands, donned a size-19 neck and could even run a 10.3 100-yard dash. He literally became the fullback no one could tackle and the tackle no runner could escape. As a sophomore, Bronko first got noticed by the national press when he forced and recovered a late-game fumble against a heavily favored Notre Dame team, which led to a game-tying Gopher touchdown. During his junior year, wearing a steel plate to protect a couple of broken vertebrae, he almost single-handedly defeated Wisconsin when, in addition to intercepting three passes and making numerous touchdown-saving tackles, he forced a fumble and ran it in for the game-winning score.

So talented was the powerful Nagurski that he would go on to earn All-America honors at three different positions. Sportswriters decided after his senior season in 1929 that he was the best fullback and tackle in the nation, making him the only player in college football history ever to be named a first-team consensus All-American at two different positions in the same season. Incredibly, he was even named as a defensive end on a few other All-America teams. Over his illustrious three year career in Gold Country, the Gophers lost a total of just four games, and none of them by more than two points.

In the fall of 1930, Bronko graduated and became THE "Monster of the Midway," literally, when he signed on with the NFL's Chicago Bears for the then-pricey, Depression-era sum of $5,000. The Bronk went on to reach superstar status in the Windy City, where he would lead the team to three NFL championships during his eight-year gridiron tenure.

It was also in Chicago where the bruising fullback's exploits soon took on legendary proportions. Papa Bear Halas, the team's owner, recalled a game against Washington at Wrigley Field, where Nagurski barreled up the middle, sent two linebackers flying in different directions, trampled two defensive backs, ran through the end-zone and bounced off the goalpost, finally bulldozing into the brick wall that bordered the dug-out used by the Chicago Cubs — even cracking it. "That last guy hit me awful hard...", the dazed Bronk would say upon reaching the sidelines.

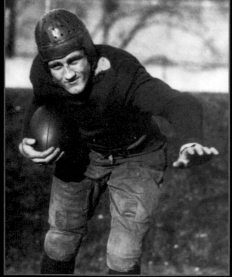

One tall tale had him falling out of bounds during a game once, and toppling a policeman's horse standing along the sideline. Another had the Bronk missing a wild tackle and shearing the fender off a Model-T Ford that was parked near the sidelines.

As a runner, Nagurski didn't bother with dazzle and finesse, and as a lineman he never bothered to learn great technique. Instead, he simply used his brute strength to overpower his opponents. In other words, he was about as subtle as a Mack Truck. When he ran, he simply tucked the ball under his arm, lowered his giant shoulders, and charged full speed ahead — ramming through anything in his way.

"I was OK, I guess," Bronko said years later. "I wasn't pretty, but I did all right. Our teams won most of the time, so that was good. I know I'd love to do it all over again. I never enjoyed anything as much as I did playing football. I felt like it was something I was born to do."

Bronko wasn't the only star running back on the team though, as future Hall of Famer Red Grange was also in the Bears' backfield as well. In fact, Bronko even took over in that same Bears backfield for another future Hall of Famer, former Duluth Eskimo great, Ernie Nevers.

"Halas stockpiled backs and he believed in spreading it around," Nagurski told Sports Illustrated in 1984. "Plus, he wanted to keep me fresh for defense, where I'd put in a full afternoon."

"I have said it a thousand times, Nagurski was the greatest player I ever saw, and I saw a lot of them in my lifetime," Red Grange would later say. "Running into him was like getting an electric shock. If you tried to tackle him anywhere above the ankles, you were liable to get killed."

Overall, Nagurski was a clutch player who did whatever it took to get his team a victory. He threw the winning touchdown pass in the 1932 playoff game against the Portsmouth Spartans, and that next season he led the Bears to another NFL championship when he tossed a pair of touchdown passes in Chicago's 23-21 victory over the New York Giants.

In 1937, Nagurski, still upset about his salary being decreased throughout the 1930s from $5,000 to $4,500 in 1931, and down to $3,700 by 1932, decided to retire, and pursue a career in pro wrestling. The Bronk had gotten into wrestling a few years earlier, but found it tough to juggle both careers. In one three-week stretch that year, he played in five Bears games and wrestled in eight cities: Portland. Vancouver, Seattle, Phoenix, L.A., Oakland, Salt Lake City and Philadelphia. Life in the ring was not as glamorous as he had hoped, but it was a living.

"I wrestled guys like Jim Londo and Strangler Lewis," said Bronko. "But they weren't in their prime then. I never liked wrestling. At that time, there wasn't a lot of money in it. And it was a sport where you worked every night and traveled a lot. I had a family at the time and didn't want to be away from home. But we were just getting out of the Depression in those days and we needed the money. The promoters told me I would make a million in no time. But it didn't happen."

Then, in 1943, because of player shortages caused by World War II, the Bears issued an S.O.S. to Nagurski to return for one final season. He agreed, and fittingly, at the age of 35, even scored the game-winning touchdown of the NFL title game against the Redskins. He hung em' up for good after that season though, finishing his amazing NFL career with 242 points scored on 4,301 yards rushing. The six-time All-Pro also averaged nearly five yards per carry, a remarkable feat.

"My greatest thrill in football was the day Bronko announced his retirement," said Green Bay Hall of Fame fullback Clarke Hinkle. "There's no question he was the most bruising fullback football has ever seen. I know, because I've still got the bruises!"

After wrestling professionally for more than a dozen years — a career he would later call "degrading," Nagurski returned to International Falls with his wife Eileen to raise their six children. (One of his boys, Bronko, Jr., played football at Notre Dame and later in the CFL.) There, quietly and unassumingly, he became the most famous gas station owner in America. (The running joke in the Falls was that once you went to Bronko's gas station, you were a customer for life... because he was the one who put the gas cap back on and nobody but the Bronk could possibly unscrew it again!) In the Falls he could finally live in peace and privacy, and enjoy the fruits of his labor. He loved the outdoors, and was an avid hunter and fisherman.

"We don't have summer," Bronko quipped, "just a season in the middle of the year when the sledding is poor."

He would later do some endorsements, including a couple of $50 deals for promoting Wheaties and Camel Cigarettes — which included a carton of smokes a week. "I bought Kools and gave the Camels away," he later said jokingly.

Sadly, on Jan. 7, 1990, Bronko died at the age of 81. His awards and honors are many and include being named as a charter member of both the Pro Football and College Football Halls of Fame, as well as being elected to the Football Writers Association of America's All-Time team. In 1995 that same group also voted to have his name attached to college football's Defensive Player of the Year award, called the "Nagurski Trophy."

In 1979 his No. 72 was retired by the U of M, and Sports Illustrated later named Bronko as Minnesota's Greatest Athlete of the 20th Century. In addition, in 1992, International Falls honored its most famous son by opening the "Bronko Nagurski Museum," the only museum in America dedicated to a single player. That same year the Gophers' practice facility was renamed as the Gibson-Nagurski Football Complex, after Bronk and his Gopher teammate, 1928 All-American guard George Gibson. Perhaps the biggest honor came years ago though, when his old high school renamed themselves as the International Falls "Broncos" in his honor.

Legendary Notre Dame Coach Knute Rockne called him "the only football player I ever saw who could have played every position," and George Halas said he was "the greatest fullback who ever lived. He was absolutely unstoppable."

Bronko was larger than life, and his size 22 NFL Championship ring, the biggest ever made, was proof. Perhaps no name has become more synonymous in the history of the sport than his. Nothing says leather helmets and high-top cleats louder than Bronko Nagurski. With his barrel chest and tree trunk legs, he became one of America's most colorful all-time characters and greatest sports heroes.

Perhaps Grantland Rice, once the most respected football authority in the nation, summed him up best when he was asked to select an all-time All-Star team.

"That's easy," said Rice. "I'd pick 11 Bronko Nagurski's. I honestly don't think it would be a contest. The 11 Nagurski's would mop-up. It would be something close to murder and massacre. For the Bronk could star at any position on the field — with 228 pounds of authority to back him up."

consin, 13-7, North Dakota University, 57-10, Oklahoma Aggies, 40-0, and Drake University, 27-6, to round out the season.

In 1928 Bronko single-handedly beat the top-ranked Wisconsin Badgers, terrorizing them up an down the field with ferocious hits and bone crunching running. He forced and recovered the fumble that set up his 6-0 game-winning touchdown, then saved the day by running down from behind Wisconsin's speedy Bo Cusinier, who was bound for the end-zone late in the game. Then, with time running out, Nagurski intercepted a Wisconsin pass to ice it for the Gophers. Needless to say, Nagurski played the entire game with his back in a metal brace to protect several broken ribs, and perhaps a broken vertebrae as well. More than 5,000 Gopher fans took trains to Madison to watch the big game and weren't disappointed to say the least.

Despite the brilliant efforts of All-Americans Nagurski, End Ken Haycraft and Guard George Gibson, a pair of third place conference finishes in both 1928 and 1929 were not enough to satisfy the Maroon and Gold faithful. (The Gophers lost only four games in those two seasons by a total of just five points.) As a result, the colorful Dr. Spears, after five respectable seasons in Minnesota, resigned to become the head coach at the University of Oregon. University President Lotus Coffman then shocked everyone by announcing that Herbert Orrin (Fritz) Crisler, an assistant to Amos Alonzo Stagg at the University of Chicago, would become the Gopher's new coach and athletics director. The selection was once again a controversial one, as the football faithful in Minnesota were unsure of a man who had no head coaching experience.

Crisler scored big points with the alumni, however, in naming his assistant coaches: Bert Baston, Sig Harris and Frank McCormick — all former Gophers. His first season would prove to be a trying one though, as he remained under the intense media pressure that went along with having the top sports coaching position in the Midwest. The players would have a hard time adjusting from Spears' military-like practices, compared to Crisler's quiet and subtle style — which included no profanity.

In 1930 Fritz had some promising rookies in Fullback Jack Manders and Tackle Marshall Wells, as well as some solid holdovers from the Spears era, including: All-American Guard Clarence (Biggie) Munn, Elmer (Bull) Apmann, Pete Somers, Allen (Tuck) Teeter, Lloyd (Snapper) Stein and Clint Riebeth. The team wasted little time in making a name for itself by spanking South Dakota State, 48-0, in its season opener. But, after a 33-7 loss to a very mediocre Vanderbilt squad, Fritz found himself in the proverbial hot-seat. To make matters worse, Pop Warner's top-ranked Stanford Indians were coming to town that next Saturday to battle his Gophers. Crisler remained calm though, and thanks to the efforts of All-American triple-threat Guard Biggie Munn, who punted, ran, and passed, Minnesota held the Indians to a scoreless tie in what was considered as one of the biggest upsets of the day. (Munn was named as the MVP of the Big Ten in 1931 as well.)

The Gophers squeezed out a 6-0 victory over Indiana that next week, but then lost, 27-6, to a great Northwestern team which had tied Michigan for the Conference title. The highlight of the Northwestern game was Kenny MacDougall's 51-yard touchdown run through the entire Wildcat defense. After smashing South Dakota, 59-0, the Gophers lost a heartbreaker to Michigan 7-6, only to drop a 14-0 decision

1934 National Champions - Front Row (l-r): Maurice Johnson, Bob Tenner, Phil Bengtson, Bill Bevan, Francis "Pug" Lund (Capt.), Dale Rennebohm, Vern Oech, Ed Widseth, John Roning. **Second Row (l-r):** Whit Rork, Art Clarkson, Milt Bruhn, Dick Smith, Stan Kostka, Bill Proffitt, Selmer Anderson. **Third Row (l-r):** Glenn Seidel, George Roscoe, Leslie Knudson, Bud Wilkinson, Jay Bevan, Bill Freimuth, Bud Smith, Frank Dallera, Ray Antil, Dick Potvin. **Back Row (l-r):** Julius Alfonse, George Svedsen, George Rennix, Babe LeVoir, Sheldon Beise, Bernie Bierman (Head Coach), Frank McCormick, Paul Berggren, Oscar Munson. **Missing:** Frank "Butch" Larson.

to Wisconsin in the final game of the season.

Minnesota closed out the 1931 season with a fifth place, 3-2 conference finish. Perhaps their biggest game of the year came against Ohio State, in what was considered to be the first ever post-season charity game. More than 40,000 fans showed up to watch Jack Manders score a pair of TDs as the Gophers beat the Buckeyes, 20-7, at the Brick House. Proceeds raised from the game then went to the families of thousands of needy unemployed men and women during the Great Depression.

The Arrival of the "Grey Eagle"

With the mediocre season, Crisler, after just two years at the helm, was replaced by one of Minnesota's most famous of prodigal sons, Litchfield's Bernie Bierman. (Crisler would later coach at Princeton and then at Michigan, where he became one of the conference's most successful all-time coaches.) Bierman, who had been the captain of the 1915 Gopher squad, had previously coached at the University of Montana, Mississippi A&M and Tulane. In fact, he had just led Tulane to a 21-12 loss to USC in the Rose Bowl only the year before. Bert Baston, the two-time All-America End, stayed on as an assistant with Bierman, as did former teammate George Hauser.

By 1932 the country was mired in the Depression and unemployment was running wild. It was during this troubled time, however, that the Gophers would emerge as "America's Team." Perhaps it was because people found a new sense of pride in following the Gophers as a form of cheap entertainment, but for whatever the reason they would undoubtedly emerge as the team of the decade.

A brilliant football tactician, Bierman was a strict disciplinarian and a perfectionist at his trade — so much so that his hair turned prematurely gray, thus earning him the nickname of the "Grey Eagle." Bernie demanded a lot out his troops that first season, immediately putting them on a conditioning program like they had never seen before. Bierman refused to allow his players to make stupid mental mistakes and ran them through months of grueling practice sessions to make sure that they got it right.

At the beginning of training camp, Tailback Myron Ubl suffered an injury. His replacement would be a small, speedy kid from Rice Lake, Wis., who, after four years in Dinkytown, would go down as one of the all-time greats — Francis "Pug" Lund. The Pug would play a big role in the team's success that season, as the Gophers opened the Bierman era with a 12-0 win over South Dakota. Minnesota then dropped a 7-0 decision to Purdue, only to rebound for a 7-6 victory over Nebraska on a touchdown by Jack Manders. Manders, who would go on to become one of the Chicago Bears' greatest all-time place kickers, also added the extra point.

Lund and Manders tore it up that season. In a 21-6 win over Iowa, Lund hit Brad Robinson for a pair of touchdowns, and in a 7-0 victory over Northwestern Lund connected with Bob Tenner for the game-winner. Then, along with Pug's 233 yards rushing, Manders scored three touchdowns in a 26-0 victory over Mississippi. After losing to Wisconsin, 20-13, on a last-second play, followed by a 3-0 loss to Michigan, in a game played in below-zero temperatures, the Gophers finished their season with a respectable 5-3 record. That loss was significant for one reason and one reason only. It would be the last Gopher loss over the better part of the next four years.

Bierman came back with a renewed vigor in

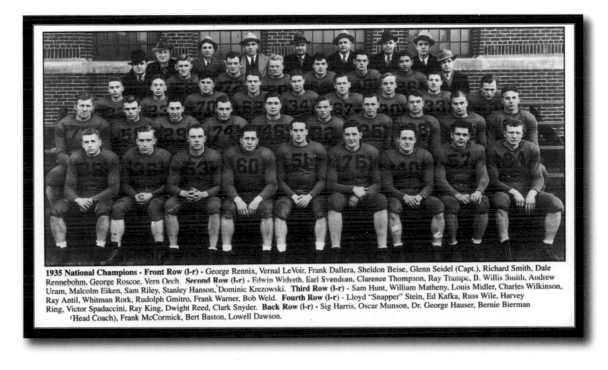

1935 National Champions - Front Row (l-r) - George Rennix, Vernal LeVoir, Frank Dallera, Sheldon Beise, Glenn Seidel (Capt.), Richard Smith, Dale Rennebohm, George Roscoe, Vern Oech. Second Row (l-r) - Edwin Widseth, Earl Svendsen, Clarence Thompson, Ray Trampe, D. Willis Smith, Andrew Uram, Malcolm Eiken, Sam Riley, Stanley Hanson, Dominic Krezowski. Third Row (l-r) - Sam Hunt, William Matheny, Louis Midler, Charles Wilkinson, Ray Antil, Whitman Rork, Rudolph Gmitro, Frank Warner, Bob Weld. Fourth Row (l-r) - Lloyd "Snapper" Stein, Ed Kafka, Russ Wile, Harvey Ring, Victor Spadaccini, Ray King, Dwight Reed, Clark Snyder. Back Row (l-r) - Sig Harris, Oscar Munson, Dr. George Hauser, Bernie Bierman (Head Coach), Frank McCormick, Bert Baston, Lowell Dawson.

GEORGE GIBSON

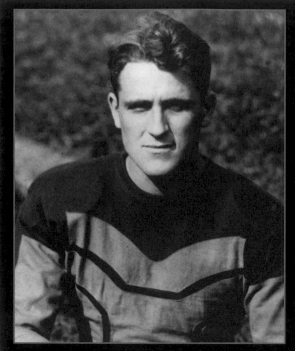

George Gibson was born in New York and raised in Medford, Okla. He came to the University of Minnesota in 1926 to play football and would emerge as a star guard with the Gophers, later becoming team captain in 1928. Back then it was the captain who, along with the quarterback, called the plays. On offense Gibson played running guard on the single wing and would ultimately earn All-American honors alongside Bronko Nagurski — who was also his best friend and roommate.

"It meant nearly everything to me to be a Gopher," said Gibson. "It was such a thrill to play for such a great program and it was something I will never forget. To play with Bronko Nagurski was also a thrill. We were roommates one year and boy was he one whale of a player. He was so modest and really such a decent person. The Gophers were a fine ball club back then and it was a real privilege to play for them. I have since donated some money to their program to build the Gibson/Nagurski indoor practice facility and that meant a lot to me to be able to do that. I love the Gophers."

George graduated in 1929 with an degree in geology. But he wasn't done with football just quite yet. After graduation, he accepted a job as the player/coach with the Minneapolis Red Jackets, one of Minnesota's first NFL teams. Gibson received a total salary of $3,900 as player-coach of the Red Jackets, which was big money back in the day. Times were tough because of the Great Depression, however, and the team went broke after just a season and a half. When the club folded, the Red Jackets actually combined forces with the Frankford Yellow Jackets, the professional team in suburban Philadelphia, for the remainder of the 1931 season. Gibson would serve as their player-coach as well.

In 1934 George moved back to Minnesota, where he earned his doctorate in geology at the U of M. From there, he went on to teach geology and coach football at Carleton College until 1938. One of the highlights of his Carleton coaching career came in 1936 when his boys barely lost to a tough Iowa team which they had held scoreless through three quarters. Gibson would stay for just five years in Northfield, but did manage to lead his team to an undefeated co-championship of the Midwest Conference in 1936.

In the late 1930s Gibson went to work for the Socony Vacuum Oil Company, looking for oil in the Egyptian desert. George recalled that one evening when he was out in the desert "about 100 miles from nowhere," he turned on his short-wave radio and much to his surprise, he picked up the Nebraska-Minnesota football game. To make it even better, the voice he heard broadcasting the game was that of his older brother William, who had become the editor of the U of M Alumni Weekly newspaper and also served as a football analyst on the side.

By 1940 World War II was heating up and all Americans were ordered out of the Egypt. During his last days in Cairo, George witnessed daily air raids from his hotel window. He knew it was time to go. His trip home took two months though. Because of the war in Europe, he had to go the long way home by train, plane, and ship via Jerusalem, the Persian Gulf, Bombay, Capetown and Trinidad. That entire time, his wife, who had already returned home with their two sons, had no idea where he was. When he finally got home Gibson decided to move to Midland, Tex., where geologists were needed to map the Permian Basin and find oil for the war effort. Nearly a dozen years later he became an independent geological consultant, and made a fortune.

George went on to become one of the most respected and successful geologists in the world. He has also given back to the University of Minnesota in a huge way. His generosity was most evident in 1985, when the $5.5 million "Gibson-Nagurski Football Complex" was opened adjacent to the Bierman Field Athletic Building in his honor. Dedicated to education and football, the facility set the standard to which many others around the nation were compared. Then, in 2000, another $5 million facelift of the building was completed, all thanks to George. He also gave a good sum of money to the Geology Department at the University as well.

"I still think back on my time in college," George recalled. "What I remember most is how well I was treated by both the athletic and geology departments. They went overboard to help me and push me along. Over the years, I've tried to repay that help by giving something back. That's why I endowed, with my late wife, the George and Orpha Gibson Chair in Hydrogeology, and have also supported men's athletics. I've never forgotten that my success started at the University of Minnesota."

Sadly, Gibson died in 2004 at the age of 98 in Midland, Texas. At the time of his death he was the oldest ever living NFL alumnus.

1933. His practices became more intense, he became more demanding, and he simply wouldn't tolerate ineptitude. If a player screwed up, the "Prussian General," as he became known, would simply say, "Take a lap around the field and make up your mind if you're going to do it right!" He even ended each practice by lining up the offense on the 20-yard line and have them run 15 perfect plays right down the field. If someone goofed during the drill on play No. 14, the whole team would start all over again from the 20. In addition, the last formality of the day meant having the entire team run laps around the field. As players passed Bierman, he would call out their names in the order with which they could hit the showers. If you practiced hard that day, your name got called early. If you messed up... you ran! It was an exhausting ritual that forced the players to try harder than ever to get it right.

The 1933 season was a pivotal one for the Gophers, as they definitely turned the corner into becoming one of football's greatest all-time dynasties. One of the first things that Bernie did that year was to change the color of the squad's uniforms to gold. That year the "Golden Gophers," as they were tabbed by local sports radio legend Halsey Hall, hit the gridiron with a new sense of purpose. (Incidentally, not

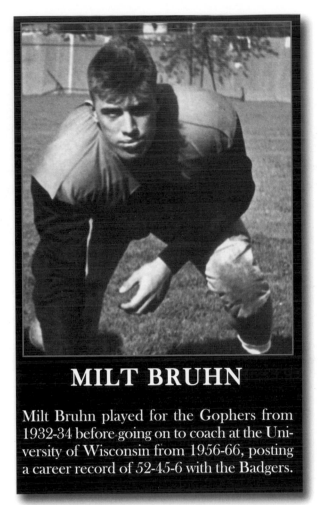

MILT BRUHN

Milt Bruhn played for the Gophers from 1932-34 before going on to coach at the University of Wisconsin from 1956-66, posting a career record of 52-45-6 with the Badgers.

only did Bierman change the uniforms to give the team a new sense of pride and identity, but also, for a bit of camouflage! "It was hard for teams to pick up the ball with our players wearing those mustard-colored uniforms," Bierman later quipped.)

The junior class of Lund, Milt Bruhn, Butch Larson and Phil Bengston was joined by a supporting cast of sophomores led by Fullback Sheldon Beise, Quarterback Glenn Seidel, Babe LeVoir and Dick Smith. In addition, George Svendsen and Bill Bevan returned home from Oregon, where they had gone to play for Doc Spears. Bierman also devised a new, revolutionary blocking strategy for his Gophers which entailed "hole" blocking. Rather than assigning his blockers to specific linemen, he assigned them to block in specific areas, or holes, where the play was going to be run, regardless of which defensemen were in their way. It was radical to say the least.

Led by Lund, who gained more yards than did all of his opposing teams' backfields that season, the team responded by putting together their first undefeated season since 1927 — four wins and four ties. Perhaps the biggest win was the 7-3 victory over eastern power Pittsburgh, thanks to a pair of Babe LeV-

1936 National Champions - Front Row (l-r) - Bruce Berryman, Frank Warner, Charles Wilkinson, Stanley Hanson, Earl Svendsen, Julius Alfonse (Co-captain), Ed Widseth (Co-captain), Clarence Thompson, Whitman Rork, Harvey Ring, Frank Darle. Second Row (l-r) - Ed Kafka, Dan Elmer, George Faust, Wilbur Moore, Allen Rork, Rudy Gmitro, Andy Uram, William Matheny, Sam Riley, Dale Hanson, Sam Hunt, Harold Washington. Third Row (l-r) - Louis Midler, Francis Twedell, Horace Bell, Victor Spadaccini, Marvin Levoir, Ray King, Charles Schultz, Robert Hoel, Lawrence Buhler, Robert Johnson, Robert Carlson, Warren Kilbourne. Back Row (l-r) - Robert Weld, Florian Klick, Oscar Munson, Lloyd Stein, Bert Baston, Sig Harris, Dr. George Hauser, John Kulbitski, Dwight Reed, Ray Bates, Bernie Bierman, Frank McCormick, Sheldon Beise, Dominic Krezowski, Ray Antil.

FRANCIS "PUG" LUND

Born and raised in Rice Lake, Wis., Francis "Pug" Lund headed west to the University of Minnesota in 1931, where he played football and ran track for the Gophers from 1932-34. On the gridiron, Lund was a two-time All-American in 1933 and 1934, earning Big Ten MVP honors those same years as well. The speedy halfback also served as the captain of the 1934 national championship team, averaging almost six yards per carry that season. Perhaps his most memorable game that season came against the University of Pittsburgh, when he took a lateral and then threw the game-winning touchdown pass to Robert Tenner late in the fourth quarter to give the Gophers a thrilling 13-7 win and their first undefeated national title. Tough as nails and never one to back down from an opponent, Lund rejected many offers to play pro football, and instead chose a career in the automotive insurance industry. Among his many honors, Lund was inducted into the College Football Hall of Fame in 1958.

oir interceptions and Bob Tenner's late TD. As for the biggest tie, that would be the 0-0 stalemate against undefeated Michigan, whereupon a Bill Bevan's game-winning field goal attempt fell short in the game's final moments. The final game of the season was a wild one as the Gophers, on Pug Lund's one yard TD plunge late, beat Wisconsin, 6-3, in a freezing, and windy blizzard at Memorial Stadium. The 4-0-4 Gophers finished in second place in the conference that year, with the cream of their young crop of talent ready to rise up and take over.

With team captain and Center Roy Oen as the only 1933 regular lost to graduation, the '34 Gophers — two-deep at literally every position — knew that they were on the verge of something special. "You men have it in you to be champions," said Bierman before the start of the 1934 season. So dedicated were the

players, that Pug Lund, after badly breaking his often-dislocated finger in training camp (from a prep pole-vaulting accident), even opted to have it amputated so that it wouldn't slow him down and hurt the team.

A couple of new additions were thrown into the mix that year as well. One was a bone-crushing fullback by the name of Stan Kostka, a large Polish kid from South St. Paul, who joined the Gophers after spending a year in Oregon. (Like a runaway tank, Kostka quickly became known as the "Hammer of the North.") The other was a big kid by the name of Ed Widseth, who had grown up in the tiny potato farming town of Gonvick, in Northwestern Minnesota. Widseth, whose family immigrated from Norway, was too busy helping out on the family potato farm to attend high school, so he never got around to enrolling until he was 19. When he finally graduated from

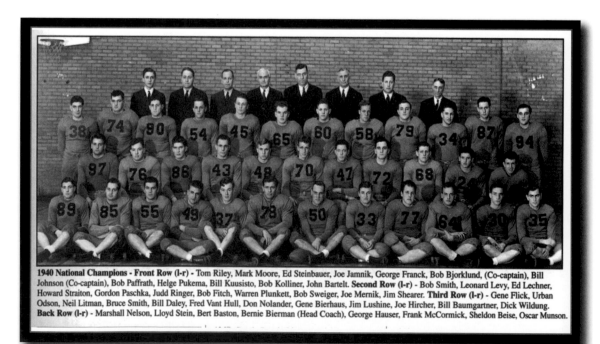

1940 National Champions - Front Row (l-r) - Tom Riley, Mark Moore, Ed Steinbauer, Joe Jamnik, George Franck, Bob Bjorklund, (Co-captain), Bill Johnson (Co-captain), Bob Paffrath, Helge Pukema, Bill Kuusisto, Bob Kolliner, John Bartelt. Second Row (l-r) - Bob Smith, Leonard Levy, Ed Lechner, Howard Straiton, Gordon Paschka, Judd Ringer, Bob Fitch, Warren Plunkett, Bob Sweiger, Joe Mernik, Jim Shearer. Third Row (l-r) - Gene Flick, Urban Odson, Neil Litman, Bruce Smith, Bill Daley, Fred Vant Hull, Don Nolander, Gene Bierhaus, Jim Lushine, Joe Hircher, Bill Baumgartner, Dick Wildung. Back Row (l-r) - Marshall Nelson, Lloyd Stein, Bert Baston, Bernie Bierman (Head Coach), George Hauser, Frank McCormick, Sheldon Beise, Oscar Munson.

Crookston High School, he made his way south to Minneapolis, where the future three-time All-American would go down as one of the greatest tackles in the history of college football.

North Dakota State was the team's first casualty, losing by the score of 56-12. Kostka was the story in this game, as he came in to spell Beise, and finished with four touchdowns. George Roscoe, backup to Pug Lund, also scored a pair of touchdowns, including a 76-yard punt return. Kostka didn't stop there though, scoring another pair that next week in a 20-0 romp over Nebraska. All-American Guard Bill Bevan also intercepted a pass and took it 28 yards for a touchdown in this one as well. (Just how tough was Bevan? He was the last known player in the Big Ten to play without a helmet!)

After that, Minnesota boarded the train for Pittsburgh, where their upcoming clash with the Panthers was billed as the undisputed "game of the year," with national championship implications riding on its outcome. Ever the psychologist, Bierman's true colors came out for all to see in this epic game. Knowing that Pittsburgh was unofficially considered as a "semi-pro" program back in those days, due to the speculation that its kids received some form of "compensation" for playing, Bierman figured that many of them weren't as dedicated to the game as his tired,

Dwight Reed

hungry and broke Gophers were. With that, he devised a game plan wherein he would simply punish the Panthers by giving them the ball over and over again, until they cracked under his team's enormous defensive pressure. By the start of the third quarter Pittsburgh was up 7-0 on Mike Nicksick's 64-yard touchdown run, while the Gophers hadn't even made a first down. In fact, they were punting the ball on third and even second downs just to tire out Pittsburgh's offense. Never fretting though, Bierman knew his gamble would pay off. Eventually, when his Gophers laid their blocks, they could hear their opponents across the line groan in pain.

Late in the third, Pug Lund, who was somehow playing with a severely injured thigh, punted his 13th ball of the game deep into Panther territory and into the arms of an awaiting receiver. It just so happened that at that exact moment Ed Widseth showed up to say hello, as he delivered one of the hardest hits in Gopher history on the poor, unsuspecting sap. The ball flew out and into the arms of another All-American End, Butch Larson. This time the Gophers, with great field position, marched into the end-zone behind a trick play from Lund, who faked an end-around, and instead pitched the ball to End Julie Alphonse on a naked reverse that turned into a 22-yard touchdown. Bill Bevan then converted to knot the score at seven points apiece.

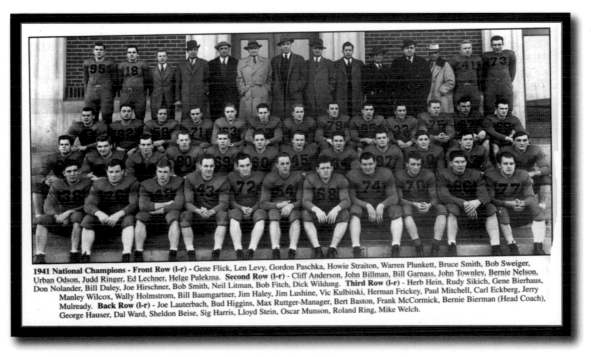

1941 National Champions - Front Row (l-r) - Gene Flick, Len Levy, Gordon Paschka, Howie Straiton, Warren Plunkett, Bruce Smith, Bob Sweiger, Urban Odson, Judd Ringer, Ed Lechner, Helge Pulekma. **Second Row (l-r)** - Cliff Anderson, John Billman, Bill Garnass, John Townley, Don Nolander, Bill Daley, Joe Hirschner, Bob Smith, Neil Litman, Bob Fitch, Dick Wildung. **Third Row (l-r)** - Herb Hein, Rudy Sikich, Gene Bierhaus, Manley Wilcox, Wally Holmstrom, Bill Baumgartner, Jim Haley, Jim Lushine, Vic Kulbitski, Herman Frickey, Paul Mitchell, Carl Eckberg, Jerry Mulready. **Back Row (l-r)** - Joe Lauterbach, Bud Higgins, Max Ruttger-Manager, Bert Baston, Frank McCormick, Bernie Bierman (Head Coach), George Hauser, Dal Ward, Sheldon Beise, Sig Harris, Lloyd Stein, Oscar Munson, Roland Ring, Mike Welch.

After more punishment by the Gophers defense, which had knocked just about all of the steam out of the Panthers offense, Minnesota got the ball back and headed downfield. Then, on fourth down, from the Pitt 17-yard line, Kostka took the snap and faked a run, only instead he handed off to Quarterback Glenn Seidel, who then pitched it to Lund around the right end. Pug then pulled up short and fired a bullet to Bob Tenner, who trotted into the end-zone from the 10. This classic variation of the famous "buck lateral" made it 13-7 in favor of the Gophers. Pittsburgh rallied late, but after being stopped four straight times by Bevin up the middle, this one was over. It would go down as a classic.

After rolling Iowa, 48-12, in a game which saw Kostka score three touchdowns and Julius Alfonse rush for two more, the Gophers then pounded Michigan, 34-0, thanks to touchdowns from five different players. Michigan, which was led by future U.S. President, Center Gerald Ford, was a team that required yet another tactical adjustment by Bierman, as his club went into half-time tied at 0-0. That's when the Grey Eagle went to the blackboard, as he did so often, and diagrammed out each adjustment that needed to made to counter the Wolverine defense. With that, the superbly conditioned Gophers, which held the

Francis Twedell

Wolverines to just 56 total yards of offense, cruised to the shut-out victory.

After blanking Indiana, 30-0 (The Hoosiers got a whopping zero yards of total offense on the day!), and rolling Chicago, 35-7, the Gophers wrapped up their undefeated season by white-washing a Wisconsin team coached by Dr. Clarence Spears, 34-0. Lund, the featured attraction in Bierman's single-wing attack, had now earned the label "Iron man of the Big Ten." He proudly ended his collegiate career in style by scoring a pair of touchdowns on the cheese-heads, including a 59-yarder up the gut. Dick Smith also scored on 25-yard tackle-eligible pass from George Roscoe, while Babe LeVoir and Whitman Rork each tallied against the Badgers as well.

(In making his annual All-American announcement, famed scribe Grantland Rice wrote of Lund: "As a ball carrier, passer, kicker, blocker and tackler, he has carried out a heavy assignment. He has been battered and broken up — teeth knocked out, finger amputated, thumb broken — but through all this blasting barrage, Lund has carried on." Later, in 1959, Sports Illustrated named Lund as a Silver Anniversary All-American.)

With that, for the first time in school history,

ORVILLE FREEMAN

Orville Freeman played football for the Gophers from 1937-39 and was a member of the 1937 and 1938 Big Ten title teams. From there, Freemen joined the United States Marines during World War II, where he served in the South Pacific and attained the rank of Major. Upon his return, Freeman earned his LL.B. degree from the University of Minnesota Law School in 1946 and then went onto a life of politics and business. In fact, he was elected Governor of Minnesota in 1954 and was re-elected in 1956 and 1958. He later was appointed to serve as the Secretary of Agriculture by President Kennedy and later by President Johnson. Freeman was also the founding chairman of the U.S. India Business Council and was also appointed as a member of the Board of Trustees of the Medeleev Chemical Institute in Moscow.

BILL BEVAN

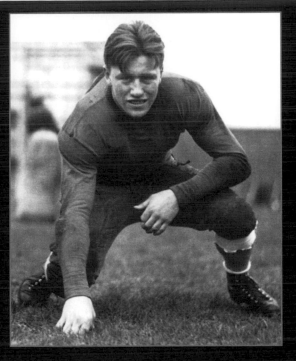

William "Arnold" Bevan came to Minnesota after attending the University of Oregon his freshman year and went on to star as a guard for the Gophers during the early 1930s. In fact, Bevan played a big role in leading the team to a pair of undefeated seasons in both 1933 and 1934, as well as the program's first National Championship in 1934. Bevan, who earned All-Conference honors both seasons, was also named as a consensus All-American in 1934. The 1934 team is considered by many to be one of the greatest collegiate football teams of all time. Bevan also kicked off and was one of the best drop kickers of his era as well. Despite being declared ineligible for the 1935 season because he played freshman football at Oregon, Bevan was elected as the alternate captain for the 1935 Gopher team that won the school's second national championship. So tough was Bevan, that he was one of the last major college football players in the nation to play without a helmet — and he had the scars to prove it. Not only was Bevan tough, he was also a proven winner. His undefeated streak in the Land of 10,000 Lakes started at St. Paul Central High School, went through his tenure with the Gophers, and finally ended as a senior when he played for the College All-Star team in 1935 and wound up losing to the NFL's Chicago Bears. In addition to excelling on the gridiron, Bevan was also a decorated boxer for the Gophers and even won a light-heavyweight boxing title in 1934 as well. Following his career at the U of M, Bevan went on to coach at Iowa State, Tulane, Dartmouth and Pittsburgh, before joining the U.S. Army, where he served as a lieutenant colonel from 1941-47. Although he became a successful businessman, Bevan continued to share his love of football as a volunteer coach at the Minnesota High School All-Star Game and also at Chisago City, Shattuck and Carleton College.

Minnesota was declared as national champions. They also captured their first conference title since 1915, as Lund, Larson and Bevan were all named as All-Americans. So awesome were the 1934 Gophers that they needed to pass just 36 times throughout the entire season, completing 15. Conversely, their defense allowed only 28 pass completions over the season, en route to intercepting 21. Oh yeah, the offense, which outscored its opponents that year 270-38, and averaged better than five touchdowns per game, also pounded out 300 yards of rushing each Saturday as well.

Bierman knew how to recruit in his own backyard and Minnesota was producing some serious talent back in the day. So deep were the Gophers at every position that no longer did they have to platoon each player to play both offense and defense for all 60 minutes — giving them a much needed rest to recharge their batteries between plays. (This revolutionary system of two offensive and defensive units, didn't catch on

John Mariucci

with the rest of the football world until the mid 1940s.) So good was the second team, that, in an attempt to get bumped up to the first team, they used to have bloody scrimmages after practice which often led to fist-fights.

"My job could be much simpler in selecting the 1934 Collier's All-America team," wrote Grantland Rice, "by naming the entire University of Minnesota eleven, one of the greatest, if not the greatest, football teams I ever saw." The team, which Rice dubbed the "Destroyers," had officially ushered in the most amazing period in Minnesota's gridiron history — the "Golden Era," which, over the next decade would bring the Gophers a total of five national championships and six Big Ten Conference titles.

Back to Back

The prospects for the 1935 season were rough, as the team found itself behind the eight-ball even before the team

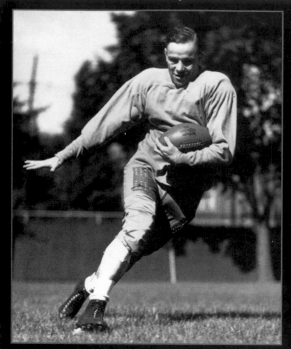

ANDY URAM

Andy Uram grew up in Minneapolis and went on to graduate from Marshall High School. From there, the speedy fullback came to the U of M and played on the 1935 and 1936 National Championship teams for the Gophers. Uram's biggest game in Gold Country came early in the 1936 season in a game against Nebraska. The game was scoreless until he took a lateral from Bud Wilkinson and scored the game-winner on a 76-yard punt return with just over a minute to play. Minnesota won, 7-0, en route to a 7-1 season and a national title. Uram would earn All-Big Ten and All-American honors in 1937 before going on to play six seasons in the NFL for the Green Bay Packers. He played for the Packers from 1938 to 1943 and was inducted into the team's Hall of Fame in 1973. Among his many claims-to-fames, Uram shared an NFL record for the longest touchdown run (97 yards against the Chicago Cardinals in 1939), until Dallas Cowboys Hall of Famer Tony Dorsett broke it with a 99-yard run against the Minnesota Vikings in 1982.

played its first down. Fully 11 lettermen were not to be seen when Fall practice got under way. While seven players had completed their three years of eligibility (Pug Lund, Butch Larson and Bill Bevan, along with Bob Tenner, Phil Bengston, John Ronning and Maurice Johnson), three more lost their eligibility due to a Big Ten transfer rule. The players, George Svendsen, Stan Kostka and Art Carleson, were all ruled ineligible that season by the conference eligibility board for playing a year of freshman football at Oregon before transferring to Minnesota. The 11th player was Halfback Julie Alphonse, who failed to make the team due to scholastic difficulties.

The revamped line, which featured Ray King and Dwight Reed at Ends, Dick Smith and Ed Wid-seth at Tackles, Vern Oech and Shattuck's Bud Wilkinson at Guards and Dale Rennebohm at Center, never missed a beat though, as the Gophers ventured out to repeat as national champions. After beating North Dakota State, 26-6, with Halfback George Roscoe tossing a pair of TDs to both Ray King and Dwight Reed, the Gophers headed to Lincoln to do battle with the Cornhuskers. There, in the sizzling heat, the Gophers played in what would become one of the classics. George Roscoe quieted the capacity crowd of 37,000 screaming Husker fans by taking the opening kickoff 74-yards deep into Nebraska territory. Sheldon Beise and Roscoe then pounded it down to the three-yard line, only to see the Nebraska line thwart off three touchdown plunges. Then, on fourth

RICHARD SMITH

Richard Smith starred as a tackle for the Golden Gophers from 1933-35, and played a big role in the team winning a pair of national championships in 1934 and 1935. Smith earned All-American and All-Big Ten honors in 1935 and then went on to play in both the College All-Star game as well as the East-West Shrine game. Smith was later drafted in the seventh round by the NFL's Chicago Bears.

LARRY BUHLER

From 1936-38, Larry Buhler did it all on the Gopher gridiron. The rugged fullback from Windom, Minn., was the team's leading scorer, a top backfield defender and even a part-time punter. As a rusher, he would post a gaudy 4.8 career rushing average under the tutelage of legendary Gopher coach Bernie Bierman. As a sophomore in 1936, Buhler led the team in rushing and average yards per carry, with 6.66, as the team won its third straight NCAA National Championship that season. As a senior, Buhler earned Honorable Mention All-America honors, was voted the Chicago Tribune Gopher MVP and was even named as the team's MVP. In addition, he placed third in the Big Ten MVP voting and was also selected to play in the prestigious East-West Shrine game. Incredibly, Buhler would finish second in the All-Big Ten voting for three straight seasons to Wisconsin's Howard Weiss, a unanimous All-American. During the "golden era" of 1932-41, Buhler was the program's fourth-leading career rusher, behind only Pug Lund, Bruce Smith and Harold Van Every. He also ranked in the top 10 in career total points as well as 100-yard rushing games during that time as well. From there, he

would go on to become just the second Gopher ever to be chosen in the first-round of the NFL Draft, when the Green Bay Packers selected him with the ninth overall pick in 1939. He would play for three years in the NFL before retiring to Windom as a hometown hero. A statue of him in his 1938 MVP uniform now sits in front of the southern Minnesota town's courthouse lawn.

down, Seidel lateralled to Beise, who faked a dive into the line and instead lateralled it back to Seidel. Seidel then pitched it over to Roscoe, who ran it in around the right end to score. Bud Wilkinson failed to convert, but the Gophers were up 6-0.

Nebraska's defense hung tough in this one, preventing Minnesota on several occasions deep in their own end. The Huskers took the lead on a second quarter 33-yard Jerry LaNoue touchdown run, only to see the Gophers rally behind Roscoe's punt that pinned Nebraska inside their own five-yard line.

Then, after holding their offense in check, the Gophers forced a poor punt and got the ball back on the 15-yard line. From there, LeVoir and Roscoe drove it down to the five, as Roscoe, who ran for 128 yards that day, took it in for his second score of the afternoon in what would turn out to be the game winner. Wilkinson again failed to convert, but this Gopher defense hung on, despite a desperate rally in the fourth quarter which included a fumbled punt recovery on the Gopher one-yard line. That's when future All-American End Ray King zoned in like a missile and

BUTCH NASH

Butch Nash came to the U of M via Edison High School in Minneapolis and played basketball and football for the Gophers from 1936-38. Nash was a forward on the hardwood and then lined up as a defensive end opposite hockey legend John Mariucci on the gridiron. There, he helped lead the Gophers to a National Championship in 1936. After graduating Butch got into teaching and coaching. Then, after serving in WWII, Nash was hired as a Gopher assistant by Bernie Bierman in 1947. The Edison High School grad would remain as an assistant in Gold Country for 37 years until finally hanging it up in 1984. He would stick around as a volunteer assistant, however, until 1991 — making him a fixture in the program. He was later honored by the Gopher football program with an award given annually to a student who is both competitive on the field and in the classroom. Over his illustrious career in Gold Country, Nash lived through the hiring of seven different head coaches and seemingly saw it all. From a national championship to a Rose Bowl to iron-man football, Nash became synonymous with Gopher Football.

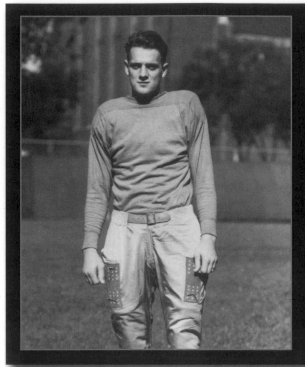

RAY KING

Ray King was a two-way offensive and defensive end for the Gophers from 1935-37. King, who also served as the team's punter, played a big role in leading the Gophers to three straight Big Ten Championships as well as two National Championships in 1935 and 1936. The captain of the 1937 team, King earned All-Big Ten and All-American honors that same season. In addition, King was also a three year starter as an outfielder and pitcher on the Gopher baseball team from 1936-38. King posted a career batting average of over .300 and helped guide the Maroon and Gold to a pair of Big Ten Championships on the diamond as well.

blitzed Husker Halfback Lloyd Cardwell for a loss, even knocking him out cold. Finally, on the fourth down, Dale Rennebohm batted the ball away from Husker Receiver Gus Scherer on a sure touchdown to ice the game.

The victory over Nebraska was short-lived though, as the Gophers received another jolt just that next week when Quarterback Glenn Seidel suffered a season-ending broken collarbone on a late touchdown saving tackle, in a 20-0 win over Tulane. Tuffy Thompson and Sheldon Beise each tallied in the game, while Bud Wilkinson gave Minnesota its other touchdown by blocking a punt and then scooping it up and trotting 35 yards into the end-zone. Bierman

revamped his backfield for the upcoming game against Northwestern by moving Babe LeVoir to Quarterback, George Roscoe to Left Half from Right Half, while George Rennix was put in at Right Halfback. Roscoe, like his predecessor, Pug Lund, was playing a mean left half — the key position in Bierman's single-wing attack.

Minnesota then went on to defeat Northwestern, 21-13, behind Thompson's two touchdowns, and Purdue, 29-7, thanks to touchdowns from Thompson, King and Roscoe. Minnesota, now feeling the week-in and week-out pressure of having every team bring their A-Games in an attempt to knock-off the defending national champs, then ventured south to Iowa

SHELDON BEISE

Mound, Minn., native Sheldon Beise came to the University of Minnesota in 1932 and went on to become one of the best blocking fullbacks of his era. "Shelly," as he was affectionately known, did a lot of the dirty work for All-American halfback Pug Lund, sacrificing his body to open holes for him to score touchdowns. As modest as he was tough, Beise's leadership helped guide the Gophers to three consecutive undefeated seasons and a pair of NCAA National Championships in 1934 and 1935. Behind Beise, the Gopher rushing attack averaged 295 yards and 33.7 points per game in 1934. The three-time All-Conference fullback scored nine touchdowns in 1935, earning first team All-American honors in the process. In addition, Beise was selected to every All-Midwest and All-Conference Team. After graduating, Beise was selected to play in the 1936 College All-Star Game and East-West Shrine Game. In 1935, he was even chosen to have his picture appear on the Wheaties box. From there, Beise went into coaching, first at Holy Cross and later at the College of St. Thomas in St. Paul. He also worked three separate stints as an assistant coach with the Gophers as well.

BUD WILKINSON

Bud Wilkinson grew up in Minneapolis but went on to graduate from the Shattuck Military School in Faribault. There, he quickly emerged as a brilliant student-athlete both on the gridiron, as a quarterback & guard, and on the ice, as a hockey goaltender. So good was Wilkinson as a goalie, that in 1932, he led Shattuck to an undefeated record and in the process, he went unscored upon over the entire season. He graduated in 1933 Cum Laude with the rank of First Lieutenant, and headed north, to the U of M, where he would emerge once again as one of his school's all-time greats.

Wilkinson distinguished himself in football and hockey in Gold Country, even finding time to also letter in golf. As a guard on the 1934 and '35 undefeated national championship teams, he was termed by the famous writer Grantland Rice as "The best offensive guard in college football." Due to injuries, Bernie Bierman asked Wilkinson if he would switch from guard to quarterback that next year. He did, and in 1936, Bud directed Minnesota to their third straight undefeated national championship. When it was all said and done, Wilkinson had done it all. Not only was he an All-American goalie on the Gopher Hockey team, but he had also garnered back-to-back All-American honors on the gridiron. In addition, he also won the school's highest honor for scholastics and sports — the Big Ten Medal of Honor.

"To be a Gopher meant a great deal to me," said Wilkinson. "I grew up wanting to be a Gopher, so when it happened it was quite a marvelous experience. Athletics taught me a lot about life and about how to be a good leader. I will always look back at my days in Minnesota fondly."

Following graduation, Wilkinson played in the college All-Star game, quarterbacking the collegiates to a 7-0 victory over the Green Bay Packers, the first time in history the All-Stars had beaten the pros. He also played on the Galloping Gophers, an all-star basketball team that traveled around the Midwest playing independent teams, including the Harlem Globetrotters — whom they defeated. From there, Wilkinson went on to Syracuse University, where, in addition to serving as an assistant football coach under Ossie Solem, he earned his Masters Degree in English. He then briefly returned to Minnesota as an assistant to Bernie Bierman before being commissioned in the US Navy.

After the war, Wilkinson was considered for the Gopher coaching job, but he turned it down and instead went to the University of Oklahoma, where he would become the team's head coach in 1947. At OU Wilkinson would forever change the game, and in the process become one of college football's greatest ever coaches. After tying for the 1947 championship, the Sooners won 12 straight conference crowns. Additionally, in between 1953 and 1957, his teams won 47 consecutive games over five straight undefeated seasons — an all-time national record. His teams also appeared in eight Sugar & Orange Bowl games, and he was named as the Coach of the Year on numerous occasions as well. His record at OU was an astounding 145-29-4, with three national titles to boot. At the time of his retirement, in 1963, Bud had become the winningest coach in college football.

Wilkinson was also an innovator. He is credited for creating the "swinging gate" formation and a 1950s version of the "no-huddle" offense which he called the "go-go offense." He also didn't believe in red-shirting but still managed to graduate an incredible 90% of his student-athletes. Although his national coaching honors and accolades are too many to mention, among his major ones include being inducted into the College Football and National Football Coaches Hall of Fames; being elected president of the American Football Coaches Association; and receiving the Sports Illustrated Silver Anniversary All-American Award in 1962.

After retiring, Wilkinson even ran for senate in 1964, where, despite winning the Republican primary, he lost in the general election. Then, after a career in TV broadcasting, among other business interests, Wilkinson later coached in the NFL with the St. Louis Cardinals in 1978 and 1979. He hung em' up after just two sub-par seasons though (9-20), and returned to the TV booth, where he served as an analyst for both ESPN and ABC.

In addition to later becoming OU's Athletic Director, Wilkinson led quite a celebrated life after football. He was a consultant to President Nixon and a member of the White House Staff from 1969-71. He was also a special consultant to President Kennedy on physical fitness from 1961-64, and he later served as the Republican National Committeeman for Oklahoma during the late 1960s.

Sadly, Wilkinson died in 1994 at the of 77 after battling heart problems. He will always be regarded as one of Minnesota's greatest all-time athletes, coaches and humanitarians. He is arguably America's greatest ever college football coach.

ED WIDSETH

Ed Widseth grew up on a dairy farm in the sleepy northwestern Minnesota town of Gonvick, just outside of Crookston. Despite having very little prep football experience, he came to the University of Minnesota and quickly emerged as a star tackle. He became the anchor of an amazing defensive line that led the Gophers to three national championships from 1934 through 1936, of which he was twice named as an All-American. The captain and MVP of the 1936 team, Widseth took great pride in the fact that his teams went an amazing 24-1 during his tenure in Gold Country. In addition, Widseth also won two baseball letters as a first baseman and pitcher for the Gophers. After playing in the 1937 College All-Star game, the fearsome tackler went on to play five seasons with the NFL's New York Giants, winning All-Pro honors three of those years. In 1953 he was inducted into the College Football Hall of Fame, and he was the only Minnesota player named to the National Football Foundation's 11-man All-America squad for the 25 seasons from 1924 through 1948. After his gridiron career ended in 1941, Widseth spent some time as a recreational specialist in the military. Upon returning home, he became head football coach at St. Thomas University, where he coached the Tommies to a pair of MIAC Conference titles before entering the wholesale food business in Minneapolis.

City, where they took on a very talented Hawkeye squad. Now, Iowa's fans were still upset about their loss from the year before, when they felt that Sheldon Beise deliberately knocked their star Halfback, Ozzie Simmons, out of the game with a cheap-shot. This, of course, was false, as many speculated that the Oz was just acting — but it led to some good drama nonetheless. Amidst the hostility, Iowa's Governor Clyde Herring added fuel to the fire when he made a statement to the Associated Press that went out to newspapers throughout the country the day before the game. His quote said in effect, that if any Gophers tried to injure Simmons, or any other Hawkeye player this year, that Iowa's spectators at the game would act accordingly.

This statement shocked Coach Bierman, as well as the hoards of Minnesotans who made the trek to Iowa to watch the game. Fearing a mob would break out, Minnesota's Governor, Floyd Olson, stepped in. While many were demanding that he rush National Guardsmen to Iowa City to protect our boys, cooler heads prevailed. In a diplomatic attempt to ease the pre-game tension that had turned into a border war, Governor Olson sent Governor Herring a

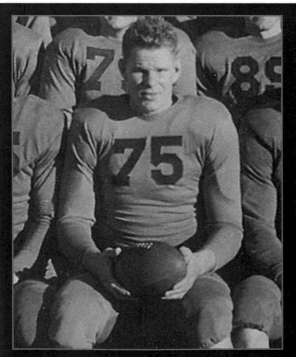

PAUL MITCHELL

Paul Mitchell grew up in Minneapolis and went on to graduate from Edison High School. From there, Mitchell came to Minnesota and starred as an All-Big Ten tackle on the Gopher's 1941 National championship team. In 1943, he was voted as the team captain and was also named as the team MVP. He earned All-American honors that same year and for his efforts was invited to play in the East-West All-Star Game. After a stint in the service, Mitchell then turned pro. Originally drafted by the NFL's Chicago Cardinals, Mitchell played pro ball from 1946-51, first with the Los Angeles Dons and New York Yankees of the AAFC, and then with the NFL's New York Yanks.

BABE LEVOIR

Vernal "Babe" LeVoir was born in the Iron Range town of Bovey, Minn., but graduated from Minneapolis Marshall High School in 1932 with 16 varsity letters. LeVoir played halfback and quarterback with the Gophers under coach Bernie Bierman in the undefeated glory years of 1933, 1934 and 1935 on teams that compiled a 20-1-4 record and won three consecutive Big Ten titles and two national championships. LeVoir was named to the 1935 All-Big Ten first team after quarterbacking the Gophers to an 8-0 record and a national championship that year. The team MVP went on to play in the 1936 College All Star Game and was later drafted in 1936 by the NFL's Brooklyn Dodgers.

telegram that read: "I will bet you a Minnesota prize hog against an Iowa prize hog that Minnesota wins." Herring enthusiastically accepted, and thus was born the "Floyd of Rosedale" traveling trophy. The Gophers, who went on to beat the Hawkeyes on a pair of Beise and Thompson touchdowns, then became the proud owners of an award-winning prized porker which was donated by the owner of Rosedale Farms, near Fort Dodge, Iowa. (The hog, who was actually the brother of the celebrity swine from the Will Rogers movie "State Fair," was then named after our beloved Governor, Floyd!) Some years later, after Floyd (the pig) passed on to hog-heaven, a St. Paul artist named Charles Brioschi was commissioned to create a bronze statue of the pig. Today, the last Saturday of every college football season means that the winning team will be able to bring Floyd home with them for one year of bragging rights.

Minnesota then handed Michigan their most lop-sided defeat in team history, crushing the Wolverines, 40-0, in Ann Arbor. Andy Uram and little Rudy Gmitro ran wild in this one, tallying three touchdowns on an amazing 460 yards of offense, while Biese and Thompson, who returned a kick-off for an 85-yard TD, also tallied in this blowout as well. The Gophers then finished the season undefeated and ran their

SONNY FRANCK

George "Sonny" Franck played halfback for the Gophers from 1938-41, earning All-Big Ten and All-American honors in 1940. Franck teamed up with fellow Hall of Famer Bruce Smith to become one of the greatest halfback duos in college football history that year. Frank, who was a key contributor on the Gopher team that went undefeated and won the Big Ten title as well as the national championship that year, finished third in the Heisman Trophy voting that year. Playing in the days of single-wing, one-platoon football, Franck was a multi-talented player who ran, passed, caught passes, kicked, returned kicks and played defense. Franck even called the signals for coach Bernie Bierman. The Davenport, Iowa, native who also lettered three times in track and field as a sprinter, was named as the MVP of the College All-Star Game in 1941 to boot. From there, Franck was selected as the first pick (third overall), of the NFL's New York Giants. He wound up playing pro ball for four seasons, 1941, 1945-47, while serving time in the military as well. As a fighter pilot in World War II, he earned nine battle stars in the South Pacific. Franck later got into teaching and coaching at the high school level. He was later inducted into the College Football Hall of Fame in 2002.

BUTCH LEVY

Leonard "Butch" Levy grew up in Minneapolis and went on to star as a guard on the University of Minnesota's Golden Gopher Football team from 1939-41. There, Levy helped to lead the Gophers to a pair of NCAA National Championships in both 1940 and 1941. As an All-Conference lineman in 1941, Levy's undefeated Gophers outscored their opponents 186-38. From there, the six-foot, 260-pound behemoth went on to play in the College All Star Game. As a wrestler, Levy also won a national championship as a heavyweight in 1941, en route to earning All-American honors that same year as well. Levy was then selected in the fourth round (27th overall) of the 1942 NFL Draft by Cleveland. He did not play professional football until 1945, however, as he spent the next three years serving in the U.S. Navy during World War II. In 1945, Levy suited up for the Rams and helped anchor a tough offensive line which played a huge role in defeating the Washington Redskins in the NFL championship game. He remained with the Rams the following season when they moved to Los Angeles, finishing second in the NFL West. In 1947, Levy moved to the newly-formed All-American Football Conference and played for the Los Angeles Dons, earning All-AAFC first team honors that next year. He retired from professional football after that season though, and turned to professional wrestling, where he would become one of the most feared wrestlers in the 1950s, competing in Verne Gagne's American Wrestling Association.

string of victories to 17 straight by defeating Wisconsin, 33-7, before a capacity crowd at the Brick Yard. While Biese and Uram each scored, it was once again the 150-pound halfback, Rudy Gmitro, who was the hero, as he electrified the crowd by returning a kick-off 80 yards to pay-dirt. (Incidentally, in the win over Wisconsin, Minnesota scored what might have been the ultimate football play. The next morning's paper showed a photo of Biese's touchdown run, in which all 11 Badgers were on the ground at the same time after being pancaked by their Gopher blockers.)

With the win, Minnesota won its second consecutive Big Ten title and was again named as national champions. Dick Smith, Bud Wilkinson and Ed Widseth all earned unanimous All-American honors, while Sheldon Beise and Ray King were named to several mythical squads as well.

Three in a Row

With Washington and Texas being added to the Gophers' schedule, Minnesota had a serious task ahead

HAROLD VAN EVERY

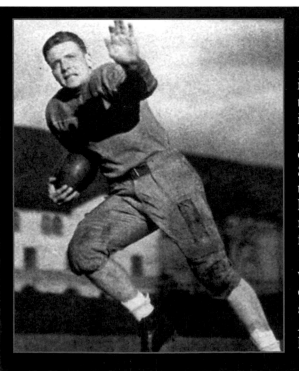

In 1937 Harold Van Every seemingly did it all for the Gophers, leading the team in passing, running, kick-off and punt returns, interceptions, and punt average. In 1939 Van Every led the nation in interceptions with eight, thus establishing a new school record for most interceptions in a season – a record that stands today. For his efforts, the outstanding two-way player later earned Sports Illustrated Silver Anniversary All-American honors. Van Every was injured in the 1938 season opener against Washington, but came back strong for his senior season. From there, the speedy halfback became the first round draft pick of the NFL's Green Bay Packers, where he played for two seasons. Among Van Every's many honors and accolades, in 1939 he won the prestigious Big Ten Scholastic Award. In 1941 he was drafted into the Army. He transferred into the air corps, however, and served as a bomber pilot. During World War II he was shot down over Germany, captured and imprisoned in a POW camp. After the war, he was forced to retire from football because of his health. He was the epitome of scholar-athlete and veteran.

BUTCH LARSON

Duluth, Minn., native Frank "Butch" Larson was one of college football's first truly dominant players. The feisty defensive end became only the fourth player in Gopher history to earn All-American honors in back-to-back seasons, 1933 & 1934. A tireless worker and extremely hard hitter, Larson was a tight end on the offensive side of the ball as well. In addition, he covered punts and was fearless as a special teamer who was never afraid to sacrifice his body for the greater good of the team. Behind Larson's leadership, the Gophers garnered back-to-back undefeated seasons in 1933 and 1934, winning their first national championship in 1934. Larson, who served as the 1934 team captain, then went on to play in the 1935 College All-Star Game and East-West Shrine Game, even winding up with his picture on the Wheaties box. After graduating, Larson coached at Duluth Central High School before serving in the U.S. Military, where he received nine battle stars. Upon his return, Larson guided Duluth Junior College (now UM-Duluth) to the National Junior Rose Bowl. In 1950, Larson turned pro and coached the Canadian Football League's Winnipeg Blue Bombers to the 1950 Grey Cup. He came home shortly thereafter, however, and took over as the coach at International Falls High School, where, over the next 22 seasons, he produced nine conference champions and a state championship team in 1954. Among his many honors and accolades, Larson was inducted into the Minnesota Coaches Hall of Fame in 1977 and has also been recognized as one of Duluth's Top 10 Athletes of the 20th Century.

of them in 1936. With Roscoe, Beise and LeVoir gone to graduation, Bierman once again rebuilt his backfield with a little creativity. This time, he took All-American Guard Bud Wilkinson and moved him to Quarterback, where he could guide Julie Alphonse (who had now regained his scholastic eligibility), Uram, Vic Spadacinni and Gmitro in his backfield. The backfield was also bolstered by a couple of impact sophomores in Larry Buhler and Wilbur Moore.

The season started off on a wild and crazy adventure and almost didn't even make it off the ground.

You see, on their way to the University of Washington for their season opener, the Gophers, who were spending the night in Missoula, Montana, woke up to find that their hotel was on fire. While the Gophers luckily escaped without incident, the players were forced to return to their train where they spent the remainder of the evening. Perhaps inspired by their near-death experience, Minnesota rallied in the fourth to beat the Huskies, 14-7, thanks to a pair of touchdown passes from both Alfonse to Wilkinson and the other from Uram to Ray King. Alfonse also inter-

DICK WILDUNG

Dick Wildung was a three-year starter at right tackle for Minnesota from 1940-42, and was an anchor on back-to-back national championship teams in both 1940 and 1941. Wildung earned All-American honors in both of those seasons and was named as the team's captain and MVP in 1942. Upon graduating, the Luverne, Minn., native played in the East-West Shrine and College All-Star Games. From there, Wildung served as a Navy lieutenant in World War II. When he got home he made his way back to the gridiron, however, by suiting up for the Green Bay Packers from 1946-1951 and 1953. There, he served as the Packers' captain for four years. He was later inducted into the Packer Hall of Fame in 1973. When his football days were over he moved back to southwestern Minnesota, where he ran a hardware store in Redwood Falls. Referred to by Coach Bernie Bierman as "the best tackle ever," Wildung was inducted into the College Football Hall of Fame in 1957.

cepted three passes in the victory as well.

The Gophers then narrowly beat a veteran Nebraska team, 7-0, when Wilkinson caught a short Husker punt and then pitched it to Uram, who bolted down the sideline for a dramatic 78-yard game-winning touchdown with less than a minute to go. After that, Minnesota rolled over Michigan, 26-0, and blanked Purdue, 33-0, as the team ran its unbeaten streak to 28 games and counting. Next up was Northwestern, in Evanston, where the Gophers rolled up 243 yards to the Wildcats' 120, but still wound up on the losing end of a 6-0 wet and windy grudge-match. The Cats, who won the game on a late fourth quarter touchdown plunge from Running Back Steve Toth, wound up on the receiving end of a very controversial 15-yard roughing penalty by Ed Widseth, that put the ball on the one-yard line. Northwestern then held off three frantic Minnesota drives that all ended inside their 20-yard line, to preserve what was considered at the time to be one of the biggest upsets in college football history. After the game Widseth insisted that he had not deserved the penalty, and Coach Bierman, after studying the game films, agreed. To put the game into perspective, the A.P. stated that the biggest shock in the world of sports that year was Max Schmeling's knock-out of Joe

Urban Odson

Louis. No. 2 was Northwestern's upset of the Gophers.

Determined to come back, the Gophers rallied that next week to squash Iowa, 52-0, before closing out the season with wins over Texas, 47-19, and Wisconsin, 24-0. Now, with the team's strong finish, coupled with Northwestern's 26-0 drubbing by Notre Dame, the Associated Press voted that the Gophers were indeed once again the best in the land. So, despite their controversial loss to the Big Ten champion Wildcats, the Gophers, who were rewarded for playing a tough non-conference schedule, had made the improbable national championship three-peat a reality. (Even today, no team has won three consecutive national titles since the Gophers from 1934-36!) Leading the post-season award barrage that year was Ed Widseth, who for the third time in his collegiate career, was named as a unanimous All-American. Joining him on other All-American squads were Bud Wilkinson, Andy Uram, Ray King and Julius Alfonse. Notably absent from the list was George Roscoe, who was one of the best natural athletes Minnesota ever produced.

Minnesota finished undefeated in the Big Ten in 1937, but losing non-conference games to Nebraska and Notre Dame eliminated them from making it four

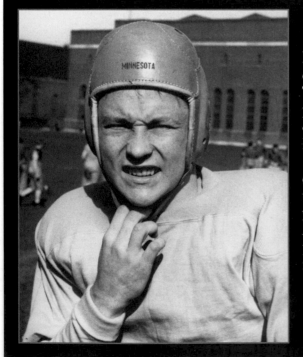

BILL DALEY

Running back Bill Daley holds the distinction of earning All-American honors at two different schools. Daley, who was a two-time All-Big Ten honoree in 1941 and 1942, was also a member of the 1940 Gopher National Championship team. Daley earned All-American honors in 1942 and then had to fulfill his military obligation with the Marine Corps. So, Daley reported to Ann Arbor, Mich., after the 1942 season to attend an officer's training school located there. Daley decided to play for the Wolverines as long as he was there and wound up as the nation's fourth-best rusher in 1943, averaging nearly seven yards per play. For his efforts, he was named as a back-to-back All-American at two different universities. Incidentally, Daley is the only player to ever win the Little Brown Jug while playing for both Minnesota and Michigan.

national championships in a row. Led by a couple of sophomore running backs, in Marty Christiansen and Harold Van Every, the Gophers came out with a season opening 69-7 mauling of North Dakota State. Van Every led the team with 147 yards, including a dramatic 76-yard touchdown run.

Minnesota then only got nine points against Nebraska, those coming on a touchdown pass from Uram to Spadacinni, and a field goal by Horace Bell, as the Cornhuskers scored a pair of touchdowns on key fumble recoveries and came from behind to win, 14-9. From there, the Gophers beat Indiana, 6-0, on Wilbur Moore's TD, and then creamed Michigan, 39-6, for Bierman's fourth straight Little Brown Jug. In that game Gmitro scored twice and Van Every hit

Spadacinni for the clincher. The downside to that game was that Andy Uram broke his arm and was done for the season. To add insult to injury, the team then lost a 7-6 heart-breaker to Notre Dame. They rallied for a second quarter touchdown on a buck lateral pass that went from Christiansen to Gmitro to Van Every, who then hit All-American Ray King, only to see kicker George Faust's try for the tying point get blocked. It was a crushing defeat.

After rolling over Iowa, 35-10, Minnesota eked out a bitterly contested match against Northwestern, 7-0, on a touchdown pass from Van Every to King. Wisconsin was then beaten, 13-6, on touchdowns from Bill Matheny and Marty Christiansen, to end the season as Big Ten champs.

BRUCE SMITH

Perhaps famed Minnesota author F. Scott Fitzgerald was thinking of Bruce Smith when once wrote the famous line: "Show me a hero and I will show you a tragedy." Smith grew up in Faribault, Minn., and like his father, Lucius, had done back in 1911, went on to stardom as a halfback at the U of M from 1939-41.

Three times in 1940 alone he scored game-winning touchdowns, including his now legendary 80-yard weak-side reverse through the mud and rain to beat Michigan, 7-6, which made him a virtual household name. Against Iowa in 1941, an injured Smith, after begging to come in late in the game, incredibly, passed or ran for every Minnesota touchdown in a 34-13 win.

The marquis triple-threat tailback of his era, Smith epitomized the single-wing offense and could seemingly do it all. In 1941 the team captain led the Gophers to their second consecutive undefeated season and national championship. For his efforts, Smith became Minnesota's first, and only, Heisman Trophy winner, beating out Notre Dame running back, Angelo Bertelli. After graduating, the All-American halfback went on to garner MVP honors in the College All-Star game against the Chicago Bears that summer.

That next year, before going off to fight in WWII, Smith first went to Hollywood, where he starred in the movie "Smith of Minnesota," about a small-town family whose son becomes an All-American halfback. (A book on his life was also written, appropriately entitled "The Game Breaker.") Smith went on to become a Navy fighter pilot, and also played service football for the Great Lakes Navy team. He returned home in 1945, and signed on with the Green Bay Packers and later with the Los Angeles Rams. He played for four years in the NFL, mostly on defense, but injuries prevented him from performing up to his unbelievable collegiate standards. In 1947 he nearly died when he suffered a ruptured kidney during a Chicago Bears game. He was even rushed to the hospital and read his last rites by a priest. He survived, but his less than stellar football career didn't.

With that, he retired at the young age of 29, and moved back to his native Faribault, where he and his wife Gloria raised a family. Then, in 1964, he moved to Alexandria, to take over a Hamms distributorship. Tragically, that same year he was diagnosed with terminal cancer. Despite his fighting efforts, he soon dwindled from 200 to 90 pounds. On August 26, 1967, at the tender age of 47, Smith finally succumbed to his disease. It was a true tragedy for a real American hero. He was inducted into the College Football Hall of Fame in 1972, and in 1977 Smith's No. 54 became the first Minnesota number to be officially removed from the roster.

"I only have to tell you that when I played against Bruce Smith at Minnesota, he was a powerful, hard running back of 205 pounds, and a magnificent specimen of a man," said Michigan All-American Running Back Tommy Harmon. "In fact, I don't know of a man who would better fit the description of an All-American than Bruce Smith. Not only was he a great talent as a football player, but he was a clean living, religious, fine guy off the field as well. He was a champion in the true sense of the word."

BERNIE BIERMAN

Born in 1894 to German parents on a farm near Springfield, Minn., Bernie Bierman grew up in Litchfield. As a youngster, Bierman had to overcome a bone infection in his leg that kept him bed-ridden and on crutches. But, after going through several operations to correct the problem, he quickly emerged as a prep star in football, baseball, basketball and track at Litchfield High School. (His family later moved to Detroit Lakes, and as evidence of his stature as a local legend, all three communities: Springfield, Litchfield and Detroit Lakes have claimed him as their own home-town hero!)

From there, Bierman decided to follow in his big brother Alfred's footsteps and play football at the University of Minnesota. There, as an All-Conference halfback, Bernie captained the undefeated 1915 Big Ten title team. Bierman was a three-sport letterman at the U of M, also starring on the basketball team and running track as well. After graduating, Bierman went on to become a successful high school coach in Billings, Montana, before going off to fight in World War I as a Captain in the Marines.

"The Marine Corps taught me discipline, organization and to love life," Bierman would later say. Returning from the Service in 1919, Bierman took over as the head coach at Montana University, where he remained until 1922. Bierman left coaching after that season to work for a Minneapolis bond house, but came back that next year to become an assistant under former Gopher teammate, Clark Shaughnessy, at Tulane University. After a couple of seasons in New Orleans, Bierman took over as the head coach at Mississippi A&M. Two years later, he returned to serve as the head coach of Tulane. He guided the Green Wave from 1927-32, posting a 39-10-1 record and even leading the squad to a 1931 Rose Bowl appearance.

In 1932 Bierman came home to be named as the head coach the University of Minnesota, where he became a living legend. Known as the "Grey Eagle," for his prematurely gray hair, Bierman could flat-out coach. He could also recruit, which he did like no other in the program's history. His rosters were loaded with big Minnesota farm kids and leather-tough kids from the neighborhoods of Minneapolis and St. Paul. Bierman trained them mercilessly, sometimes six days a week, for as long as he felt necessary. His boys were going to be in shape come game day. Period.

During Bierman's first 10 years as Minnesota's head coach (1932-41), better known as the "Golden Era," the Gophers not only won seven Big Ten titles, they also won five national championships as well (1934, 1935, 1936, 1940 and 1941). During one amazing span, the Maroon and Gold went three straight seasons and half way through a fourth without a defeat, and lost just eight conference games during the entire Golden Era. With five undefeated teams in all, there was no other team in the country that could match Minnesota's dominance in that 10-year span. Under Bernie, Minnesota ruled the college football world, much like Miami and Florida State do today.

"Bernie was a task master and you had to survive to play for him," said former player Bud Grant. "You were tested all the time and the people who survived, played. It was like the Marines. A lot of people went by the wayside. If you could survive the practices and scrimmages and not get hurt, then you could play. Bernie was from a different era of football back then."

Bierman's players were schooled in practice and on timing to such a degree that Bierman would inspect their footsteps in the grass to see if they went where they were supposed to go as blockers, tacklers or runners. They also got a good dose of Bierman's philosophy, whether they wanted it or not: "There's only one thing worse than going into a game convinced you can't win," said Bierman. "That's going into a game convinced you can't lose."

In 1942, Bierman rejoined the military for a three-year stint to serve in W.W.II. He returned to coaching in 1945 but never adapted to two-platoon football which had become the norm following the war. He would coach the Gophers for six more seasons before finally retiring from coaching in 1950. With a 93-35-6 coaching record at Minnesota, Bernie was without question the greatest college football coach in Gopher history. He would ultimately retire with a 146-62-13 career record in his 25 years of coaching. A recipient of numerous Coach of the Year awards, he was later inducted into the College Football Hall of Fame.

Asked about the secret to his success, the Grey Eagle said this: "There's nothing secret about blocking, tackling and hard charging. That's fundamental. Given a reasonable share of material that has speed, brains, some brawn and a burning desire to give — and school it as thoroughly as possible in these fundamentals — then, with a few good breaks, you're bound to win once in a while."

Upon his retirement, Bierman spent some time as a color commentator on Gopher radio broadcasts. Bernie later moved to California, where, in 1977, he died at the age of 82.

BILLY BYE

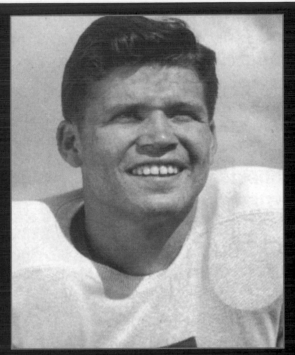

Billy Bye was a star halfback for the Gophers from 1946-49. Bye is perhaps the most prolific and versatile athlete in the state's history. In four years at Thief River Falls High School and two years at Anoka High School, Bye earned 21 letters in six sports: hockey, golf, football, basketball, baseball and track. On a spring day in his senior season, Bye won the district golf championship in the morning, played on the championship baseball team in the afternoon and qualified for regional competition in five track and field events in the evening. As a Gopher, the speedster led the team in rushing during his freshman and sophomore seasons with 900 yards and 10 touchdowns, collectively, and was the team's leading scorer all four seasons. He was even named as the team MVP during his freshman season, something almost unheard of in those days. During his senior season, 1949, Bye rushed for 561 yards and a record seven touchdowns. The "49ers" as they were known, finished in third place in the Big Ten that season for the third straight year. In all, Bye gained 1,784 rushing yards and ran for 21 TDs over his illustrious career in Gold Country. Bye then played professionally with the Winnipeg Blue Bombers in the Canadian Football League for three years before returning to Minnesota to teach, coach and launch a successful business career. Sadly, Bye passed away in a boating accident at his home on Bay Lake in the Summer of 2009. One of the most popular and giving alumnus in Gopher football history, he had recently been selected to serve as one of five honorary captains for the opening of TCF Bank Stadium.

With Van Every, Christiansen and Moore returning on offense, combined with a solid defense built around Captain Francis Twedell at Guard, and All-American Butch Nash at End, the Gophers looked to repeat as Big Ten champs in 1938. After beating Washington and Nebraska in their first two games, Minnesota opened their conference schedule by beating Purdue, 7-0, thanks to a Marty Christiansen and Wilbur Moore's 80-yard touchdown march. The Gophers then eked out a 7-6 victory over Michigan, who's new coach was none other than former Gopher skipper Fritz Crisler. The defense was the key in this one, as Eveleth's John Mariucci (the future Godfather of Minnesota hockey) blocked the extra point of Michigan's early touchdown. Wayzata's Harold Van Every, playing with a ruptured kidney, then led the come-from-behind victory by first forcing and recovering a fumble, which led to him throwing a nine-yard tying touchdown pass to Wilbur Moore. George Faust then kicked the game-winning extra point for the rights to the coveted Jug.

The Gophers then met up with their old neme-

GORDIE SOLTAU

Gordie Soltau starred as a pass catching end and kicker for the Gophers from 1946-49, earning All-Big Ten honors as a senior. After being selected to play in the East-West Shrine game, College All-Star game and Hula Bowl, Soltau, who also played hockey for the Gophers, went on to play pro football with the NFL's San Francisco 49ers. There, the Duluth, Minn., native led the league in scoring in both 1952 and 1953. During his nine seasons as a 49er he led the team in scoring with 644 points, 25 touchdowns, and 70 field goals. For his efforts he was named as an All-Pro in 1952, 1953, and 1954. Among his career highlights: scoring 26 points in a victory over the Rams in 1951; catching 10 passes for 190 yards against the Giants in 1952; and kicking four field goals to beat the Rams, 33-30, in 1956. Soltau is a member of the Bay Area Sports, Duluth and Norwegian Halls of Fame. In addition, he was also voted onto the 49ers all-time team at two different positions, end and kicker.

BUD GRANT

Harry "Bud" Grant was born on May 20, 1927, and raised in Superior, Wis. Bud grew up playing sports and became a tremendous prep athlete. After playing football, baseball and basketball at Superior's Central High School, Bud joined the Navy in 1945 and was stationed at the Great Lakes Naval Station outside Chicago. Bud continued his athletic prowess at Great Lakes, where his team played Big Ten clubs under football Coach Paul Brown and basketball Coach Weeb Ewbank, both hall of famers. In 1946, Bud was discharged and he enrolled at the U.

There, even without a scholarship (because he was in the service, the G.I. bill paid for his tuition), he would excel in three sports, earning nine letters from 1946-49. He was a two-time All-Big Ten end on the football team, he starred as a forward and was the team MVP on the basketball team, and also played centerfield and pitched for the baseball team — where he even led the team in hitting as a freshman. On the gridiron under coach Bierman, Bud played with Gopher greats such as Leo Nomellini, Clayton Tonnemaker, Gordie Soltau, Billy Bye, Jim Malosky and Vern Gagne. Then, to earn spending money in the summers throughout college, Grant became creative. Since he could pitch three days a week and bat clean-up, he played baseball as a "ringer" for several small town-teams around Minnesota and Wisconsin, where he could mop up as much as $250 bucks in a good week.

"Being a Gopher kind of grows on you a little bit," said Bud. "It wasn't anything that I felt particularly strong about when I got there, but now it means a lot. Back then, the Gophers were the only game in town and we always played before a packed house. It was a tough time, with no scholarships and little money, but we had a lot of fun."

By 1950, Bud had finished his tenure at the U of M, and was considered by most to have been the most versatile athlete ever to compete there. (That was affirmed when he later beat out Bronko Nagurski and Bruce Smith to be named as the "Top Athlete at the University of Minnesota for the First 50 Years of the Century.") From there, he joined George Mikan and Jim Pollard as the newest member of the Minneapolis Lakers dynasty. In joining the Lakers, Bud also became the NBA's first "hardship case," meaning he could leave college early and play professionally. (Lakers general manager and good friend Sid Hartman petitioned the league and made it happen for him.) As a Laker, Grant averaged 2.6 points per game in each of the two years he played for the club, both of which were NBA championship teams.

Anxious to try something different, Bud left the Lakers and joined the NFL's Philadelphia Eagles, who had made him their No. 1 draft pick that year. So talented was Grant, that in 1952, after switching from linebacker, where he led the team in sacks, to wide receiver, he finished second in the league in receiving and was voted to the Pro Bowl. After two years in Philly, he decided to take a 30% pay-raise and head north of the border to play for the Winnipeg Blue Bombers of the Canadian Football League. In so doing, Bud became the first player in NFL history to play out the option on his contract. He dearly missed hunting and fishing, something he figured he could readily do in up in Winnipeg.

There, he played both ways, starting at corner and at wide receiver. He led the league in receiving for three straight years and also set a record by intercepting five passes during a single game. Then in 1957, after only four years in the league, and in the prime of his career, the front-office offered the 29-year-old the team's head-coaching position. He accepted and proceeded to lead the Blue Bombers to six Grey Cups over the next 10 years, winning four of them.

On March 11th, 1967, Grant came home again, this time to take over the NFL's Minnesota Vikings. It was a position that former Lakers owner, Max Winter, who now ran the Vikings, had originally offered to him, but had declined back in 1960. Bud took over from Norm Van Brocklin, and although he only won three games in his first season, that next year he led the purple to the division title. The year after that, in 1969, they made it to the Super Bowl, and Bud was named the league's Coach of the Year. It would be his first of four.

That was the beginning of one of the greatest coaching sagas in all of sports. Bud could flat out coach, and his players not only respected him, they also liked him. Bud treated them like men. He didn't work them too hard in practice and his players always knew they could count on that post-season playoff check. He was tough, but fair.

Grant, who coached for 28 years, won a total of 290 regular season and post-season games, 122 as coach of the Winnipeg Blue Bombers of the CFL from 1957-66, and 168 as coach of the Vikings from 1967-83 and 1985. At Minnesota, his teams made the playoffs 12 times, and won 15 championships: 11 Central Division (1968-71, 1973-78, and 1980), one NFL (1969) and three NFC (1973, 1974 and 1976). In 1994 Bud was inducted into the Pro Football Hall of Fame. With it, he became the first person ever to be elected to both the NFL and the Canadian Football League Halls of Fames. In a word, Bud Grant is truly a Minnesota treasure.

"There were people who could run faster, jump higher, throw harder and shoot better than me, but I don't think anybody competed any harder than I did," said Grant. "I felt that I always had an advantage over my opponents because I never got tired. The longer we played, the stronger I got. Then I could beat you. And I applied that same theory to coaching. That was the type of player who I was always looking to get to play for me. Also, one thing that most coaches can't say, is that I've never been fired. I've always left whatever I was doing on my own accord, and I am proud of that. Every dollar I have ever made was from professional sports. I've had no other business or profession, and the only investments that I've got are six kids with college educations. Other than that, I don't have much."

CLAYTON TONNEMAKER

Clayton Tonnemaker played for the Gophers from 1946-49, earning All-America honors as a center and linebacker in 1949 while serving as Coach Bierman team captain. Tonnemaker, like the great Pudge Heffelfinger before him back in the late 1800s, unofficially played for the Gophers even as a high school student. The recruiters had spotted him absolutely dominating his Minneapolis Edison High School team's opponents, and wanted to get him up to play with the big boys as soon as possible.

With that, the young Center took the street car down to campus to get a taste of spring football. Being that it was not legal to allow a high schooler to train with a college team, the Gophers did not mention or acknowledge him being there. Once, in a Saturday scrimmage, Tonnemaker intercepted a pass and run it back for a touchdown. Excited, he ran out that night to pick up a copy of an early edition of the Sunday newspaper to read about his accomplishments. When he opened it up though, all he read about was how another "different" center on the team made a spectacular interception return for a touchdown!

The Ogilvie, Minn., native later went on to serve as the co-captain of both the College All-Star squad as well as the East-West Shrine All-Star Game. From there, Tonnemaker played professionally with the Green Bay Packers, who had selected him with their No. 1 pick (fourth overall). After just one season with the Pack, however, Tonnemaker was called to duty and served for 30 months as a first lieutenant with the Army in the Korean War. Upon his return, Tonnemaker rejoined the Pack and played for them until 1954.

He retired that same year to start what would turn out to be a very successful business career, first with Cargill and later as the president of the Coal Creek Mining Co. in Billings, Mont. In 1949 the Minneapolis Star named him as Minnesota's greatest center in football history. Among his many honors and accolades, Tonnemaker was inducted into the College Football Hall of Fame in 1980.

sis from Evanston, the Northwestern Wildcats, who once again had Minnesota's number — this time winning, 6-3. Minnesota went on to beat Iowa for the eighth consecutive time, 28-0, on a pair of Sonny Franck and Bob Paffrath touchdowns, before falling once again to Notre Dame. In a game that clearly defined what is meant by the "luck of the Irish," Notre Dame posted more touchdowns (three) than it did first downs (two). The Gophers played solid football, but lost, 19-0, on three well executed touchdown plays. (The jinx ended when the schedule makers finally took the Irish off of Minnesota's schedule — it would be 40 years until the two teams met again!) Bierman punished his players mercilessly that week. As a result, the team then took out their frustrations on Wisconsin, with Larry Buhler leading the charge on a 27-yard TD run up the middle to guide the Gophers to a 21-0 victory, and their fourth Big Ten title in five years. Bierman's mind tricks worked every time.

Despite the return of Van Every, Bob Paffrath and Sonny Franck, along with the arrival of a sophomore Running Back named Bruce Smith, 1939 would have to be considered a disaster. After all, it was the beginning of W.W.II. and people's minds were on other, more important issues. While football took a back-seat during the late 1930s and early 1940s, the game, as they say, "must still go on." With that, the season opened with the Maroon and Gold annihilating Arizona, 62-0, as Bruce Smith and Franck each got a pair of touchdowns in the win.

The Gophers then dropped a 6-0 decision to Nebraska that next week, followed by a 13-13 tie with Purdue. Shortly thereafter, Minnesota lost to Ohio State, 23-20, as Joe Mernik's tying field goal attempt in the final minutes hit the crossbar. The wheels had come off this well-oiled machine, and before they knew it, they had lost to both Northwestern, 14-7, and Iowa, 13-9. In the Iowa game, Van Every intercepted a pass late in the fourth which had apparently clinched the victory for Minnesota, but a controversial interference penalty was called from 50 yards away from the play and the Hawkeye's scored on the next drive to win it.

They did manage to shut down Michigan's star Running Back Tommy Harmon, as Van Every, Franck and Smith each found the end-zone to secure a 20-7 victory over the Wolverines. A 23-7 comeback win over Wisconsin in the final game was inspired by touchdowns from Marty Christiansen, Bruce Smith and Bob Sweiger, as well as a blocked punt for a safety by Bob Fitch. Despite the strong finish, the Gophers finished with a 3-4-1 record and an ugly 7th place conference standing. (Van Every, who earned all-conference honors, would later be named as a Silver Anniversary All-American by Sports Illustrated.)

Back to the Promised Land
The 1940 season was a big turn-around in Gopher Country, as Minnesota rebounded to finish with an undefeated 8-0 record, another Big Ten title, and yes, their fourth national championship. It would be a storybook season for the Gophers, as they would once again return Bernie Bierman to the promised land. The line was solid this year with Bill Johnson and Bob Fitch at Ends, Dick Wildung and Urban Odson at Tackles, Bill Kuusisto and Helge Pukema at Guards and Bob Bjorkland at Center. In the backfield were Bruce Smith and George Franck, followed by Bob Paffrath at Quarterback and Bob Sweiger at Fullback.

The season opened with Washington coming to town, as Sonny Franck's second touchdown of the afternoon, a 98-yard kickoff return, iced a 19-14 victory. Nebraska was next as they came to the Brick House and shut-down Franck and Smith, only to see William Daley and William Johnson gain nearly 300 yards on the ground in leading the Gophers to a 13-7 victory. Then, at Ohio State, Smith took over, scoring both of Minnesota's touchdowns en route to racking up 134 yards rushing. Franck might have been the hero though, as he made a game-saving play by tackling Buckeye Quarterback Don Scott out of bounds on the Gopher one-yard line as the clock struck zero.

Franck then showed why he was a unanimous All-American selection that year by scoring four touchdowns, two of them on passes from Bruce Smith, in a 34-6 scorching of the Hawkeyes. The celebration would not be long-lived, however; as pesky Northwestern was on deck — a team that had owned the Gophers over the past few seasons. In another barn-burner, the Gophers finally got the monkey off their back though, by rallying to beat the Cats, 13-12, thanks to a pair of Bob Sweiger touchdown runs combined with a Joe Mernik place-kick. Amazingly, it was Minnesota's first victory at Dyche Stadium in 11 years.

Next up were the undefeated Michigan Wolverines. Led by Bruce Smith's 205 total yards and game-winning 80-yard weak-side reverse touchdown (followed by what would prove to be the game-

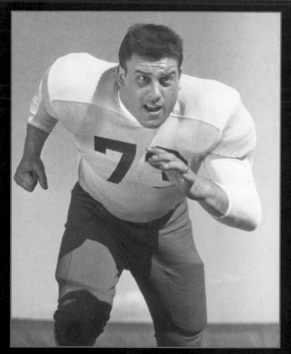

LEO NOMELLINI

Born in Lucca, Italy, Leo Nomellini grew up in a tough neighborhood outside of Chicago, where, incredibly, he never played high school football. He went on to enlist in the Marines, however, and eventually learned the rules of the game while stationed in North Carolina. After serving active duty in the invasion of Saipan and Okinawa, Nomellini enrolled at the U of M as a 22-year old freshman in 1946. In 1949, the tackle led the Gophers to a No. 1 ranking, anchoring a defense that allowed just 80 points all season.

Nicknamed "The Lion," Nomellini would go on to earn All-American honors for the second time in as many years that season. So good of an athlete was Nomellini that he even took up wrestling, where, after just one year, he wound up winning the Big 10 championship as a heavyweight. Nomellini was also on the track team as a shot putter and anchor man on the 440-yard relay team.

The three-time All-Big Ten tackle graduated in 1950 and went on to become the first-ever draft pick of the upstart San Francisco 49ers. There, he would go on to star for 14 seasons in the NFL as a two-way lineman, playing in 174 consecutive regular season games along the way. At six-foot-three and 265 pounds, he was the third fastest player on the team, making him the true prototypical lineman of his era.

When it was all said and done, the 10-time Pro Bowler became one of the few players ever to be named All-Pro both on offense and defense, winning offensive honors in 1951 and 1952, and defensive laurels in 1953, 1954, 1957 and 1959. Later in his career, he hooked up with his old buddy Verne Gagne, and the two of them then teamed up to become tag-team partners in the ring. He even won the world championship in 1956, a title he held for seven months. In 1969 Nomellini was inducted into the Pro Football Hall of Fame and in 1977 he was inducted into College Football Hall of Fame. He was also named to the National Football League's all-time team in 1970. Furthermore, the 49ers retired Nomellini's No. 73 as well.

VERNE GAGNE

Verne Gagne was born in Corcoran, Minn., and grew up in Hamel during the Depression, attending a onc-room school house. Later he transferred to Wayzata High School for one year, ultimately graduating from Robbinsdale High School in 1943. There he earned all-state honors in football, and, even though he weighed only 185 pounds, he also won the state heavyweight wrestling championship.

During the early 1940s, because of World War II taking so many young men, the University needed football players. So, Gagne was recruited by Bernie Bierman to play for the Gophers. But his main sport quickly became wrestling. After winning the Big Ten heavyweight wrestling title in 1944 as a freshman, he went into the Marine Corps. Stationed in Santa Ana, Calif., Gagne played football for the El Toro Marine team for the next two years while also teaching the art of hand-to-hand combat to his fellow soldiers.

He returned to the U of M to continue playing football, where, in 1949, the star end was selected to play in the College All-Star Game. As a wrestler, Verne became arguably the greatest grappler to ever come out of Minnesota. Gagne would claim three more conference wrestling titles from 1947-1949, thus becoming the first-ever four-time Big Ten champion. He also won a pair of NCAA championships, first as a 191-pounder in 1948, and then as a heavyweight in 1949. The three-time All-American won the 1949 AAU Wrestling Championship as well. In addition, Gagne was also a member of the 1948 U.S. Olympic Greco Roman wrestling team.

After college he was drafted as a defensive end by the Chicago Bears. But, because Halas wanted him to give up a year of eligibility and sign a contract as a junior, Gagne passed and that next season signed with Curly Lambeau's Green Bay Packers. Verne played for the Pack throughout the 1949 pre-season, but just before the first regular season game, Lambeau informed him that because the Bears still owncd his rights and wouldn't release him, he was ineligible to play. Gagne then said "to heck with football" and went into the sport that would make him one of the most celebrated and recognizable athletes of his day, professional wrestling.

Verne spent a life-time participating and promoting the sport that he loved, a sport that was born in Minneapolis, "All Star Wrestling." Verne was a local celebrity and became a local hero to a lot of people around the country. He was a daily feature in all the old newspapers and became synonymous with the sport.

"In pro wrestling back then, there were a lot of great wrestlers like myself, who came out of major universities and wanted to continue in the sport," said Gagne. "Sure there were famous guys we wrestled, like Gorgeous George back in the late 40's and early 50's, but back then it was more like collegiate wrestling. Today there are no 'wrestlers' in wrestling."

"We did a TV show called All Star Wrestling that we broadcasted from the old Calhoun Beach Hotel, starting in 1950 and going all the way until 1992, never missing a week. The program was syndicated all over the United States, in the far east and all over the world. During the 60's, 70's and 80's it was the highest rated television show in Twin Cities, period. With a 26-share rating, we beat every sit-com, the Vikings, the Twins, everybody. We had no idea that it would grow as big as it did. We even drew the biggest crowd ever at Madison Square Garden. I was traveling the country and making more money than Joe DiMaggio and Mickey Mantle."

The grand grappler retired in 1981 but had more than a few come-backs with his son, and tag-team partner, Greg — who also briefly played Gopher football back in '70s. Verne was an entertainer and one of the most successful ones at that. Verne was always one of the "good guys," making him one of the sport's all-time favorites. Among his many honors and accolades, he is a member of the Minnesota Wrestling and Gopher M-Club Halls of Fames.

"Gopher Football was pretty exciting back in those days," said Gagne. "When we were growing up as kids and listening to the Gopher Football team winning the national championships in the 30's and 40's, every kid wanted to play football for the Gophers. I never dreamt that I would have a chance to go to college. I was very fortunate."

winning extra-point by Mernik), Minnesota held off the Wolverines by the final score of 7-6 in front of nearly 60,000 Brick House fans. This one came down to a missed Wolverine point-after attempt by Harmon, as the Gopher defense, which fought off four drives that began on a first down inside their own five-yard line, hung on to preserve the victory amidst a memorable Armistice Day blizzard. While Michigan's Heisman Trophy winning running back, Tommy Harmon, did manage to throw a TD pass to Quarterback Forest Evashevski (later to become Iowa's greatest coach) to give Michigan the lead at 6-0, he was once again shut-out, incredibly having never scored against the Gophers in his three varsity seasons as a Wolverine. He did have one last shot at ending the Minnesota jinx, when Michigan End Ed Frutig blocked a Franck punt to give his team the ball on the Gopher three-yard line. But, after three Harmon plunges up the middle, the score remained 7-6, with Minnesota once again keeping the Little Brown Jug.

(The wonderful part about this particular game was that it finally vindicated Bruce Smith's father's 1910 vow of revenge. You see, the "Myth of Smith" was a legend that began 30 years prior when Smith's dad, Lucius, played End for the Gophers. That year, because of Lucius' missed block while playing Tackle, a position he was thrown into that afternoon due to an injury, Michigan scored the only touchdown of the day and beat Minnesota, 6-0. Lucius took the big game so hard that he vowed to have a son who would one day avenge the tragic loss. His promise came true in 1940 on his son's 80-yard game-winning touchdown. In fact, it was such a compelling story that a Hollywood screenplay writer decided to make a movie about it a few years later, entitled: "The Smiths of Minnesota.")

The Gophers then went on to beat Purdue, 33-6, behind Franck's 85-yard opening kick-off return for a touchdown. In the final game of the season Minnesota defeated Wisconsin, 22-13, as Bill Daley and Bruce Smith each scored on touchdown runs, while All-American George Franck added another on a 20-yard interception return. With the win, Minnesota had earned its fourth national championship in seven years. Just how much did this 1940 title team rely on its running game vs. the passing attack? Well, consider this, in the three-game stretch that featured Nebraska, Ohio State and Iowa, Minnesota threw a grand total of three passes... for a grand total of three touchdowns.

With Franck gone to the NFL to play for the New York Giants, the 1941 team was all Bruce Smith's. The Captain would lead the defending national champs back to the promised land once again that year, accomplishing something that had never been done before. Along the way, he became the first and only Gopher ever to win the Heisman Trophy, emblematic of the nation's best collegiate player.

Smith kicked off the season by scoring both of Minnesota's touchdowns in the team's 14-6 victory,

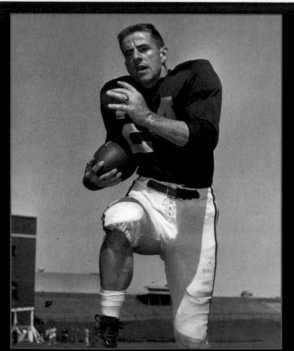

RICHARD "PINKY" McNAMARA

Richard "Pinky" McNamara came to the University in the early '50s, worked tirelessly to earn a scholarship as a halfback and cornerback, and became a three-year letter winner for Coach Warmath's Golden Gophers from 1953-56. Pinky and his older brother Bob, an All-American halfback, were teammates together at Minnesota from 1953-54. The Hastings, Minn., native had many highlights over his collegiate career, including an outstanding performance in the 1956 Blue-Gray All-Star game. After graduating that same year, McNamara, who was drafted in the 23rd round by the Baltimore Colts, went on to an extremely successful business career. He would later found Activar Inc., a company specializing in restructuring failing companies and bringing them to profitability. With that success came kindness, and Mac has certainly gone on to become a well known and respected philanthropist. McNamara, who served as a member of the University's Board of Regents from 2001-05, has been one of the institution's most generous donors, giving the school $10 million in 1998 to help fund the McNamara Alumni Center and to support students in the College of Liberal Arts as well as student-athletes. At the time, it was the second largest gift ever received by the U from a living alumnus. In addition, he has worked tirelessly to raise money for several Gopher athletics programs, and has generously donated a considerable amount of time and money towards the new football stadium.

and fourth straight over Washington. The Gophers then pummeled Pittsburgh, 34-6, with Smith's understudy, Bud Higgins, scoring three touchdowns. From there the team rolled over the Illini in the Big Ten opener, as Fullback Bill Dalcy's 72-yard opening-drive touchdown run was just the beginning of a 39-0 thrashing.

Then, as was the case the year before, Michigan and Northwestern proved to be the team's biggest foes. The Wolverines were eliminated thanks to sophomore Herman Frickey's game-winning touchdown, while Halfback Bill Daley also intercepted a pair of key passes down the stretch to ice it for the Gophers. The Michigan victory proved costly though, as Smith wound up injuring his right knee during the game. He did manage to play briefly in the first quarter of the Northwestern game, but with Frickey also sidelined, Bierman was forced to concoct a makeshift backfield which featured a pair of Fullbacks in Bill Daley and Bob Sweiger, along with a pair of Quarterbacks in Bill Garnaas and Warren Plunkett.

The Gophers got on the board first in this wild one, thanks to a safety on a poor snap from center. Northwestern took the lead late in the opening quarter when future NFL great Otto Graham hit Bud Hasse on a touchdown pass to take a 7-2 lead. The game roared back and forth until Bierman, who needed to do something desperate to get his team back in it, instructed his quarterback to run the "Talking Play." The now-infamous "talking play" was a gadget play intended for use only in a desperate scoring emergency. Such was the case at that very moment late in the third quarter after Ed Lechner had blocked a Bill DeCorrevont punt on the Wildcat's 41-

yard line. The play started inconspicuously enough when, as planned, the Gophers' first play in the series was just "teaser" run with Bob Sweiger running for no gain over to the left sideline. What this did was necessitate bringing the ball in to the center hash mark to start the next play. At this point the Northwestern defensive players were loose and were even engaging in casual conversation while they waited for the Gophers to simply set up at the line of scrimmage.

To assist in Northwestern's relaxed mood, the Gophers stood around "talking" and ultimately distracting the officials. Then, without warning, Minnesota quickly lined up with everyone standing totally still on the line to the right of Center Gene Flick, who stood nonchalantly facing his own end-zone. Suddenly, Flick grabbed the ball and pitched a shovel-pass to Bud Higgins (a scat back from Minneapolis Washburn who weighed not too much more than the football), who then raced clear across the length of the field before he got an opening to make the 90-degree turn toward the end-zone. Once he got open, he flew by the stunned and flat-footed Wildcat defense and into open field. Tackle Urban Odson made a couple of key blocks along the way on the final two defenders as Higgens went on to score what would become one of the most controversial touchdowns in college football history. Northwestern, now furious, complained in vain to the officials, who had been pre-warned in advance by the Gopher coaches that they may run the play that afternoon. The extra point was missed, but the Gophers hung on to win by a narrow 8-7 margin.

After the big win, Minnesota made sure not to let their guard down against Nebraska. Bob Sweiger's first half touchdown run followed by Bill Garnaas'

BOB GRAIZIGER

One of the best athletes ever to don the Maroon and Gold, Bob Graiziger earned a total of ten letters (four in football, two in baseball and four in hockey) during his tenure in Gold Country from 1942-45 — a record that still stands. On the gridiron, Graiziger was named as the team captain and played in the College All-Star Game, earning honorable mention All-American honors as a guard that same year. Graiziger was also an outstanding hockey player who led the team in scoring his junior and senior seasons. For his efforts he was named as the team captain in 1942-43, earning MVP honors that season as well. In addition, Graiziger was an All-Big Ten catcher on the baseball diamond — making him Minnesota's ultimate triple threat athlete. He was later selected in the seventh round of the NFL draft by the Brooklyn Dodgers.

fourth-quarter field-goal would be all the offense the Gophers would need as they rolled to a 9-0 victory. Bruce Smith returned with a vengeance that next week against Iowa, where he ran or passed for all the Gopher scores, including a couple of TDs to Bill Daley, in the 34-13 win. Incredibly, Smith, who was still injured, begged Bierman to put him in the game after the Gophers hadn't produced a single yard of offense on the ground.

Minnesota then pounded the hapless Badgers, 41-6, winning not only the undisputed Big Ten title, but also their fifth national championship. With the win, Bernie Bierman also became the winningest coach in school history. Bruce Smith, the great triple-threat star, was later awarded the prestigious Heisman Trophy. In addition, Tackle Dick Wildung and Quarterback Bill Garnaas were also selected to various All-America squads.

From the Great Depression to the second World War, this was truly the "Golden Era" for Minnesota football. In the 10-year span from 1932-41, Bierman's Gophers won six Big Ten championships, five NCAA national championships and had five undefeated seasons en route to posting an amazing 63-12-5 record.

The Turbulent War Years

World War II would deny Minnesota their sixth national championship in nine years due to the fact that most of the players were forced to enlist in the armed services. Even Bierman himself, who was a Captain in W.W.I, joined the Marine Corps, where he coached a training camp team called the Iowa Seahawks. Assistant Coach George Hauser handled the coaching duties in his absence, trying to salvage something out of a season which saw some 350 college and universities around the country suspend their athletic programs altogether during the war. Incredibly, the Gophers, who, after beating Pittsburgh 50-7, thanks to Bill Daley's four touchdowns, in their 1942 season opener, had their string of 18 straight victories over the past four seasons broken by none other than their own coach, Bernie Bierman. That's right, Bierman's service team, the Seahawks, who won the game 7-6, were even led by a bunch of former Gophers including George Svendsen, Gene Flick, Judd Ringer and Charlie Schultz, as well as a number of professionals.

(During the war period many collegiate players transferred to schools that had Naval programs, which permitted them to finish their careers before going overseas. As a result, a lot of the countries' premier players found themselves playing on rival teams. Among them was Fullback Bill Daley, who was transferred to a military base in Ann Arbor in 1942 and later earned All-American honors at Michigan. In addition, End Herb Hein, who, after playing the 1942 season with the Gophers, became an All-American at Northwestern in 1943.)

From there, the Gophers lost to Illinois 20-13, beat Nebraska 15-2, and then beat Michigan, 16-14, for the ninth straight time behind Bill Garnaas' im-

BOB McNAMARA

Bob McNamara was such a versatile running back with the Gophers that he actually earned All-American honors in 1954 as both a fullback as well as a halfback. In addition, the Hastings, Minn., native was All-Big Ten in both 1952 and 1954, and was also named as the team MVP during his senior year. From there, McNamara spent four years with the Winnipeg Blue Bombers of the Canadian Football League. He earned All-Pro honors in 1956, the same year he scored six touchdowns against Vancouver, a record that still stands. He later played two seasons with the Denver Broncos in the American Football League. Incidentally, in addition to being outstanding on the gridiron, McNamara also won an amazing 13 National racquetball titles over his career as well. Today "Mac" is an avid supporter of everything Maroon and Gold. In fact, he spearheaded the 2002 grassroots fundraising campaign that saved the school's golf and men's gymnastics programs from elimination. He and his brother, "Pinky," a former gridiron teammate who is also a member of the Hall of Fame, have done a considerable amount of work raising money and endowing scholarships for many Gopher athletics teams, especially the U's tennis programs. Most recently, however, they have focused their efforts towards the new on-campus football stadium, a dream which was realized in the Summer of 2006.

promptu drop-kick. They would beat Iowa but lose to both Wisconsin and Indiana to finish the season with a very modest 5-4 record, good for just fourth in the Big Ten. Tackle Dick Wildung was honored as an All-American that year, as the country really had more important things to worry about other than football. The 1943 season should also be remembered as the year Minnesota's line was anchored by a young kid named Vern Gagne, who would go on to put the sport of wrestling on the map, both collegiately, where he won two national championships as a heavyweight for the Gophers, but also professionally, where he helped to pioneer a form of entertainment that today generates billions in revenue.

The Gophers were anything but a football power through the mid-1940s, averaging just five wins per year through 1947. There were highlights along the way though, like in 1943, when Wayne "Red" Williams led the nation in total yards, with 1,467, while averaging 167-yards per game. In one of those games, against Iowa, he tallied four touchdowns. In 1944 Minnesota eked out some fourth-quarter heroics over Indiana and Wisconsin. The Hoosiers were beaten, 19-14, with Merlin Kispert scoring the winning touchdown, while the Badgers were edged, 28-26, in a wild one that ended in the final moments with Bob Kasper finding Bill Marcotte in the end zone.

In 1945 Bernie Bierman returned home from the Marine Corps to find that college football had changed. Freshmen were now rubbing elbows with 25-year-old servicemen who had been toughened by both combat as well as the rigors of Army football. This new, older athlete, was also much less receptive to stern discipline — long the hallmark of Bierman's coaching philosophy. For the most part, these young men were sick and tired of being ordered around and wanted to just have fun. As a result, Bierman was less connected with his new Gopher squad and the record book reflected that. Struggling with the transition to the new T-formation from the old single-wing was one of the major reasons that the team posted just a 4-5 record that year. After beating Missouri, Nebraska, Fort Warren and Northwestern, the bottom fell out as the Gophers lost the rest of their games to Ohio State, 20-7, Michigan, 26-0, Indiana, 49-0, Wisconsin, 26-12, and Iowa, 20-19.

The "49ers" Hit Campus

In 1946 a new batch of freshmen hit the campus who would later become known as the "49ers," emblematic for the year in which they were to graduate. They were mixed in with an unusual crop of talent to say the least, with many of them playing on the varsity as freshman under a World War II ruling making first year men eligible for Big Ten competition. (Prior to the war, freshmen hadn't ever been allowed to play.)

Players like Bud Grant and Billy Bye, who hadn't played collegiately but did play for the Great Lakes Naval Station, were joined with pre-war college

LLOYD "SNAPPER" STEIN

Lloyd "Snapper" Stein grew up in Two Harbors, Minn., and played center for the Gopher football team from 1928-30. Stein graduated from Minnesota in 1932 with a degree in Physical Education. From there, he went on to serve as the freshman athletic trainer from 1932-34 and in 1935 he became the U of M's head athletic trainer. In 1942, Stein enlisted in the U.S. Navy and served as athletic trainer at the Iowa Preflight School in Iowa City. Stein returned to the U of M in 1945 and later earned a degree in Physical Therapy. Stein also worked as a part-time research consultant at a local sports medicine center as well. Stein, who was a mentor and colleague to countless other Athletic Trainers in Minnesota and across the nation, has been referred to as the "Grandfather of Athletic Training" in Minnesota. Having cared for literally thousands of youngsters on and off the athletic field, Stein was one of the country's true pioneers of athletic training. After more than 40 years of loyal service, Stein eventually retired in 1975, but would remain a fixture on campus nonetheless as a volunteer with the football program. Among his many honors and accolades, Stein was a charter member of the Minnesota Athletic Trainers' Association (MATA) Hall of Fame in 1993, and is also a member of the National Athletic Trainers' Association Hall of Fame. In addition, he was also the first ever recipient of the Minnesota Viking ring for his many contributions in athletics to the state of Minnesota.

PAUL GIEL

As a young boy, Paul Giel grew up playing football and baseball on the sandlots of Winona during the Great Depression. There, he would often try to emulate the smooth moves of his childhood hero, Heisman winning Gopher Halfback Bruce Smith. Paul's imagination was refueled every Saturday morning, when he religiously listened to his beloved Gophers on the radio. Soon he grew into an incredible prep athlete in his own right, starring in football, baseball and basketball at Winona High School. By 1950, not only was he one of the most celebrated prep football prospects in Minnesota history, he also had an opportunity to sign on with several major league baseball teams right out of high school as well. Lluckily for us though, he had decided long ago that he too was going to wear the Maroon and Gold.

"Coming out of high school in Winona, I was really steeped in the tradition of the Gophers, and because of guys like Bruce Smith, I wanted to be a Gopher," said Giel. "Also, because I could play both football and baseball there, it was even better. It meant everything for me to be a Gopher."

Giel came in and literally took the Gopher sports world by storm. By the time he had finished his illustrious career in Minnesota, he had shattered most of Bruce Smith's records, while single-handedly rewriting the record books. All in all, he rushed for 2,188 yards, caught 281 passes for 279 yards, and posted 417 return yards on both punts and kicks, for a total of 3,165 career all-purpose yards. He also had 22 touchdowns — a number that still ranked in the top-10 all-time more than 50 years later.

In addition to all of that, he also starred on the baseball diamond, where, as a pitcher on Coach Dick Siebert's Gopher Baseball teams, he dominated. In fact, Siebert said "Pitching Paulie" Giel was the hardest-throwing pitcher he had ever coached. From 1952-54 he was named to the All-American and All-Big Ten teams. On the mound, he earned 21 wins, and had the same number of complete games. His record for the most career strikeouts, 243, stood for more than 50 years and he remains fifth all-time for the most single season strikeouts, with 92. He finished his brilliant career with a 2.16 ERA.

So, with a resume like that, what was Paul to do after graduation? "I knew in my heart that I wanted to play baseball over football, and I was trying to be realistic about myself," said Giel. "I wondered where in the heck I would play in pro football. I mean I wasn't fast enough to be a halfback in the pros, and I couldn't have made it as a pure drop-back quarterback. So, I thought I still had a shot to make it in baseball."

His tenure as "Mr. Everything" at the U of M would ultimately prove to be a springboard for bigger and better things to come in the world of sports. With that, despite being drafted by the NFL's Chicago Bears, Giel opted to instead try his hand at professional baseball with the New York Giants. He would make his big league debut for legendary Manager Leo Durocher on June 29, 1954, striking out the side in the 9th inning of a 10-7 loss at home to the Pirates. It would be the beginning of a steady six-year Major League career, interrupted only by a two-year stint to serve his country in the military. From New York he went to San Francisco, and then to Pittsburgh for two seasons before finishing up his pitching career with his hometown Twins in 1961. He would hang up the spikes for good that same year, finishing his career with an overall record of 11-9, and a modest ERA of 5.39.

From there, Giel simply did it all, working first for the Vikings doing public relations and game management; followed by an eight year career as Sports Director of WCCO Radio — broadcasting prep, college and pro sports throughout Minnesota. In 1972 he was asked to return to his alma mater and serve as the University's Athletic Director, a position he would gladly accept and perform masterfully for more than 17 years. When that was up he even became a Vice President with the North Stars. Having seemingly covered every sport possible in the Land of 10,000 Lakes, in 1990 Giel settled down and took over as the Vice President of the Minneapolis Heart Institute Foundation, where he raised millions for heart health research and education. It was only fitting that a man with a heart as big as Paul's round out his illustrious career at such an appropriate place.

Tragically, Paul died in the Summer of 2002, leaving behind a legacy that will never be equaled in Minnesota sports history. A true legend at the University of Minnesota, Giel was one of those players who comes around once in a millennium. He played the game like no one will again, and did it with an unpretentious demeanor, earning the respect of his teammates and his opponents alike. It has been more than a half century now since he first lived out his dream of playing football and baseball for his beloved Golden Gophers. The old brick stadium is gone and so is that old baseball diamond, but memories of the "Winona Phantom" will live on forever.

"Being a Gopher meant so very much to me that it is really hard to put it into words," said Giel. "It had been a dream of mine since I was a kid and it was without question the wisest decision I ever made in my entire life. The opportunities that it afforded me both academically and athletically were immeasurable. It truly made me who I am today. To play for my home-state school, in front of so many wonderful fans who supported me so much through all those years was an honor I can't even begin to describe. Sometimes I have to pinch myself because it seems like a dream come true."

guys such as Chuck Avery, Herman Frickey, Herb Hein, Bill Baumgartner and Judd Ringer. Veterans Bill Carroll, Warren Beson, Dean Widseth and Bill Elliott were also joined by newcomers such as Gordy Soltau, Ken Beiersdorf, Bill Thiele, Buster Mealey, Gene Fritz and Jim Malosky. Then, there were true freshmen, like Clayton Tonnemaker, and Leo Nomellini, who hadn't even played high school football, but was encouraged to walk-on by former players that they knew from the service. The enormously big and tough Nomellini wound up starting at tackle when an injury to the incumbent thrust him into the lineup. Incredibly, "Leo the Lion" found himself starting for the Golden Gophers in what would prove to be the first football game of his life!

Bierman started out using the veteran players but with freshmen still eligible under the war-time rules, he began to play the youngsters. They would prove to be instrumental in three upset wins in the team's final three Saturdays over Purdue, Iowa and Wisconsin — where Billy Bye scored the game's only touchdown to give the Maroon and Gold a 6-0 win. They finished the season with a 5-4 record.

In 1947 Minnesota opened the season with wins over Washington, Nebraska and Northwestern. In the Washington game, End Bud Grant provided the heroics when he took a Husky fumble into the end zone for what would prove to be the game-winner. From there the Rose Bowl champions from Illinois whipped the boys in gold by the final score of 40-13. Michigan, despite Running Back Ev Faunce's big day on the ground, which included Minnesota's only touchdown, narrowly escaped with the Little Brown Jug by winning, 13-6. Meanwhile, victories over Pittsburgh, 29-0, Purdue, 26-21, and Wisconsin, 21-0, plus a 13-

Bob Rutford

7 loss to Iowa, left Minnesota with a 6-3 season. Against Purdue it was all Billy Bye and Bud Hausken, who each scored a pair of TDs, while Hausken and Bill Thiele each returned interceptions for touchdowns against the Badgers.

Ev Faunce kicked off the 1948 season with a 67-yard TD run to lead the Gophers past Washington, 20-0. They then went on to beat Nebraska in the home-opener, 39-13, followed by a 19-16 loss to Northwestern, which featured a couple of scores from Dale Warner and Ken Beiersdorf. After beating Illinois, 6-0, on a fourth quarter 53-yard pass from Bemidji's Dick Lawrence to Vern Gagne, the Gophers lost to the defending national champs from Michigan, 27-14. The Wolverines won despite being held to just 22 yards rushing by Nomellini and Tonnemaker. Minnesota then rallied from behind in a pair of wins over both Indiana and Purdue, 30-7, and, 34-6, respectively, and went on to beat Iowa, 28-21, thanks to Billy Bye's three touchdowns and Faunce's game-winner. In the finale, the Gophers blanked Wisconsin, 16-0, in the rain and sleet, behind Beiersdorf's two touchdowns and Gordy Soltau's field goal, to finish with a 7-2 record. Nomellini was named to the All-American team that year as the Gophers knew that they were on the verge of turning the corner.

(Incidentally, after beating Wisconsin, a new tradition was started for one of college football's greatest rivalries — "Paul Bunyan's Axe," honoring the Midwest's greatest lumberjack. While the teams, which first played one another back in 1890, had been vying for a "Bacon Slab" since 1930, the schools decided to create a new traveling trophy in 1948 that was symbolic of their competitive traditions. Today the six-foot long handle proudly displays the scores of all 118 games, the longest rivalry in the

Wes Fesler

history of Division 1-A football.)

By 1949 those 49er kids were finally all grown up and ready to take on the world. And while the expectations were running high for this talented bunch of over-achievers, in the end, they would turn out to be the right men in the wrong place at the worst possible time. Although this was primarily a senior-laden team, some pretty good sophomores had moved up in the depth chart throughout the year, including Dick Gregory, Wayne Robinson, Dick Mundinger, George Hudak, Bob Thompson and Art Edling.

The group, which had come so far, frustrated and even angered Bierman, who, due to philosophical differences, felt that they never reached their full potential. Times were different after the war, and kids of this era simply did not consider football to be the most important thing in lives, considering what they had lived through and seen overseas. Bierman's authoritative approach to the game also didn't hold much water with this group, who, unlike the kids from years past, never had to rely on the University for a good campus job to live on. In the post-war economic boom, jobs were plentiful, and, along with the G.I. Bill, student-athletes were enjoying a new sense of independence rarely seen before.

With that, Minnesota opened the season with a 48-20 drubbing of Washington. The Huskies were led by future NFL Hall of Fame Running Back Hugh McElhenny, who ran back the opening kickoff 98 yards for a touchdown. They were simply no match for the Gophers however, as Billy Bye and Ralph McAllister each scored a pair touchdowns on the afternoon. Minnesota then rolled over Nebraska, 28-6, thanks to junior Fullback Dave Skrien's two touch-

downs; Northwestern, 21-7; and Ohio State, 27-0; as Billy Bye, Dick Gregory, Jim Malosky and Ken Beiersdorf all scored to give the Gophers a No. 3 national ranking.

Michigan upset the Gophers that next week, 14-7, but still left them hope for the Rose Bowl since every Big Ten team had lost at least one game up to that point. Bierman, upset with his boys' attitudes, worked them mercilessly in practice that next week. But instead of inspiring them, like in years past, it backfired, and it showed on the field. "I've never gone through such a tough week of practice in my life," Tonnemaker would later say. "He absolutely killed us in practice that week."

The 26-point underdogs from West Lafayatte then came to Memorial Stadium and pulled off one of their program's biggest upsets of all-time, piling up 354 yards of offense en route to a 13-7 shocker. Lawrence was able to tally a touchdown late, but it wasn't enough as the Gophers suddenly saw their Rose Bowl dreams all but evaporate. Embarrassed and upset, Bierman tried a different tact that next week. "We will have fun the rest of the way," he said, and his Gophers responded by crushing Iowa, 55-7, that following Saturday. They didn't stop there either, as they went on to beat Pittsburgh, 24-7, and then closed out their season with a 14-6 victory over Wisconsin.

The sad footnote to an underachieved 7-2 season came on Jan. 1, 1950. That's when Ohio State, whose only loss that year, a 27-0 butt-kicking courtesy of the Gophers, beat the University of California, 17-14, to win the Rose Bowl. Tonnemaker joined Nomellini that year as unanimous choices for every All-American team, as both would go on to brilliant

BOB HOBERT

Bob Hobert was an outstanding football player as well as an outstanding student-athlete for the Gophers from 1954-56. On the gridiron, Hobert earned All-Big Ten and All-American honors in 1956 as a tackle. Joining him on that first team were fellow Gopher halfbacks Paul Giel and Bob McNamara. Furthermore, Hobert earned Academic All-American honors that same year as well. In fact, Hobert became the first Gopher football player ever to earn Phi Beta Kappa academic honors. Hobert was later selected in the sixth round of the 1957 NFL draft by the New York Giants. He also played two seasons with the Winnipeg Blue Bombers of the Canadian Football League and was a member of the Blue Bombers Grey Cup championship team.

pro careers with Green Bay and San Francisco, respectively. Gordy Soltau also ended up in San Francisco as a kicker, and Bud Grant, in addition to playing pro basketball with the Minneapolis Lakers, went on to play with the Philadelphia Eagles, where he became a star receiver. (Bud earned nine letters during his tenure at the U of M, starring on the basketball and baseball teams as well. He, of course, would later go on to become a Hall of Fame NFL coach with the Minnesota Vikings.) Wayne Robinson, Vern Gagne, Dave Skrien, Larry Olsonoski and Floyd Jaszewski all later played pro ball as well, while Quarterback Jim Malosky went on to become one of the country's winningest all-time coaches at the University of Minnesota-Duluth.

A combination of graduation and the return of the freshman ineligibility rule (this time because of the Korean War), the Gophers were looking pretty thin in 1950. You knew it was going to be bad when Washington, who had always been a doormat to the Gophers, finally ended the hex after losing seven straight, and won 28-13. They did manage to beat Purdue, 27-13, and tie the Rose Bowl bound Michigan Wolverines, 7-7, but lost seven games that year to finish with a dismal 1-7-1 record. With the future looking bleak and the press hounding him, Bierman, who was also upset about being passed over by Ike Armstrong as Minnesota's new Athletics Director, finally came to the realization that he was simply out of touch with a new generation of kids who wanted no part of his old-school regime. With that, Bierman, who had posted a modest 30-23-1 post-war record, reluctantly decided to step down as the Gopher's head coach. He would be remembered as the greatest ever to coach in Gold Country.

One of the few things Bierman was negligent of, was recruiting mostly just kids from his own backyard. Back in the day he could get away with it. There was a lot of talent in the Midwest, and kids didn't want to venture too far away from home. But in the new era of competitive college athletics, universities were now scouring the countryside armed with big scholarships in search of the best talent they could find. Minnesota finally got wise to this, and, in an effort to get the local kids to stay put, started its own scholarship program called the Williams Fund.

The Winona Phantom
In 1951 the Gophers hired former Ohio State head coach Wes Fesler, a three-time All-American End for the Buckeyes, to take over the reigns and right the ship. It would be a formidable task, but he did have one thing going for him — the Winona Phantom. One of those freshman who was ineligible in 1950 was a kid from Winona who would go on to become one of Minnesota's greatest ever athletes, rewriting the record books along the way. His name was Paul Giel, one of the first benefactors of that new scholarship fund.

The '51 squad struggled to say the least. After starting out the season with losses to Washington and California, Fesler moved Giel from quarterback to left half, where the speedster's running and passing potential could be better utilized under the team's new single-wing offense. That next week, against Nebraska, Giel scored on a short run in the first; lateralled to Fullback Ron Wallin for a second; completed

GINO CAPPELLETTI

Gino Cappelletti was one of Minnesota's first great kickers. Not only was he the team leader in kick-scoring in 1952, '53 and '54, he also scored three touchdowns in 1952 as a receiver as well. Striving for perfection, Cappelletti was 18 out of 18 on Point-After Touchdowns (PATs) in 1953 and 13 out of 13 in 1954 to make it a team record 31 straight. The Keewatin, Minn., native also led the team in punting as well, banging out a 37.9 yard average in 1954. Cappelletti then went on to play for the American Football League's Boston Patriots, where, from 1960-70, he became the team's all-time leading scorer with 1,130 points (42 TDs, 176 FGs and 342 PATs). In fact, he is the all-time leading scorer in American Football League history. In addition, Cappelletti is among the AFL's all-time top ten receivers with 292 catches for 4,589 yards. Nicknamed the "Duke," Cappelletti was the league's MVP in 1964, and was a five-time AFL All-Star. Cappelletti went on to serve as a color commentator on Patriots radio broadcasts. The New England Patriots later honored Cappelletti by retiring his No. 20.

a 53-yard pass to End Bill Foss for a third; and then busted around the end late in the game on a seven-yarder to score his second TD of the day, en route to leading the Gophers to an impressive 26-7 victory.

Giel added two more against Iowa in a 20-20 tie, and then led the Gophers to a 16-14 win over Indiana. He electrified the crowd with a 64-yard touchdown run in a 19-13 loss to Purdue, and got enough yardage in the 32-6 loss to Wisconsin to bring his total yardage for the season to over 1,000, ultimately setting a new conference record. Percy Zachary, George Hudak, Kermit Klefsaas, Don Swanson, Jerry Helgeson, John Baumgartner, Jimmy Soltau, Chuck Swanum, Gino Cappelletti and Gordy Holz all contributed that year, but the team finished with a dismal 2-6-1 record.

By 1952 Giel was having a ball... literally. He passed the ball, caught the ball, ran the ball, kicked the ball, and even held the ball for PATs. In addition, he called the plays and emerged as the leader both on and off the field. That season the Gophers improved to finish with a 4-3-2 record, highlighted by a couple of big upset wins and last-minute thrillers. After losing a couple of non-conference games to Washington and Cal, the Gophers rebounded to beat Northwestern. Giel hit Don Swanson for the tying touchdown in the last 17 seconds of the game and then Kicker Gino Cappelletti added the winning point for the victory. Minnesota then upset the nationally ranked defending champs from Illinois, 13-7, as Giel hit Bob McNamara for one touchdown and Mel Holme ran for another.

After losing to Michigan, 21-0, Minnesota upset Iowa, 17-7, at Memorial Stadium. Down 7-0 in the fourth, Giel made a leaping one-handed catch from Swanson and sprinted 38 yards for the tying touchdown. After recovering a pair of Iowa fumbles that resulted in both a field goal and a touchdown pass by Swanson, the Gopher defense simply hung on for the win. That next Saturday the Gophers had to settle for a 14-14 tie against a tough Purdue team, which could've been beaten had Cappelletti's field goal attempt late in the fourth not missed by a foot. Giel then led his squad past Nebraska, 13-7, by throwing for one and running in an-

Perry Gehring

other.

In the season finale against Wisconsin, Giel handled the ball 54 times and either passed or ran for all of Minnesota's touchdowns in a thrilling 21-21 tie. In a game filled with fumbles and interceptions, the ball, incredibly, switched hands five times in the last two minutes of the game. For Giel, who was selected as the conference MVP and received All-American honors, the loss was bitter knowing that if his squad had won they would've taken the Big Ten title. (Incidentally, at the end of the season, the football gods decided to legislate against platoon football, something which had been allowed in the post-war years.)

Optimism was running high in the Land of 10,000 Lakes in 1954, as the Gophers looked poised to finally make a run for the roses. Minnesota got off to a slow start that year — losing to USC, 17-7, Michigan State, 21-0, and Illinois, 27-7, while finally getting into the win column with a 30-13 victory over Northwestern. Next up was Michigan. The game was significant because it was the Silver Anniversary of the Little Brown Jug and many of the stars from 1903, including Sig Harris and Ed Rogers, were on hand for the festivities. Fesler knew it was a big game and came down hard on his players that week. He knew that if they were to win though, it would come down to the play of one man — Paul Giel.

Giel, who had the power to call his own plays and audible at the line whenever he felt necessary, was ready to make history, and turn the season's misfortunes around that Saturday. In what many have called the greatest-ever single performance in Gopher history, Giel single-handedly crushed the Wolverines.

The game opened with Minnesota kicking off and it got exciting early when Gordy Holz recovered a Michigan fumble on their own 29-yard line. Just four plays later Giel called his own number, and after deking out several Wolverines, he found himself standing in the end-zone with his squad up 7-0. He would repeat that feat yet again in the first quarter, leading a 62-yard drive which was capped by another run around the end to make it 14-0.

Giel provided more heroics in the third when he returned a punt 41 yards down to the Michigan 34-yard line.

SANDY STEPHENS

Sandy Stephens grew up in Uniontown, Pa., in a household where his parents strongly encouraged his academic and athletic endeavors. Upon graduating from high school, more than 50 colleges and universities, eight from the Big Ten alone, recruited him. Sandy felt pretty strong about his football roots: "We always felt that those of us who lived in Western Pennsylvania had the best high school football in the country, bar none — including Ohio and Texas too."

Stephens was a tremendously gifted all-around athlete, earning nine letters in football, basketball and track. He garnered high school All-American honors in football, was an All-State basketball player, and, although he never played high school baseball, was a good enough pitcher and centerfielder to be romanced by several major league baseball teams — including his home state Philadelphia Phillies, who tried to sign him out of high school.

With assurances that he would be given a shot at quarterback, as well as the opportunity to play baseball, Stephens enrolled at the University of Minnesota in the fall of 1958. So did an old friend and high school rival from Clairton, Pa., who would be his roommate for the next four years, running back Judge Dickson. In so doing, the two became pioneers for all young African American men who wanted to play college athletics in the predominantly white northern schools.

Still considered by many to be one of the top five all-time greatest players ever to wear the Maroon and Gold, Stephens is a football legend in Gold Country. From 1959-61, he threw for nearly 1,500 yards, rushed for a record 20 touchdowns, and twice he led the team in punting. In 1961, he led the Gophers to their second consecutive Rose Bowl and defeated UCLA by the score of 21-3. He also led the team in rushing that year with 534 yards while throwing for nine touchdown passes as well. For his efforts in leading the conference with 1,151 yards of total offense that year, he was named as the Big Ten MVP. In addition, he was also named as an All-American, becoming the first-ever African American player ever to be so honored. He also won College Back of the Year and finished fourth in the balloting for the Heisman Trophy as well.

"He was a hell of a great football player, but he was never given the publicity and acclaim he deserved," said Coach Warmath. "He was one of the greatest football players I ever saw. He was a great running back, a good passer and an excellent defensive player. He could do everything and do it well."

After college, Sandy was drafted in the first round by the New York Titans of the American Football League. "At the time," Sandy said, "the Titans didn't want a black man playing quarterback. Cleveland had my NFL rights, but the NFL still wasn't ready for a black quarterback. So, I was forced to play in Canada." With the promise that he would be given a chance to play quarterback, Sandy then went north of the border to the Montreal Alouettes. Montreal had finished last in the Canadian Football League the year before, but with Stephens at the helm, he led the Als to the CFL Finals.

After three years in Canada, Sandy's life was abruptly changed when he was involved in a nearly fatal car accident. The doctors said that he would never walk again, but Sandy was determined. In 1966, Sandy's old teammate and friend, Bobby Bell, asked his Kansas City Chiefs coach, Hank Stram, to give his old buddy a shot at a comeback. Sandy overcame the odds and went on to play in the Chiefs organization for two seasons, both as a defensive halfback as well as a quarterback. He retired from the NFL in 1970.

Among his many honors, in 1997 Stephens was inducted into the Rose Bowl Hall of Fame. "Getting this honor now, after all these years, is thrilling and definitely a high point in my life," he said. In addition, Sandy's No. 15 jersey was retired at half-time of the 2000 Minnesota vs. Iowa game which celebrated the 40th anniversary of the 1960 national championship.

Before his tragic death in June of 2000, Sandy had been recognized as a major influence in the breakthrough of African American athletes in collegiate athletics. He was a real pioneer both on and off the field and a was a true trailblazer in life. Long considered the greatest quarterback to ever wear the Maroon and Gold, he blessed the University of Minnesota football program with his talents and leadership like no other, before or since.

"I hope that they'll remember the championship teams that we had," said Stephens. "That's my biggest thing. I have always been a team player. The only reason that you achieve accolades is because of the teammates that you have, and I had great teammates all the way through. We were all champions."

From there, after nice runs by McNamara and Holme, Giel hit Bob Rutford in the end-zone to make it 20-0. The Gophers added a late safety to make the final score 22-0, and with that they had regained the precious Jug that had eluded them for a decade. Giel set a Big Ten record that day by handling the ball on 53 of 63 offensive plays, of which he ran for 112 yards. He also completed 13 of 18 passes for another 169 yards, returned one kickoff for 24-yards, and four punts for 59-yards. Oh yeah, on defense he also intercepted a pair of Michigan passes to end a couple of key drives. It was an unbelievable performance from an unbelievable player.

"They had kicked us around pretty good in those previous years and I really wanted to beat them badly," Giel later said. "From a personal standpoint, I would have to say that it was my best all-around game ever."

Giel was a throwback. Not only was he an unbelievable halfback, he was also an tremendous quarterback, defensive back, punter, punt returner, kick

GOPHERS IN THE COLLEGE FOOTBALL HALL OF FAME

Name	Pos.	Years	Inducted
Bert Baston	E	1914-16	1954
Bobby Bell	T	1960-62	1991
Bernie Bierman	Coach	1919-50	1955
Tom Brown	G	1958-60	2003
Fritz Crisler	Coach	1930-47	1954
Carl Eller	T	1961-63	2006
George Franck	HB	1938-40	2002
Paul Giel	HB	1951-53	1975
Lou Holtz	Coach	1969-2004	2008
Herb Joesting	FB	1925-27	1954
Pug Lund	HB	1932-34	1958
Bobby Marshall	E	1904-06	1971
John McGovern	QB	1908-10	1966
Bronko Nagurski	T/FB	1927-29	1951
Leo Nomellini	T	1946-49	1977
Eddie Rogers	E	1896-03	1968
Bruce Smith	HB	1939-41	1972
Clayton Tonnemaker	C	1946-49	1980
Ed Widseth	T	1934-36	1954
Dick Wildung	T	1940-42	1957
Henry Williams	Coach	1891-21	1951

returner and kicker. Giel's offensive regime is often credited for developing what was then called the "spread formation," which by today's NFL standards is called the "shotgun." It was that set-up that defenses feared most. In it, Giel lined up five yards back from center. This is where he could do the most damage. Having the advantage of not having to take a seven-step drop to get set to throw, he could see the defense from the pocket, giving him valuable time to raise holy hell in the backfield. Often he would pass, lighting up the secondary. Other times he would follow his fullback up the middle or his halfback around the end. He could hand-off the ball to Gopher All-American Bob McNamara or split wide in the single wing formation to run the option. Sometimes he would line up at the running back position behind either quarterback Geno Cappelletti or Don Swanson in the power-T formation and blast full speed ahead. Occasionally he would fool the defense and pull a quick kick or even punt the ball. When-

JUDGE DICKSON

Judge Dickson lettered three times at halfback for the Golden Gophers from 1959-61 and was a key member of the 1961 squad which captured the Big Ten title and the national championship. The Clairton, Penn., native also played a key role in helping to lead Minnesota past UCLA in the 1962 Rose Bowl as well. In addition, Dickson was a first-team Academic All-Big Ten selection and a second-team Academic All-America selection in 1961. He was later drafted by the NFL's St. Louis Cardinals and AFL's New York Titans (later renamed as the New York Jets). After a successful career with IBM, Dickson now serves as the co-chair, along with former teammate Bobby Bell, of the Sandy Stephens Scholarship Fund called "Building Bridges." He and Stephens were childhood friends who both came to Minnesota back in the late 1950s.

BOBBY BELL

Growing up in Shelby, N.C., Bobby Bell played quarterback for his high school six-man football team, until his senior year when he finally piloted an 11-man team. Bobby originally came to Minnesota with every intention of playing quarterback for the Golden Gophers. As a sophomore, he could run as fast and throw farther than all the quarterbacks in practice. But Coach Warmath had already begun to mold the great Sandy Stephens as his quarterback, and since the talented Bell was too good to keep on the bench, as Stephens' replacement, the coach put him in the line-up as an offensive and defensive tackle. Bell, who just wanted the chance to play, accepted the role and eventually became one of the greatest tackles not only in Gopher history, but in Big Ten history.

"Bobby was probably the most versatile player that I ever had the pleasure of playing with," said Sandy Stephens. "I don't know of anyone else who could have gone from quarterback to tackle. When he came in, the only place we had open was at left tackle, and coach Warmath realized that since he was such a good athlete, he had to play him somewhere. Bobby said that he just came here to play and didn't care where it was that he lined up. He was one of the only guys that could throw a football further than me, and I could throw it 80 yards.

The 6-4, 220-pounder's transition from signal-caller to tackle was hailed by sportswriters of the day as one of the modern wonders of college football. He led Minnesota to a 22-6-1 record during his tenure, including a national championship and Rose Bowl victory. There aren't many All-American tackles today that could boast to have the same sized 28 inch waist as Bell did back in 1961.

Bell is one of only eight Minnesota football players to earn consensus All-America honors in two different seasons, 1961 and 1962. He was awarded the prestigious Outland Trophy his senior year by a landslide vote, recognizing him as the nation's top interior lineman. During his career at the University, Bell won the conference MVP in 1962 and was All-Big Ten in both 1961 and 1962 as well. He was later elected to the College Football Hall of Fame in 1991.

Bell was such a fantastic athlete that he was actually recruited by several other U of M athletics programs in addition to the football team, including the gymnastics and baseball squads. Wanting to do more, he even became the first African-American to play a varsity game for the Gopher basketball team. Gopher Hockey Coach John Mariucci even tried to talk him into playing goalie. "He told me that I had the quickest reflexes that he'd ever seen and that I was going to be the first black hockey player in the country," said Bell. "Now, coming from North Carolina I had never even seen hockey before. So, when we got out on the ice and someone nearly took my head off with a puck, I told him that the only way I'd get out there is if he turned the net around in the other direction!"

As a professional in the NFL, Bell made another transition, this time to linebacker, where he guided the Kansas City Chiefs to two Super Bowls. In fact, Bell was one of the stars of the team that stopped the Vikings, who were led by his old teammate and friend Carl Eller, in Super Bowl IV in 1970. He would go on to play 13 years in the NFL, was an all-pro for eight consecutive seasons, and became the Chiefs' first inductee into the Pro Football Hall of Fame in 1983. Bobby Bell was undoubtedly the greatest lineman and one of the greatest athletes ever to wear the Maroon and Gold.

"I thought I had died and gone to heaven when I arrived at the University of Minnesota," said Bell. "Coming from North Carolina, I remember the first time I ever saw snow, it was so exciting. Being on campus as a Gopher was one of the most exciting things in my life. Playing in those Saturday football games was just so great. The fans and everybody were just really involved in the game. The night before our games we would stay at a hotel in St. Paul. Then, on Saturday, we would drive down University Avenue with a police escort, and it was just wall-to-wall people everywhere yelling and screaming for us. My heart started to pound like crazy. I was so excited, and my stomach was churning. I couldn't wait to get my uniform on. Getting off that bus and seeing all the people hanging out of the frat house windows was incredible. Seeing all that excitement in one place was fantastic. Everybody was so into it! Tickets to our games were nowhere to be found. I had so much fun there, and to this day I have a real love for the University of Minnesota."

ever he got into trouble, he would scramble — and boy could he scramble. On the other side of the ball Giel played cornerback, constantly making spectacular tackles. And with a quarterback's instincts, he could anticipate pass patterns to force timely interceptions. He was simply unstoppable.

Giel averaged more than 100 yards per game that year and for his efforts was again unanimously named as an All-American. In addition to being awarded the prestigious Big Ten Medal of Honor, he was given the Walter Camp Award for "Back of the Year," and was chosen UPI's "Player of the Year." The highlight, however, was his runner-up finish to Notre Dame Halfback Johnny Lattner in the Heisman Trophy race. It was so tight that it remains the closest balloting ever recorded. Many felt he would've won the nation's top honor had the Gophers won more games. It didn't matter. Minnesotans knew that he was the best all-around player in college football that season, regardless of the final voting. In his three seasons at Minnesota he scored 22 touchdowns, threw 13 touchdown passes, and racked up 5,094 all-purpose yards. What's even more amazing was that Giel was also named as an All-American Pitcher on the Gopher baseball team. In fact, after his senior year, he even decided to forego a certain star-studded career in the NFL to instead play major league baseball — first with the New York Giants and later with his hometown Minnesota Twins.

The Gophers went on to beat Pittsburgh, 35-14, behind Giel's three touchdowns, and Indiana, 28-20, before getting shut out by Iowa, 21-0. They ended the season by once again tying Wisconsin, 21-21, this time fumbling on the Badger two-yard line with just a minute to go, to finish with a 4-4-1 record — far short of pre-season expectations. At the end of the season Coach Fesler resigned his post to accept an executive position with a Minneapolis radio station. And with that, for the second time in three years, Minnesota found itself looking for a new head football coach.

Enter the "Autumn Warrior"

With the resignation of Fesler as Minnesota's football coach, rumors ran wild about reports that former Gopher star Bud Wilkinson, who was coaching at Oklahoma at the time, was going to be named as the team's new skipper. It never happened, however, and in late January of 1954, Gopher Athletics Director Ike Armstrong announced that Mississippi State Head Coach Murray Warmath had been selected to fill the vacant post. The choice of Warmath, a virtual unknown, was unacceptable to many Gopher fans, who, in addition to being upset about hiring a coach who was not a member of the Big Ten family, were reeling about the University's inability to lure their native son, Wilkinson, back to campus.

Warmath, who had played at Tennessee under

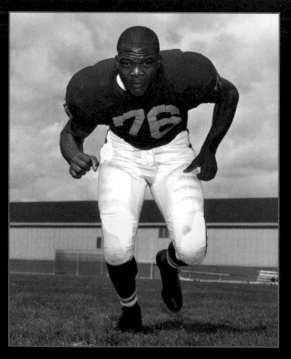

CARL ELLER

A native of Winston Salem, N.C., Carl Eller starred as a two-time All-American defensive tackle for the Gophers from 1961-63. The six-foot-six 260 pound terror was then selected by the Vikings with the sixth overall pick of the first round of the NFL draft. He went on to play 225 regular-season games over 15 years for the Vikings before spending one final season with the Seattle Seahawks in 1979. He was named All-Pro six times, was the NFL's Most Valuable Defensive Lineman twice, and played in six Pro Bowls. He was also voted as the NFL's Defensive Player of the Year in 1971.

Eller would retire as the Vikings all-time sack leader, with 130, and a whopping 44 from 1975-77 alone. He also recovered 23 fumbles, a number that still ranks in the top five in NFL history. Eller's leadership and abilities were a big reason for the Vikings 11 division titles, three NFC crowns and four Super Bowl appearances. He retired after 16 professional football seasons in 1979 but probably could've kept right on playing if he really wanted to. He was just that good. Known for his outstanding speed, power and agility, Eller was elected to the Pro Football Hall of Fame in 2004.

"Being a Golden Gopher was great," said Eller. "Going to the U was one of the better choices that I made in my life. Being on a metropolitan campus and being a part of the Saturday football scene at Memorial Stadium were wonderful experiences for me. Sure, it was a culture shock because I had come from a segregated town in North Carolina. But I did all right. Everything at the U was a new and incredible experience for me, and it was my first exposure to big-time football. Yes, it means a lot for me to be a Gopher."

TOM BROWN

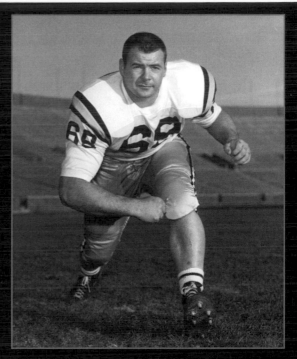

Tom Brown, who played football and ran track at the U of M from 1958-60, was one of the all-time greatest offensive and defensive linemen ever to wear the Maroon and Gold. Brown grew up loving sports and went on to star in football, track, and swimming at Minneapolis Central High School. After winning the state championship in the shot-put and discuss, the heavily recruited prep football and track star decided to attend the U of M, where he not only ran track, but also played offensive and defensive tackle on the football team.

In 1960, Tom's senior year, the Gophers tied for the Big Ten title, were voted national champions and went to the Rose Bowl. The defensive unit allowed only 88 points that entire season. One of the stars of that team was the "Rock of Gibraltar," Tom Brown. His Herculean strength was legendary, and his ability to blast holes in opposing defensive lines made him an easy pick for the Outland Trophy, recognizing him as the best lineman in the country. He was also named as the Big Ten MVP, a first team All-American, and runner-up in the Heisman Trophy voting. Brown was later inducted into the College Football Hall of Fame in 2003.

"Tom Brown scared more people on a football field than any player in Minnesota history," said former Coach Murray Warmath. "He was a one-man interior line."

After his collegiate career, Tom was drafted by the Baltimore Colts in the NFL as well as the British Columbia Lions in the Canadian Football League. "I didn't want to move to Baltimore," said Brown. "I thought that the Great Northwest would fit my outdoor lifestyle much better." So he headed north of the border, where, in 1964, he led the Lions to the Grey Cup championship and was named as the team's MVP. He would win one more Grey Cup during his tenure in B.C. before having to retire prematurely due to a neck injury in 1967.

"Being a Gopher was a very prominent part of my life," said Brown. "Growing up there, I used to follow everything at the University even though there wasn't a lot of TV at the time. When I saw all of the other kids not only from Minnesota, but from other states trying to get into the University to play sports, it made me want to go there even more. I wouldn't trade my experiences there for anything."

General Bob Neyland, had also coached at Army and Mississippi State. He brought four "Dixie" assistants with him, but opted to keep Butch Nash on staff, a decision that certainly pleased the alums. A student of the split "T" offense, complete with a plethora of flankers spread out behind the line, Warmath would do pretty darn good in his first season behind the Gopher bench, even quieting a few of his critics along the way. Warmath showed his military roots too, by announcing that the team would have practice every morning at 6:30 a.m., something that went over about as good as a warm beer on a hot day with the players.

In addition to Bob McNamara, there were several other standouts from the Fesler era on the squad including Gino Cappelletti, John Baumgartner, Don Swanson and Jimmy Soltau. There were also a couple of promising young sophomores in Dick "Pinky" McNamara — Bob's younger brother, Center Dean Maas and future All-American Tackle Bob Hobert. The team rallied behind their new coach and finished with a very surprising 7-2 record that year that featured wins over Nebraska, Pittsburgh, Northwestern, Illinois, Michigan State, Oregon State and Iowa, and just

a pair of losses to Michigan and Wisconsin. Chants of "Mac and Cappy" (McNamara and Cappelletti) were abound at Memorial Stadium that year, as the Gopher faithful liked what they saw.

Leading the way for the Gophers that season was running back and team captain Bob McNamara, who had fully recovered from knee surgery just the year before to receive All-American honors. Big Mac's tough running accounted for at least three Gopher victories that year. He ran for one score in the opening 19-7 win over Nebraska, returned a punt 65 yards for a TD to turn a close game with Pitt into a 46-7 rout, scored twice in the 26-7 win over Northwestern, added another in the 19-6 victory over the Illini, put in two more in the 19-13 win over Michigan State, and tallied a pair in the 44-6 crushing of Oregon State.

Then, against Iowa, McNamara gained 209 first half yards alone, and scored the first two Gopher touchdowns — a 36-yard run around the left end, followed by an 89-yard kickoff return which Warmath later called the "greatest exhibition of one man against eleven he had ever witnessed." The game, which was deadlocked for the third time at 20-20 late, got crazy when an 85-yard Iowa touchdown run was nullified for a clipping penalty. Then, an Iowa fumble in their own end-zone gave the Gophers a safety, which, with the two points, was enough to give them a well-deserved 22-20 victory.

Warmath was pleased with his first season in Gold Country, but knew that he had a lot of work to do. His next few years at the Gopher helm would be a saga like non other. He made no bones about the fact that Minnesota's home-grown talent was simply not going to be enough to cut it any longer in the ultra-competitive Big Ten. With that, he took a big leap of faith and made the decision to recruit young African American men from out east and down south to come to Minnesota. While it proved to be an unpopular move at first, most became pretty accepting of it when,

in 1960, he brought Minnesota it's first national championship in nearly 20 years.

Warmath's second year, 1955, was a rebuilding one as his Gophers posted just three wins and twice as many losses, en route to registering a dismal 2-5 Big Ten record. Washington squashed Minnesota, 30-0, in the opener, while an errant fumble cost them a tie in the 7-6 loss against Purdue. Missed conversions were big factors in the 21-13 and 14-13 losses to both Illinois and Michigan as well. On the bright side, Fullback Dick Borstad tallied in the 18-7 win over Northwestern, while Halfback Bob Schultz scored a pair of touchdowns in the 21-6 upset victory of Wisconsin. Perhaps the highlight of the season came against mighty USC, when the Gophers upset the Trojans, 25-19, in a classic snow-fest at old Memorial. Richard Borstad scored twice and Quarter-

MURRAY WARMATH

Murray Warmath grew up in the tiny western Tennessee town of Humboldt and graduated from a nearby military prep school in 1930. From there, Warmath went on to play college football at the University of Tennessee under General Bob Neyland, where he lined up as a tight end and guard, graduating in 1934. Warmath's illustrious coaching career would span many, many years, starting as an assistant at Mississippi State from 1939-45. From there, Warmath went on to coach at Army and in 1952 he took over as the head coach back at Mississippi State, posting a 10-6-3 record from 1952-53.

In 1954 Warmath took over as the new head coach at the University of Minnesota and he would go on to make history in Gold Country. After struggling for a few seasons, everything came together in 1960, when the Gophers, despite losing to the University of Washington, 17-7, in the Rose Bowl, went on to stun the college football world by winning the national championship. (In those days the national champion was crowned at the conclusion of the regular season, so Minnesota won the title before going to the Rose Bowl.) For his efforts, Warmath was named as the NCAA Coach of the Year.

The 1961 team, behind Big Ten MVP, Sandy Stephens, went on to win the Rose Bowl, 21-3, over UCLA. They would come close again that next season, but were robbed of another run for the roses after a very controversial game in Wisconsin. The run was over. For three glorious seasons in the early 1960s, Minnesota had produced a very respectable 22-6-1 record, entitling them to a National Championship, a Big Ten title, and a Rose Bowl victory.

The next few years would take a toll on Warmath, however, as his team began the dreaded rebuilding process. They went through some ups and downs over the next couple of seasons and then put it all together in 1967 when they shared co-Big Ten honors with Indiana and Purdue. In 1971, after 18 seasons in Gold Country, Warmath resigned. A man of dignity, toughness and pride, the Autumn Warrior took a program in shambles and built it into a national champion, and for that he will always be remembered as one of the great ones.

After coaching the Gophers, Warmath served as an assistant with the Minnesota Vikings for two years and then spent another 10 years as a scout for the team. In all Warmath would spend 65 years in the game of football, playing, coaching and scouting. A true football coaching legend, Murray Warmath, now in his late 90s, lives in the Twin Cities.

"I have never been anything other than a football coach in my life and I am a lucky man for that," said Warmath. "I think that I had a good influence on a lot of people and that was important to me too. I just hope that my players had the same amount or respect and regard for me as I did for them."

back Don Swanson added another on a 65-yard keeper to "ice" it for Minnesota.

The 1956 Gophers had to face a quarterback controversy at the start of the season when incumbent QB Dick Larson was joined in the backfield by Bobby Cox, a transfer from the University of Washington. After smoking Washington 34-14, and rallying to beat Purdue, 21-14, on Ken Bombardier's fourth-quarter TD, Minnesota managed just a 0-0 tie with Northwestern. From there the Maroon and Gold went on a three-game winning streak which began with a 16-13 win over Illinois, thanks to Cox's long punt return which led to Dick Borstad's game-winning field goal. Cox again played the hero that next Saturday when he led the Gophers to a 20-7 victory thanks to his two fourth-quarter touchdowns.

While Borstad's late field goal was enough to get past Pittsburgh, 9-6, in Week Six, the unbeaten Gophers were upset by the Hawkeyes the following weekend. Fumbles and penalties plagued the Gophers all day, as Iowa hung on for a 7-0 victory at Memorial Stadium. Minnesota rebounded to edge Michigan State, 14-13, on Blakley's fourth-quarter touchdown run, but managed just a 13-13 tie with Wisconsin in the season finale. With that, the 6-1-2 Gophers painfully watched Iowa pound Oregon State in the Rose Bowl, as their successful season somehow ended in disappointment.

With Tackle Bob Hobert (who anchored a defense that gave up just 87 points in 1956), Center Dean Maas, and Halfback Pinky McNamara being the only regulars lost to graduation, the 1957 Gophers, which featured Cox, Larson, Blakley, Borstad and Jon Jelacic, were feeling good about their prospects that year. But, despite the high expectations, in the end it was a season that just wasn't meant to be. Their potent offense, which put 201 points on the board, had to contend with a porous defense that surrendered 188 points as well. When it was all said and done, Minnesota had finished the season with a 4-5 record. It would be the start of a miserable pair of seasons in Gopher land, in terms of won-lost records, which would then be followed by one of the most amazing turn-arounds in college football history.

The Good, the Bad and the Ugly

With victories over Washington and Northwestern, along with a 21-17 win over Purdue, the Gophers started out their season at 3-0. From there the team traveled to Champaign, where the Gophers were feeling confident going into their game against the Illini. They had been tabbed as 13-point favorites and even had their star player, Bobby Cox, featured on the cover of Sports Illustrated that week. When it was all said and done though, the Gophers got embarrassed, losing 34-13, and scoring only on a couple of mop-up touchdowns against the Illini's scrubs late in the fourth. To compound matters, Cox's ankles were hurt and slowed him down, while Larson was also banged up at safety to make an already thin secondary even more suspect. After losing to Michigan that next week, the team managed to beat lowly Indiana, 34-0, before dropping the rest of their games to Iowa, Michigan State, and Wisconsin to round out the season.

The next year, 1958, the bottom fell out for the Gophers, who posted the worst season in modern his-

JULIAN HOOK

Despite his relatively small size of just five-foot-nine and 189 pounds, "Jules" Hook was a defensive stalwart on both the 1961 and 1962 Gopher Rose Bowl teams. In fact, Hook is personally credited with breaking up four major plays during the Illinois game in 1960 — a game many players refer to as the season's turning point, a 21-10 victory which propelled the team to the 1960 National Championship. Known for his quickness and agility, Hook earned All-Big Ten honors at linebacker during his senior season. He excelled on the gridiron because of his quickness and toughness; skills he honed as a Gopher wrestler. Hook later went on to obtain his law degree and served in the Minnesota Legislature from 1970-74 before opening his own law office in the Twin Cities.

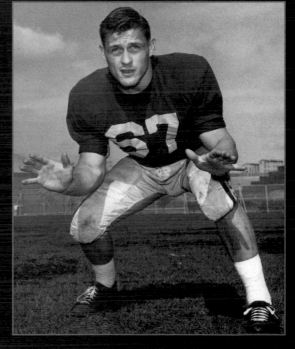

tory with just one win, against Michigan State, and eight losses. With their disappointing record, Warmath's critics had resurfaced big-time. So much was the pressure from the masses that Warmath even considered taking the head coaching position at Arkansas. Unfortunately, it didn't get any better in 1959 either, when the team went just 2-7, beating only lowly Indiana and Vanderbilt. By now there were loud cries from throughout the local sports world calling for Warmath's head. Even his own boosters, the "M" Club, felt that it would be best for both sides to part ways. If that weren't enough, a couple of local businessmen made an effort to buy off the remainder of his contract. It got so bad that Warmath's home even became a target for vandals.

Things were ugly in Gold Country all right, but somehow Warmath, ever the tactician, hung in there. He knew that he needed to not only recruit outside of Minnesota, but also recruit a new kind of player. You see, through that bad stretch he had gone out and recruited some of the most promising young African American players from around the country that college football would ever know. Among them were a crop of Pennsylvanians which included Quarterback Sandy Stephens, and a pair of Halfbacks — Judge Dickson and Bill Munsey. He also recruited a couple of future NFL Pro Bowl Defensive Ends out of North Carolina in Bobby Bell and Carl Eller.

"It became obvious," said Warmath in the

GOPHER HEISMAN TROPHY HISTORY

Name	Pos.	Year	Finish
George Franck	HB	1940	3rd
Bruce Smith	HB	1941	1st
Paul Giel	HB	1952	3rd
Paul Giel	HB	1953	2nd
Tom Brown	T	1960	2nd
Sandy Stephens	QB	1961	4th
Bobby Bell	T	1962	3rd

1972 book "Gold Glory," "that we couldn't win with just Minnesota boys, because of the small population of the state and the short season."

Joining that star-studded recruiting class for the 1960 campaign were a couple of other out-staters who would make an impact that year: Ends Bob Deegan and Tom Hall, Guard John Mulvena, Linebacker Julian Hook and Quarterback "Smoky" Joe Salem. They, along with homegrown holdovers: Guard Tom Brown, Fullback Roger Hagberg, Tackle Frank Brixius and Center Greg Larson, would join together to become a team of destiny. On the horizon was a turn-around which would become the most dramatic in Gopher history

After starting out the 1960 season with an embarrassing 19-7 pre-season loss to the alumni squad, Minnesota got its house in order by whipping the Nebraska Cornhuskers, 26-14, in Lincoln. Sandy Stephens led the charge in this one, running for one touchdown while passing to Dave Mulholland for another. Jim Rogers also scored on a short TD run following a fumble recovery, and the speedy defensive back, Bill Munsey, added a 42-yard interception return for the final score of the game. That following week Minnesota thrashed Indiana, 42-0, thanks to touchdowns from Roger Hagberg, on a short run around end, Bob Deegan, who caught a 46-yard TD from Stephens, Linebacker Jerry Annis, who returned an interception, Stephens, on a short dive over the middle, and Dave Lothner, on a pass from Salem.

1960 National Champions - Front Row (l-r) - Steve Jelacic, Dave Lothner, Jerry Jones, Bob Prawdzik, Bob Bell, Julian Hook, Paul Benson, Bill Munsey. **Second Row (l-r)** - Roger Hagberg, Bill Kauth, Lyle Skandel, Joe Salem, Larry Johnson, Jerry Annis, Frank Brixius, Greg Larson, Dick Miller, Tom Brown, Paul Gorgos, Dan Powers, Jim Rogers. **Third Row (l-r)** - Dick Larson, Dean Odegard, Wally Johnson, Dick Larson, Butch Nash, Jim Camp, Murray Warmath (Head Coach), Bob Bassons, Dick Borstad, Lloyd Stein, Milt Holmgren, Dana Marshall, Tom Robbins, Dale Halvorson. **Back Row (l-r)** - Bob McNeil, Dick Enga, John Mulvena, Tom Hall, Robin Tellor, Jim Wheeler, Bob Deegan, Jack Park, Tom Loechler, Bob Frisbee, Ted Rude, Judge Dickson, Dave Mulholland, Tom King, Sandy Stephens.

The Gophers won their third straight over Northwestern that next Saturday, 7-0. Tom Brown led the defensive surge to shut-out the Wildcats, while Sandy Stephens' lone four-yard touchdown run was enough to give Minnesota the victory. The winning drive began with Salem, who, after three successive hand-offs at midfield to Munsey, faked a draw and instead pulled up to hit Deegan on a 40-yard pass. Then, on third down, Stephens came back in and rushed it into the end-zone. Next up were the Illini, a team Minnesota would hang on to beat, 21-10, on a fourth quarter rally. Quarterback Larry Johnson led the late charge for the men of gold, as Stephens came in to cap a 66-yard game-winning scoring drive with nine-yard touchdown — his third on the day.

At 4-0, Minnesota was starting to gain some respect in gridiron circles. They would make some more believers that next week, when they blanked a very good Michigan team, 10-0, at Ann Arbor. Defense was the key to the team's big win that day, as they forced five fumbles and held the Wolverines to just 76 yards rushing and 68 yards passing. Jim Rogers finished a 44-yard scoring drive when he ran in what would prove to be the game-winner from the two yard line.

Kansas State then fell to the Gophers, 48-7, setting up an epic showdown between the suddenly No. 2 ranked Gophers and the No. 1 ranked Iowa

GOPHERS IN THE PRO FOOTBALL HALL OF FAME

Name	Pos.	Years	Inducted
Bobby Bell	T	1960-62	1991
Carl Eller	T	1961-63	2006
Bud Grant	E	1946-49	1994
Bronko Nagurski	T/FB	1927-29	1951
Leo Nomellini	T	1946-49	1977
Charlie Sanders	TE	1965-67	2007

Hawkeyes. Forest Evashevski's Hawks had owned the Gophers over the last five years, surrendering just 21 points over that time period. More than 65,000 Gopher fans somehow jammed into the 53,000-seat Memorial Stadium on that November 5th to see history. Iowa took the opening kickoff to mid-field, only to see Tom Brown so dominate the Hawkeye Center, that when it came time for him to long-snap the ball back to his punter, he nervously floated it straight over his head. Minnesota recovered the ball at the 14-yard line and made it 7-0 on Stephens' pitch it to Munsey a few plays later. Iowa came back on a field goal and later, in the second half, went 55 yards for a touchdown to take a 10-7 lead. Joe Salem then came off the bench and hit Hagberg on a couple of key passes which set up yet another Stephens touchdown run from inside the 10. Then, in the fourth, Tackle Jim Wheeler forced and recovered his own fumble, which then set up a Hagberg 42-yard touchdown run on the very next play. Bobby Bell later recovered a Hawkeye fumble deep in Iowa territory which set up a Salem touchdown run to make the final score 27-10 for Minnesota.

Against Iowa Tom Brown was simply unstoppable. "Brownie" had been stuffing the Hawkeye linemen all day and was just dominating both sides of the line. On one particular third-down play, with the ball on the Gopher five-yard line, Brown fired through the line just as the ball was snapped and he knocked the

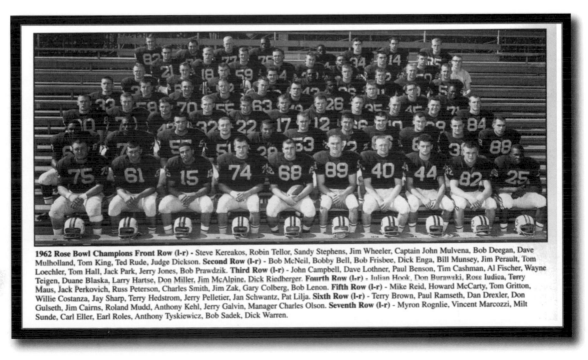

1962 Rose Bowl Champions Front Row (l-r) - Steve Kereakos, Robin Tellor, Sandy Stephens, Jim Wheeler, Captain John Mulvena, Bob Deegan, Dave Mulholland, Tom King, Ted Rude, Judge Dickson. Second Row (l-r) - Bob McNeil, Bobby Bell, Bob Frisbee, Dick Enga, Bill Munsey, Jim Perault, Tom Loechler, Tom Hall, Jack Park, Jerry Jones, Bob Prawdzik. Third Row (l-r) - John Campbell, Dave Lothner, Paul Benson, Tim Cashman, Al Fischer, Wayne Teigen, Duane Blaska, Larry Hartse, Don Miller, Jim McAlpine, Dick Riedberger. Fourth Row (l-r) - Julian Hook, Don Burawski, Ross Iudica, Terry Maus, Jack Perkovich, Russ Peterson, Charles Smith, Jim Zak, Gary Colberg, Bob Lenon. Fifth Row (l-r) - Mike Reid, Howard McCarty, Tom Gritton, Willie Costanza, Jay Sharp, Terry Hedstrom, Jerry Pelletier, Jan Schwantz, Pat Lilja. Sixth Row (l-r) - Terry Brown, Paul Ramseth, Dan Drexler, Don Gulseth, Jim Cairns, Roland Mudd, Anthony Kehl, Jerry Galvin, Manager Charles Olson. Seventh Row (l-r) - Myron Rognlie, Vincent Marcozzi, Milt Sunde, Carl Eller, Earl Roles, Anthony Tyskiewicz, Bob Sadek, Dick Warren.

center into the quarterback, who then flew back into the fullback — pancaking all three of them on their butts on one play for a five-yard loss. It was nothing short of spectacular. After that game Brown proudly hoisted Floyd of Rosedale over his head for all to see.

With the big win, Minnesota found itself as the No. 1 ranked team in the land. Then, out of the blue, last-place Purdue came to town and wrecked everything. Purdue Quarterback, and future Minnesota Twin, Bernie Allen led the Boilermakers on a pair of first half 80 and 25-yard touchdown drives to give his squad a 14-0 lead. Johnson led the Gophers back in the third on a 40-yard pass to Deegan, followed up by a 27-yard touchdown run by Munsey. Stephens then hit Munsey on a two-point conversion to make it 14-8. But after a Johnson interception, Purdue was able to drive and kick a 35-yard field goal. Minnesota rallied in the fourth behind a 27-yard, Stephens to Hall pass which set up a Hagberg touchdown. But when the Gophers fumbled in their own end-zone late in the game, Purdue was able to secure the 28-14 upset.

Down, but not out, the Gophers traveled to Wisconsin for the final game of the regular season

"Goldie" Gopher Returns To

PASADENA!

with a Big Ten title and possible Rose Bowl berth laying in the balance. Minnesota "rose" to occasion that afternoon, scoring a pair early and a pair late, as their top-rated defense shut down the Badgers to secure a 26-7 victory. With that, the Gophers found themselves at the top of both the AP and UPI final polls, declaring them as consensus national champions for the first time in two decades. And, although they had a better record, the Gophers did have to share the Big Ten title with Iowa. This was due to the fact that their early rout of Indiana, which was on probation for recruiting violations, did not count in the final standings. (The irony there was that the Hoosiers' coach was a guy by the name of Phil Dickens, who just so happened to be Warmath's roommate at Tennessee.) Fittingly, for his perseverance and courage, Warmath received full vindication by being named as college football's Coach of the Year. Bud Wilkinson would later comment on Warmath's achievement: "What he did under that pressure was one of the greatest things to happen to college coaching in a long, long time."

With their Big Ten title, their first since the in-

BOB STEIN

Bob Stein played football at Minnesota from 1966-68 and was a consensus first team All-American and All-Big Ten defensive end in both 1967 and 1968. In addition, Stein was a two-time Academic All-American, as well as a three time Academic All-Big Ten selection. Stein, who also kicked for the Gophers, broke the team record for career field goals and longest field goal (40 yards) in 1968.

In 1967, the Gophers finished tied with Indiana for the Big Ten title. But, even though they had already beaten the Hoosiers that season, Indiana was chosen to represent the Big Ten in the Rose Bowl because, according to the rules, Minnesota had played in the big game more recently, in 1961.

After graduating in 1969, Stein was selected by Kansas City in the fifth round of the NFL Draft. That season, Stein played in all 14 regular season games as a linebacker and helped lead the Chiefs past the Minnesota Vikings in Super Bowl IV. Stein played three more seasons with the Chiefs, and then moved on to play with the Los Angeles Rams for two seasons, followed by brief stints with both the San Diego Chargers and his hometown Vikings.

Stein retired following the 1975 season and went onto become a successful lawyer and businessman. He also served as the first general manager and later as president of the NBA's Minnesota Timberwolves.

vasion of Pearl Harbor, the Gophers would now have to sit back and wait to find out if, and where, they would be spending New Year's Day. You see, at the time, the Big Ten – Pacific Coast Rose Bowl pact was not in effect, which therefore allowed the PAC-10 champion, Washington, to choose its opponent. Luckily, however, they chose Minnesota, and the Gophers were off to Pasadena to face the Huskies in their first-ever Rose Bowl.

Once there, the Gophers were showered by well-wishers who simply couldn't get enough of this Cinderella story. When the game got going though, it became a different tale. Washington, unlike the star-struck Gophers, had been there before, crushing Wisconsin just the year before by the final of 44-8. Nearly 100,000 fans were on hand to watch what would later become a tale of two halves. The game got underway with the Huskies scoring early on a 34-yard field goal by George Fleming. From there they went on to score a pair of touchdowns in the second quarter, thanks in large part to the efforts of Quarterback Bob Schloredt, who threw for one and ran in the other from 31-yards out to give his squad a 17-0 half-time lead.

The Gophers, meanwhile, could muster just two first downs the entire half, while Stephens' interception didn't help much either. It was a different story in the second though, as the Gophers came out and rallied behind a Bob Deegan fumble recovery which set up an 18-yard touchdown pitch from Stephens to Munsey. Minnesota threatened to get back in the game by driving to the Washington six-yard line midway through the fourth, but were held when Stephens was sacked for a 13-yard loss. The Gophers then tried a little razzle-dazzle by going for a

GOPHER FIRST TEAM ALL-AMERICANS

Year	Name	Position			
1903	Fred Schact	Tackle	1938	Francis Twedell	Guard
1904	Moses Strathern	End	1940	Urban Odson	Tackle
1909	Johnny McGovern	QB		George Franck	Halfback
1910	James Walker	Tackle	1941	Bruce Smith	Halfback
1913	Clark Shaughnessy	Fullback		Dick Wildung	Tackle
1913	Lorin Solon	End	1942	Dick Wildung	Tackle
1914	Lorin Solon	End	1943	Bill Daley	Fullback
1915	Bert Baston	End		Herb Hein	End
	Bernie Bierman	Fullback	1948	Leo Nomellini	Tackle
	Merton Dunningan	Guard	1949	Leo Nomellini	Tackle
1916	Bert Baston	End		Clayton Tonnemaker	Center
	C.I. Long	QB	1952	Paul Giel	Halfback
1917	George Hauser	Tackle	1953	Paul Giel	Halfback
1923	Ray Ecklund	End	1954	Bob McNamara	Halfback
	Earl Martineau	Halfback	1956	Bob Hobert	Tackle
1926	Herb Joesting	Fullback	1960	Tom Brown	Guard
1927	Herb Joesting	Fullback	1961	Sandy Stephens	QB
	Harold Hanson	Guard		Bobby Bell	Tackle
1928	George Gibson	Guard	1962	Bobby Bell	Tackle
	Kenneth Haycraft	End	1963	Carl Eller	Tackle
1929	Bronko Nagurski	FB & Tackle	1965	Aaron Brown	End
1931	Biggie Munn	Guard	1967	Bob Stein	End
1933	Butch Larson	End	1968	Bob Stein	End
	Pug Lund	Halfback	1971	Doug Kingsriter	End
1934	Butch Larson	End	1997	Lemanzer Williams	Def. End
	Pug Lund	Halfback	1998	Tyrone Carter	Safety
	Bill Bevan	Guard	1999	Tyrone Carter	Safety
	Bob Tenner	End		Ben Hamilton	Center
1935	Bud Wilkinson	Guard	2000	Ben Hamilton	Center
	Ed Widseth	Tackle		Preston Gruening	Punter
	Dick Smith	Tackle	2004	Greg Eslinger	Center
1936	Ed Widseth	Tackle		Mark Setterstrom	Guard
1937	Ray King	End	2005	Greg Eslinger	Center
	Andy Uram	Fullback		Laurence Maroney	Halfback
			2006	Matt Spaeth	Tight End

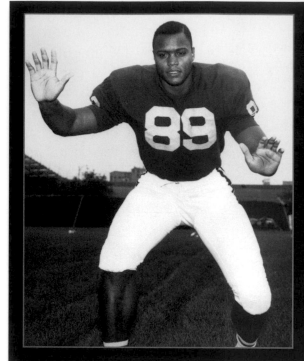

AARON BROWN

An outstanding two-way player, Aaron Brown was an All-American defensive end for the Gophers in 1965 and a two-time All-Big Ten selection in both 1964 and 1965. On the offensive side of the ball, Brown also set a then team record of 27 receptions in a season in 1964. From there, he went on to get drafted in the first round by the NFL's Kansas City Chiefs and played professionally for nine seasons, seven with Kansas City and two with the Green Bay Packers. Brown also played in two Super Bowls while he was with the Chiefs; losing in Super Bowl I to the Packers and then beating the Minnesota Vikings in Super Bowl IV.

fake field-goal on fourth-down, but came up short when Stephens, the holder, pulled up and threw an interception on a pass intended for Tom Hall at the Husky one yard line. The Gophers got the ball back late but were unable to get past the 35-yard line. Despite putting up 60 more total yards than the Huskies that afternoon, Minnesota came up on the short side of a 17-7 loss.

"We didn't play as well as we could, and on that day we played one of the best football teams I've seen in 18 years at Minnesota," Warmath would later say. "But as the game wore on, we started coming on fast and they were fading. Another 15 minutes and we maybe would have won."

"We made some stupid mistakes in that Rose Bowl game, but we knew we had a good team," said Stephens. "After the game, I recall that I had never felt so bad after losing. However, it was a fantastic experience for me. The Rose Bowl was everything I thought it would be and more. The whole first half we were sort of awe struck, but the second half we were ready to play. I think they only got one first down in the entire second half, and that was off a long quarterback sneak. We just couldn't get any offensive momentum going at that point, and we couldn't overcome Washington. I don't want to take anything away from the Huskies, they were a fine team. But they were just a better football team on that day. We lost the game, but were still national champions, and they can't take that away from us."

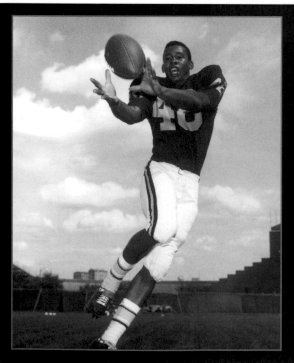

CHARLIE SANDERS

Charlie Sanders lettered for Minnesota in 1966 and 1967 as a tight end, earning All-Big Ten honors as a senior. He helped lead the Gophers to an 8-2 record and a share of the Big Ten title in 1967. Sanders moved to tight end as a senior where he caught 21 passes for 276 yards and two touchdowns. Sanders, who also played basketball for the Gophers, was drafted by Detroit in the third round of the 1968 NFL Draft and went on to play for the Lions for 10 seasons. By the time it was all said and done, he had caught 336 balls for 4,817 yards and 31 touchdowns. Among his many honors and accolades, Sanders was a two-time all-pro selection, an All-NFL selection once, seven-time Pro Bowler, and a member of the 1970s All-Decade team. In addition, he was inducted into the Pro Football Hall of Fame in 2007.

"The year before we finished near the bottom of the Big Ten, but we were actually very close to winning a lot of close games that we lost," added Tom Brown. "So, Coach Warmath got us all together and told us that we needed that extra little effort to cross that thin line between winning and losing. Beating the No. 2 ranked Nebraska Cornhuskers in a pre-season game really built our confidence, and from then on we felt like we could do some real good things that season. The Big Ten at that time was very dominant on the national football scene."

Despite losing the Rose Bowl, the Gophers still remained as National Champs, their sixth in program history, due to the fact that the voting was done prior to the post-season. When it was all said and done, Bobby Bell and Tom Brown each earned All-American honors. In addition, Brown, who also received the Outland Trophy as the best interior lineman in the nation, went on to be named as the Big Ten MVP and even finished as the runner-up in the Heisman Trophy voting — a first for a lineman.

Pasadena: Part II

The Gophers weren't going to sneak up on anyone in 1961 like they had done the year before. The team, which had lost a few key players to graduation, including Tom Brown and Joe Salem, still had a nucleus of stars in Bobby Bell, Sandy Stephens, Bill Munsey, Judge Dickson, and a new sophomore tackle by the name of Carl Eller, who stood six-foot-five and weighed in at 240 pounds. Eller and Bell, a pair of outstanding book-end tackles from North Carolina, would anchor the Gopher defense and eventually lead the squad back to Pasadena.

The team's season opener against Missouri at-

Keith Fahnhorst

Jim Fahnhorst

tracted a lot of national interest because the Tigers were the team that Minnesota had climbed over to earn the No. 1 ranking in the polls after the last week of the 1960 season. The playing conditions that day were less than desirable, to say the least. "It was the worst game in terms of weather conditions that I ever played in," said Stephens. "It was just awful, and it was so cold that I couldn't feel the ball when it was centered." The two teams battled back and forth all afternoon. Amidst constant rain and wind, however, the Tigers hung tough and upset the Gophers by the score of 6-0.

Minnesota won six in a row from there, starting with Oregon, who they rallied to beat, 14-7. Stephens scored both Minnesota touchdowns in this one, with the speedster from Fairmont, Jim Cairns, adding a two-pointer for good measure. Then, against Northwestern, Stephens tallied on a one-yarder, while Judge Dickson added a 31-yard field goal of his own to give the Gophers a 10-3 victory. In Champaign, Stephens beat the Fighting Illini all by himself, passing for four touchdowns and scoring a fifth on a short run.

In the 23-20 win over Michigan, Stephens, who was married just two days prior, played one of his best games ever, racking up over 300 all-purpose yards in another come-from-behind victory. The game started out horribly though, as Stephens coughed up two balls that led to Michigan touchdowns early on. Trailing 13-0, Stephens rolled out on his own 37-yard line, and behind the brilliant blocking of Cairns, sped 63 yards into the end-zone. He then hit End John Campbell with a two-point conversion pass. After a third quarter Wolverine touchdown to make it 20-8, Stephens struck again, hitting Jack Campbell on a 46-yard TD pass. Minnesota then had a touchdown called back on a penalty, only to have Judge Dickson re-

JULES PERLT

Julius "Jules" Perlt was a public address announcer at the University of Minnesota for more than a half century, at basketball, football, hockey and track events. Perlt announced his first football game in the Fall of 1928 and remained a fixture in Gold Country until 1987. Perlt was a throw-back and was known for his clever announcement of scores and players' names. He always tried to make the games fun for the fans and players alike, and that is what made him such a legendary figure on campus for so many years. In all, Perlt was behind the microphone for more than 400 football and 1,000 basketball games during his illustrious tenure with the Maroon and Gold. Not many people knew that Perlt was an outstanding gymnast for the Gophers. In fact, he was the 1923 and 1925 Parallel Bars Champion, 1924 and 1925 Big Ten Pommel Horse Champion, 1925 Big Ten Horizontal Bar Champion and 1926 Big Ten All Around Champion.

cover a fumble and then go in on a one-yarder to score the winning touchdown just a few plays later on a key fourth down. With under a minute to go, Stephens then hit Tom Hall for the two-pointer. Stephens even saved the day in the final seconds of the game when he deflected a sure touchdown pass on defense to ice it.

Then there was the 13-0 shutout over the then top-ranked Michigan State Spartans at Memorial Stadium, where Munsey, who had recovered from an injury that sidelined him from the Wolverine game the week before, scored both touchdowns for the Go-phers.

"I remember playing that great Michigan State team where they had the No. 1 offense in the country and we had the No. 1 defense," recalled Bobby Bell. "I think they were averaging something like 550 yards of offense per game, and at half-time they had like 26 yards — we shut them down. Carl was just unstoppable. We unbalanced the line that game so he could come down to my side and double-down. Carl would drive their guy into the ground every play and our offense took over. He was so tough and strong, that's why we named him the 'Moose.' He was the great-

NOEL JENKE

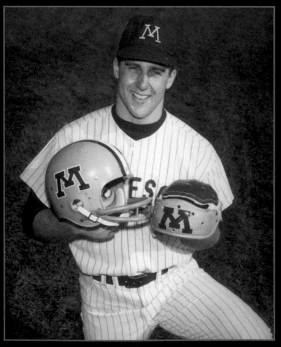

One of the top athletes ever to compete in Gold Country, Noel Jenke lettered three times in football and hockey, and once in baseball from 1966-69. In fact, he is the last three-time letter winner at the U of M. On the gridiron, Jenke wore the captain's "C" and earned All-Big Ten honors as a linebacker in 1968. He also earned Academic All-Big Ten honors in both 1968 and 1969 as well. In hockey, he was known for being a tough two-way player with great speed and power. On the baseball diamond Jenke also earned All-American and All-Big Ten honors as an outfielder.

When it was all said and done, Jenke was the first athlete in the history of U of M, as well as the Big Ten, to be drafted in three professional sports. (Baseball: Red Sox, Hockey: Blackhawks, Football: Vikings) He still holds the distinction of being the only college player to letter in three different sports and to be drafted professionally in each one. Among his many honors and accolades, Jenke also won the coveted Big Ten Medal Award Winner for Academics and Athletics in 1969.

Upon graduating, Jenke played professional baseball for nearly three seasons at the Triple A level and then played five seasons in the NFL for the Minnesota Vikings, Atlanta Falcons and Green Bay Packers.

DOUG KINGSRITER

Doug Kingsriter was an All-Big Ten and All-American tight end for the Gophers in 1971. Kingsriter led the team in receiving in 1970, '71 and '72 and went on to play in the North-South All-Star game after his senior season. An outstanding student-athlete, Kingsriter also earned Academic All-Big Ten and All-American honors in 1971-72. Among his many awards and accolades, he won the University of Minnesota's prestigious President's Cup in 1972; he was named as the Fellowship of Christian Athletes College Athlete of the year in 1973; and he was an NCAA Post Graduate Scholarship winner as well. Kingsriter was then drafted in the sixth round by the NFL's Minnesota Vikings in 1973 and went on to play for three seasons with the Purple, including stints in Super Bowls XIII and IX.

est."

Next up was Iowa. After giving up an early safety, Tom Loechler's field goal early in the second gave Minnesota a 3-2 lead. Then, in the third, Stephens tallied on a 39-yarder, followed by a touchdown on a blocked punt by Dick Enga, which was recovered in the end zone by Campbell to give the Gophers a 16-9 victory.

Purdue was next, as an all-time record crowd of 67,081 crammed into Memorial Stadium to watch the Gophers beat the Boilers, 10-7. Minnesota went ahead 10-0 on Tom Loechler's 25-yard field goal, followed by Stephens four-yard score. The Boilermakers rallied back to score, but the Gopher defense, which yielded just 27 yards of rushing on the day, stood firm in preserving the win in one of the most bruising battles in Gopher history.

Now only the Wisconsin Badgers stood in the way of the Gophers' first perfect Big Ten record since 1941. But Wisconsin coach Milt Bruhn, an ex-Gopher, had a different idea, as his Quarterback, Ron Miller, connected with Pat Richter for two touchdowns in leading his Badgers to a 28-21 win. In the loss, Stephens and Tom Hall combined for an 80-yard touchdown bomb, followed by Jerry Jones' 22-yard score. Stephens then connected with Al Fischer with just under two minutes to go, but it was too little too late.

Normally a 6-1 Big Ten record would make a solid case for winning the title, but in 1961 the undefeated Ohio State Buckeyes would receive that honor. Then, in a bizarre twist of fate, Woody Hayes' Ohio State Buckeyes, who were invited to play the UCLA Bruins in the Rose Bowl, declined the invitation. If an

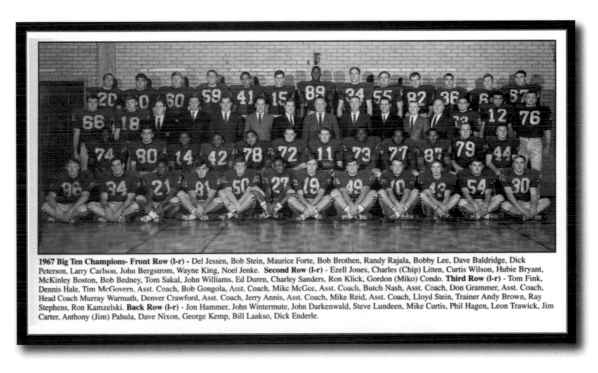

1967 Big Ten Champions- Front Row (l-r) - Del Jessen, Bob Stein, Maurice Forte, Bob Brothen, Randy Rajala, Bobby Lee, Dave Baldridge, Dick Peterson, Larry Carlson, John Bergstrom, Wayne King, Noel Jenke. Second Row (l-r) - Ezell Jones, Charles (Chip) Litten, Curtis Wilson, Hubie Bryant, McKinley Boston, Bob Bedney, Tom Sakal, John Williams, Ed Duren, Charley Sanders, Ron Klick, Gordon (Miko) Condo. Third Row (l-r) - Tom Fink, Dennis Hale, Tim McGovern, Asst. Coach, Bob Gongola, Asst. Coach, Mike McGee, Asst. Coach, Butch Nash, Asst. Coach, Don Grammer, Asst. Coach, Head Coach Murray Warmath, Denver Crawford, Asst. Coach, Jerry Annis, Asst. Coach, Mike Reid, Asst. Coach, Lloyd Stein, Trainer Andy Brown, Ray Stephens, Ron Kamzelski. Back Row (l-r) - Jon Hammer, John Wintermute, John Darkenwald, Steve Lundeen, Mike Curtis, Phil Hagen, Leon Trawick, Jim Carter, Anthony (Jim) Pahula, Dave Nixon, George Kemp, Bill Laakso, Dick Enderle.

official Big Ten-West Coast agreement been in effect at that time, Minnesota would have been ineligible to play in the big game two years in a row — but there was no such contract that year. As a result, the Rose Bowl committee selected the Gophers, and for the second time in as many years they were off to Pasadena for a run at the roses. (Incidentally, it would be the first college football game ever to be televised nationally in color.)

Reminiscent of the '61 Rose Bowl, when Washington scored a field goal on the opening drive, UCLA would also strike first in 1962. After being held deep in Gopher territory, the Bruins settled for a 28-yard field goal by Bob Smith just seven minutes into the game. The 98,214 fans that had poured into Pasadena's Rose Bowl to see the game could sense early on that Minnesota wasn't just happy to be there. That would be all the scoring the Bruins would do that day against the stingy Minnesota defense. The Gophers, haunted by the previous year's score, rallied back late in the first on a one-yard touchdown plunge by Stephens, which was made possible by Dickson's fumble recovery a few plays prior. Coach Warmath had decided early on that he wasn't going to play as conservatively this go-around, and his Gophers went for it on several pivotal fourth down plays — picking up a first down on one and scoring on another. Just before the half, Stephens marched the Gophers 75 yards for a second touchdown, with Munsey scoring on a reverse.

Dominating the game with their amazing defense, the Gophers looked poised in the second half. Stephens led the Gophers on an incredible 84-yard scoring drive late in the final period, scoring his second touchdown of the game from two yards out. The 19-play drive ate up 11 minutes off the clock, leaving little time for UCLA to do anything but won-

Marc Trestman

der what could have been. The Gophers controlled every aspect of the game, compiling 21 first downs while holding UCLA to eight. Led by the outstanding defensive play of Bell and Eller, Minnesota held the Bruins to a paltry 107 yards of total offense and a mere field goal. Minnesota would not be denied in their second run for the roses, winning the game, 21-3, for the team's first and only Rose Bowl victory. As coach Warmath was carried off the field, it was said that his smile could be seen all the way back in Minnesota.

"This time," Warmath would later say, "we were better prepared mentally because it was a team of veterans. We had a more professional attitude, and we wanted to redeem ourselves for what happened the year before. UCLA was not as good a team as Washington the year before, but we played an excellent game."

"We went out the year before and lost to Washington, so this year we were going to win the Rose Bowl, no matter what," said Bobby Bell. "We beat UCLA pretty bad, and I have to say it was amazing. It was one of the greatest things that ever happened to me in college. I was playing with cracked ribs during the game, but at the time I didn't care because I wanted to win so badly. I can remember our defensive coach was saying to us, 'Hey, if you let these guys run three or four yards up the middle, then we are not players at all, we might as well pack up, put our dresses back on, and go home.' Their running back, All-American, Charlie Smith, was a great player, but every time he got close to that line, we were all over him. We shut him down completely. It was great, and when it was over we were sitting on top of the world."

"It wouldn't have mattered who we would have played this go around," added Big Ten MVP, Sandy

Cal Stoll

RICK UPCHURCH

Rick Upchurch transferred to Minnesota after earning back-to-back All-American honors as a wide receiver/halfback/kick returner at Indian Hills Junior College in Iowa. With the Gophers, Upchurch was able to showcase his blistering speed with great success. A second team All-Big Ten honoree, Upchurch played for the Gophers from 1973-74 and once ran back a kickoff a record 100 yards. In addition to leading the team in rushing and scoring during the 1973 and 1974 campaigns, he led the team in receiving in 1974 as well. The Toledo, Ohio, native held the school record for most return yards in a season (305), and ranked tenth on the school's all-time rushing yards list (1,783) and yards in a season (942). In 1975, the receiver was selected in the fourth round of the NFL draft by the Denver Broncos. He would play his entire nine year career in the Mile High City, even earning the distinction of catching Hall of Fame Quarterback John Elway's first NFL pass. The four-time Pro-Bowler would go on to lead the NFL in punt return average twice (1978, 1982), and finished his career with 49 carries for 349 rushing yards, 267 receptions for 4,369 yards, 248 punt returns for 3,008 yards, and 95 kickoff returns for 2,355 yards. Overall, Upchurch gained 10,081 total yards and scored 35 touchdowns (8 punt return, 24 receiving, 3 rushing). At the time of his retirement, his eight punt returns for touchdowns were the most in NFL history. Furthermore, he was selected to two NFL All-Decade Teams as a kick returner.

Stephens. "I would have died before I lost that game, even if I had to win it all by myself. We just completely dominated UCLA from the point after they made that opening field goal. The game started out similar to the Rose Bowl of the year before, and that shocked us and woke us up pretty quick. That was the first and last time UCLA would score on us that day."

"I don't know if this is something that is very well known," said Carl Eller, "but I think that a lot of the senior players weren't sure if they even wanted to go back to the Rose Bowl in 1961. We actually had a team meeting on whether or not we should even go. Many of the players didn't want to go if Coach Warmath, who was a task-master, was going to lock them up in a retreat again when they were right down the street from Hollywood. Now, I was only a sophomore at the time, so I didn't have a voice on the team like the juniors and seniors did, but I felt like there was a mutiny going on. So, I stepped up and said, 'Hey guys, I don't want you to rob me of my chance to go to the Rose Bowl.' I didn't care what hotel we

MARION BARBER JR.

Marion Barber Jr. was a two-time All-Big Ten running back for the Maroon and Gold from 1977-80. The team MVP and captain finished his tenure in Gold Country with a record 3,094 yards (4.7 avg.) and 34 touchdowns. He was also a dangerous return man, adding another 700 all-purpose yards to his total as well. The Detroit, Mich., native then went on to play for the NFL's New York Jets for seven seasons from 1982-89. (Incidentally, his two sons would also play for the Gophers before going on to play in the NFL: Marion III, a Pro Bowl halfback with the Dallas Cowboys; and Dominique a cornerback with the Houston Oilers.)

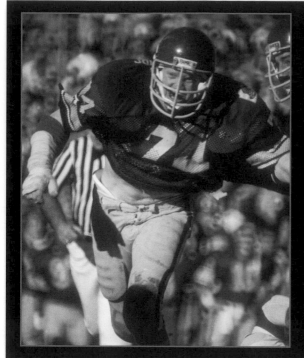

KARL MECKLENBURG

Karl Mecklenburg graduated from Edina West High School and then made the Gophers as a walk-on defensive end. He would go on to earn second team All-Big Ten honors as well as Academic All-Big Ten honors in 1982, while also receiving the Carl Eller Award that same year, given annually to the team's outstanding defensive player. From there, Mecklenburg went on to play in the NFL for 12 seasons with the Denver Broncos, where he played in three Super Bowls and became a six-time pro-bowler from 1983-94. He would finish his illustrious career with 79 sacks — second most in franchise history. "I grew up being a Gopher fan," said Mecklenburg. "My dad brought me to games in the old brick house as a kid. I used to pretend I was Gopher Tight End Doug Kingsriter when I played flag football with my friends. Getting the chance to live out my childhood fantasy of wearing the Maroon and Gold and representing the 'U' was a dream come true for me."

stayed at, I just wanted to go to the Rose Bowl! I think in retrospect, he (Warmath) probably did relax a little bit on us out there, and we had a great time that year. We had a very strong team in 1962 and we just over-powered UCLA, physically dominating them. It was a tremendous experience."

After the season several Gophers were honored, including Bell, who was once again named as a unanimous All-American, and was also awarded the prestigious Outland Trophy, recognizing him as the nation's top interior lineman. Sandy Stephens also became the first African American ever to be named as an All-American Quarterback.

Insanity at Camp Randall

With Stephens gone, Duane Blaska took over the quarterbacking duties in 1962. He was joined by a solid backfield that year as well, with Bill Munsey, Jerry Jones, Jim Cairns, Bill McMillan, Bill Crockett and Jerry Pelletier. It would be the defense, however, that would be the trademark of this team, which posted an amazing five shut-outs this season. Anchored by future Minnesota Viking's Hall of Famer Carl Eller, the Gopher defense allowed just 58 yards of rushing per game against Big Ten opposition, while surrendering a mere 61 points in nine games — more than half of which came in one game, a 34-22 upset by Northwestern.

After opening the season with a tough 0-0

MIKE HOHENSEE

Mike Hohensee was an All-American quarterback at Mt. San Antonio Junior College before transferring to the University of Minnesota in 1981. As a Gopher, he was the team's MVP and the University's Athlete of the Year in both 1981 and 1982. Despite playing just two seasons, Hohensee threw for a record 4,792 yards and 32 touchdowns. He also set several individual records in passing attempts, completions and touchdown passes, as well as records for consecutive 250-yard (4) and 300-yard (2) passing games. He also posted a record of 10 consecutive games with a touchdown pass. From there, Hohensee went on to play professionally in the Arena League, USFL and CFL, before getting into coaching.

standoff with Missouri, Minnesota went on to blank Navy, 21-0, even holding the Midshipmen to negative 31 yards rushing. After being upset by a pesky Northwestern team, they rebounded to post a pair of 17-0 shut-outs over Illinois and Michigan — the Wolverines were held to negative 46 yards rushing as well. They followed that up with wins over Michigan State, 28-7, Iowa, 10-0, and Purdue, 7-6.

With a 5-1 Big Ten record, the Gophers needed a win at Wisconsin to secure the conference title and a repeat trip to Pasadena. The Badgers, also at 5-1, were ready and waiting when the Gophers arrived at Camp Randall Stadium in Madison. Unfortunately, what followed could be considered to be one of the most bizarre and disturbing games ever played in college football history. When the dust finally settled in this one it became clear that the officials, not the players, played a pivotal role in a game that will

TONY DUNGY

Tony Dungy was born in Jackson, Mich., and went on to graduate from Parkside High School in Jackson. From there, Dungy went on to play football and basketball at the University of Minnesota. On the gridiron, Dungy quarterbacked the Golden Gophers from 1973-76, finishing as the school's career leader in pass attempts (576), completions (274), passing yards (3,577) and touchdown passes (25). In addition, Dungy rushed 413 times for 1,345 yards and 16 touchdowns, earning the team's MVP Award two times. As a senior, Dungy played in the East-West Shrine Game, the Hula Bowl and the Japan Bowl and upon completion of his career, he ranked fourth in Big Ten history in total offense behind Mike Phipps, Archie Griffin and Bob Griese.

On the hardwood, Dungy played only during his freshman year in Gold Country, averaging 2.6 points per game. Dungy graduated with a bachelor's degree in business administration in 1976. And, in addition to his incredible on-field performance, Dungy was also a two-time Academic All-Big Ten selection.

"The University of Minnesota is really where I got my start," said Dungy of his alma mater. "I owe a lot to Head Coach Cal Stoll. He helped shape some of my values and some of the things I wanted to do in my life. The 'U' is where I developed a lot of the values that I carry with me today."

"When you are playing for your school, representing them in the Big 10 Conference, playing against the best players in college football, it was a great thrill," he added. "Now, looking back as an alum, you see all the people who have come through the program and you realize that you were a part of it. That gives me a great feeling because I really enjoyed my time there at Minnesota. The school pride and school spirit was tremendous there and it was an honor to represent such a great university. I remember being recruited by both Cal Stoll and Bill Musselman and that was an exciting time. The atmosphere at the school was very positive at that time and I really liked the fact that it was a good academic school with a good business community nearby."

Following his college career, Dungy signed as a free agent with the Pittsburgh Steelers, where he was converted from quarterback to wide receiver to safety. In 1978 Dungy ranked second in the AFC with six interceptions and played in the Steelers' 35-31 victory over the Dallas Cowboys in Super Bowl XIII. That next year he was traded to the San Francisco 49ers, where he played in 15 games before being traded to the New York Giants. He would retire that next season, however, and in 1980 came back to serve as the defensive backs coach at his alma mater in Gold Country.

That next season Dungy got his first NFL coaching job with the Steelers, where he worked from 1981-88. He would serve as either an assistant or as a coordinator for the next eight years, including a four year stint as the defensive coordinator of the Minnesota Vikings, until finally landing the head coaching position with the Tampa Bay Buccaneers. There, Dungy would perform one of the greatest turn-arounds in pro football history. In 1997, after guiding the Buccaneers to a 10-6 record and a wild-card playoff victory over Detroit, Dungy was named Professional Coach of the Year by the Maxwell Football Club. Then, in 1999, the Buccaneers won the NFC Central, their first division championship in 18 seasons, and made it all the way to the conference finals.

In 2002 Dungy took over as the head coach of the Indianapolis Colts, where he led the team to a Super Bowl title in 2007 — becoming the first African-American head coach ever to do so. In 2009, after setting a new NFL record for consecutive playoff appearances by a head coach, with 10, Dungy announced his retirement, deciding to truly go out on the top of his game. Today Dungy is a sought after motivational speaker and also spends his time working with his many charities and philanthropic interests.

long be remembered for all of the wrong reasons in Gold Country.

The Gophers opened the scoring in the second quarter with Duane Blaska connecting with Jimmy Cairns on a 15 yard scoring strike. The extra point was no good. Badger Quarterback Ron VanderKelen then rallied his squad back with a 65-yard scoring drive to take at 7-6 lead. In the second half the game started to turn into a penalty-filled freak-show, capped by the Gophers being penalized 15 yards for illegally aiding the advance of a runner, Bill Munsey. Minnesota settled for a Collin Versich 32-yard field goal, and the scoreboard read: Minnesota 9, Wisconsin 7.

The Gophers later punted and the coverage team, seeing the ball clearly hit a Badger player, jumped on the loose ball rolling in the end zone and claimed a touchdown. The officials didn't see it that way, however, and returned the ball to Wisconsin out on the 20-yard line. The Gophers, dejected, assumed that the refs probably just didn't see it, and figured they would get it right the next time. Wrong! That's when it happened – an event that will live in infamy. On the Gopher 43 yard-line, VanderKelen dropped back to pass and was sacked hard by Bell. The ball then flew into the awaiting arms of Gopher John

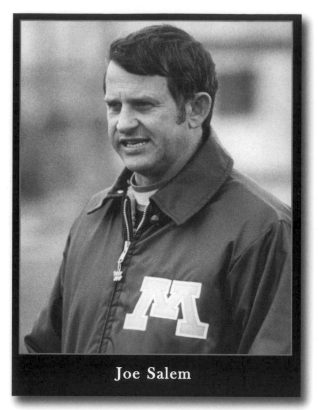

Joe Salem

Perkovich, only to have the referee, Robert Jones, nullify the interception. Incredibly, he even called Bell for roughing the passer. At this point, Coach Warmath could no longer contain himself. The 15-yard roughing call suddenly turned into 30 when the ref slapped the Gopher bench with an additional unsportsmanlike conduct penalty. So, instead of Minnesota having the ball at mid-field, the Badgers now had a first down on the Minnesota 13-yard line with less than two minutes to go. Three plays later Wisconsin scored to make it 14-9.

Then, amazingly, the officials, who were feeling the heat, decided to even things up and let the Gophers back into the contest by first calling the Badgers for a personal foul penalty on the ensuing kickoff, followed shortly thereafter by a pair of pass interference calls. Suddenly, with a minute to go in the game, the Gophers found themselves with a first down on the Wisconsin 14. Now it gets weird. Mysteriously, all communications from the press box to the Gopher bench disappeared, and the assistant coaches who had the bird's eye views were silenced with jammed head-sets. So, on first down, Blaska, not knowing otherwise, went for it all. But, his floater was picked-off in the end zone to kill the rally. Just like that, Wisconsin had won the Big

PETER NAJARIAN

By the time Peter Najarian had finished his tenure in Gold Country, the tough-as-nails linebacker had become the program's all-time leading tackler with 482. He also held the records for career assists (245), as well as solo tackles in a game (20), which happened in 1984. With a nose for the ball, Najarian led the team in tackles in each of his four seasons with the team (1982-85) and earned first team All-Big Ten honors as well as honorable mention All-American honors in 1985. The three-time Carl Eller Award winner (defensive MVP), was also an outstanding student-athlete, earning Academic All-Big Ten honors for three straight seasons (1983-85). After serving as team captain his senior year, Najarian was selected to play in the Hula Bowl, Japan Bowl and Senior Bowl. The speedy linebacker would then go on to play in the NFL from 1987-89 with the Minnesota Vikings and Tampa Bay Bucs. From there, Najarian went on to become an extremely successful businessman and co-host of his own CNBC financial television program, "Fast Money."

Ten championship. The irate Gopher fans had just witnessed their third straight Rose Bowl appearance vanish before their very eyes.

"I was called for roughing the Badger quarterback," said Bell, who would go on to receive All-American honors for the second straight year, "but you could see on the film that he still had the ball in his hands, so it couldn't have been roughing. It was a blown call. It was a mess and they ended up getting about 45 yards out of the whole thing, which ultimately led to them winning the game. It was the craziest game I ever played in. I bet that I've received hundreds of letters and newspaper clippings from around the country about that one play, and people still want to talk to me about it. The referee's name was Robert Jones. I will never forget that guy."

The run was over. For three glorious seasons in the early 1960s, Minnesota had produced a very respectable 22-6-1 record, entitling them to a National Championship, a Big Ten title and a Rose Bowl victory. Tougher times would lie ahead though as the next few years would take a toll on Warmath. The team lost a lot of key seniors from the 1962 team and 1963 was viewed as a rebuilding year. They did have Carl Eller and Milt Sunde, as well as a sophomore defensive end by the name of Aaron Brown, who would go on to become one of the great ones.

One of the highlights of the season came against the team's first-ever meeting with Army, as the Gophers spanked the Cadets, 24-8, thanks to the passing of Quarterback Bob Sadek and the running of Fullback Mike Reid. After finishing up the season with a promising 14-0 shut-out of Wisconsin, the Gophers packed it in with a humbling 3-6 record, good for ninth in the Big Ten. Carl Eller received All-American honors that year and would go on to become the

Kent Kitzmann

backbone of the Vikings' legendary "Purple People Eaters" defense.

That next year the team was led by a young quarterback named John Hankinson, who had a plethora of targets to throw to that year including: Kenny Last, Kent Kramer, Ray Whitlow, Billy Crockett and even Aaron Brown, who, platooning at tight end, caught a school record 27 balls that year. Minnesota put together a couple of winning seasons in 1964 and 1965, going 5-4 and 5-4-1 respectively. Aaron Brown, who, despite suffering a broken jaw on the opening play of the game against Washington State in 1965 — but still insisted on playing — was named as an All-American. Brown was so tough that he even finished the season with his mouth wired shut!

That 1965 team, which beat Indiana, 42-18, Iowa, 14-3, Michigan, 14-13, Northwestern, 27-22, and Wisconsin, 42-7, came on strong to finish tied for third place in the Big Ten. By the time team captain John Hankinson graduated that season, he had broken nearly every Minnesota passing record, including setting a single-season total offense plateau of 1,583 yards. ("Hank" would go on to play in the NFL with the Vikings, later producing three amazing kids who would all go on to play professional hockey in the NHL.)

Warmath was forced to rebuild yet again in 1966, this time with Curt Wilson as his quarterback. Wilson, a good running QB, was helped out that year by Warmath's decision to change to the "I" formation. The more high powered offensive attack was a struggle in the beginning, but started to take shape late in the season. Minnesota tallied wins against Stanford, Iowa, Ohio State and Northwestern, finishing their season with a 4-5-1 record, good for fifth in the Big Ten.

The nucleus of that team

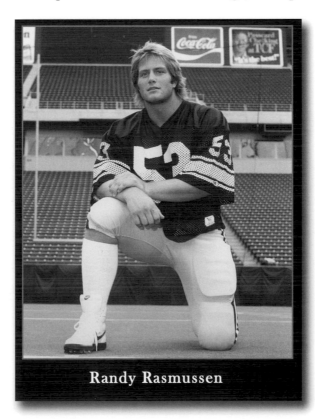
Randy Rasmussen

RICKEY FOGGIE

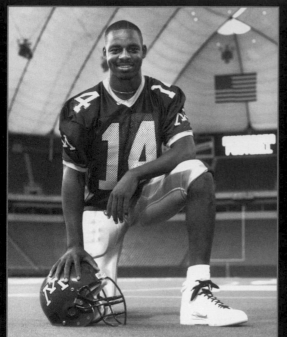

Rickey Foggie was born on July 1, 1966, in Waterloo, S.C., and grew up as one of nine siblings in a family that loved sports. At Laurens High School he was an all-conference and all-state performer in both football and basketball. As a senior, he led his high school football team to the South Carolina state championship. After being heavily recruited in both sports, Foggie came to Minnesota in 1983.

As a freshman, he led the team in both rushing and passing, and showed great promise by redefining the conventional rules of the quarterback position. For his career he was twice named as the team's MVP and twice he earned All Big Ten honors. He accounted for nearly 2,000 yards in offense in his senior season alone, passing for 1,232 yards and 8 TDs, while rushing for 714 yards and 6 TDs.

By the time it was all said and done, Foggie would leave Minnesota in 1987 as the school's all-time leader in total offense with 7,312 yards. In addition, he ranks in the top 10 all-time in rushing with 2,150 yards and 25 TDs as well. He also scored 160 points, threw a record 34 touchdowns, and ranked No. 2 all-time in career yards passing, with 5,162. Considered a threat every time he touched the ball, he became only the third quarterback in college football history to run for more than 2,000 yards and pass for more than 4,000 yards.

"Once I learned the great tradition of the school and its winning success, it all kind of sunk in," said Foggie. "Coach Holtz brought back a lot of the tradition. To be able to play in front of sell-out crowds for our first two years was great. I felt that we brought a college football atmosphere back to the U of M. The fans were great, and it always meant a lot to me that they supported me the way that they did. Maroon and Gold is something that I will never be able to get out of my system, and I am always proud to say that I am a Gopher."

"I would hope to be remembered," he added "as a guy who went out and just had fun playing the game, was part of rebuilding a program that had been down for a couple of years, and helped bring the excitement and respectability back to Gopher football."

returned in 1967, and with it came a renewed interest in Gopher football. The fans were again coming out to see this group which showed some real promise early on. Warmath had shifted Curtis Wilson, his starting quarterback from 1966, to halfback, and instead rotated Ray Stephens (Sandy's younger brother), Walter Bowser and Phil Hagen into the fold to share the duties as the team's signal caller.

The Gophers kicked off the season with a very unimpressive 13-12 win over Utah, followed by an even more unimpressive 7-0 loss to Nebraska. They rebounded though, beating SMU, 23-3, and the Illini, 10-7. Next up were the defending Big Ten champs from Michigan State, who came to campus riding a 16-game unbeaten streak. Warmath shook it up in this

John Gutekunst

one, switching Wilson back to quarterback, and letting the Spartan scouts believe that the Gophers were going to be utilizing his running skills that Saturday. Luckily for Murray, they took the bait. As the decoy Wilson torched MSU by passing for 264 yards and three touchdowns, including a pair to Chip Litten and another to Hubie Bryant, en route to a huge 21-0 upset victory. George Kemp and Jim Carter did most of the damage on the ground, combining for more than 100 yards rushing, while the Minnesota defense, anchored by All-American End Bob Stein, McKinley Boston, Dick Enderle and Del Jessen, shut-down the Spartan's high-octane offense.

Minnesota kept it going that next week, coming from behind to take a 20-15 win over Michigan, followed by a 10-0 shut-out victory over Iowa. They then suffered a mental lapse against Purdue in Week Eight, getting crushed 41-12. With the Big Ten title hanging in the balance, the undefeated Indiana Hoosiers came to town to let it all hang out. Minnesota opened the scoring in this one on Wilson's six-yard touchdown run in the second quarter. It would be just the first of four rushing touchdowns on the day for Wilson, who also passed for one as well to his favorite receiver, Charlie Sanders. Minnesota went on to win the game, 33-7.

With the win the Gophers found themselves in somewhat of a quagmire. You see, going into the last week of the season, they were in a position to win a share of the Big Ten title if they could beat Wisconsin. Indiana, which was playing Purdue, was in the identical position. However, if Minnesota lost their game, and finished second in the conference, they would get to go to the Rose Bowl. Confusing? Here's how it went down. Because Purdue was ineligible to go to the Rose Bowl that year (due to the fact that there was a rule at that time which declared that a team couldn't go two years in a row), the second place team would get to go instead. Well, the Gophers wound up beating the Badgers, 21-14, but it also so happened that Indiana upset Purdue, 19-14. With both Minnesota and Indiana now tied for the Big Ten title, along with Purdue (who was ineligible to go the Rose Bowl), the committee selected the Hoosiers to go over the Gophers because "they had never been there before." It was a tough blow to the players and fans alike, who really wanted to make another trip to Pasadena.

The season finale against the winless Wisconsin Badgers, meanwhile, was memorable to say the

GOPHER "M" CLUB
HALL OF FAME ENSHRINEES

Marion Barber Jr.	1977-80	Chip Lohmiller	1984-87
Bert Baston	1915-16	Francis "Pug" Lund	1932-34
Sheldon Beise	1933-35	John Mariucci	1938-1940
Bobby Bell	1960-62	Bobby Marshall	1904-06
William Bevan	1933-34	Earl Martineau	1921-24
Bernie Bierman	1913-15, Coach 1932-41, 1945-50	John McGovern	1908-10
Aaron Brown	1963-65	Bob McNamara	1951-54
Tom Brown	1958-60	Richard "Pinky" McNamara	1953-56
Larry Buhler	1936-38	Paul Mitchell	1941-43
Billy Bye	1946-49	Clarence "Biggie" Munn	1929-31
Gino Cappelletti	1952-54	Bronko Nagurski	1927-29
Ted Cox	1922-24	Peter Najarian	1982-85
Bill Daley	1940-42	George "Butch" Nash	1936-38
Judge Dickson	1959-61	Leo Nomellini	1946-49
Tony Dungy	1974-76	Malvin Nydahl	1926-28
Carl Eller	1961-63	Dwight Reed	1935-37
Keith Fahnhorst	1971-73	Ed Rogers	1902-03
Bob Fitch	1939-42, 1945	Glenn Seidel	1933-35
Rickey Foggie	1984-87	Bruce Smith	1939-41
George Gibson	1926-28	Richard Smith	1933-35
Paul Giel	1951-53	Lorin Solon	1913-15
Bob Graiziger	1942-45	Gordon Soltau	1946-49
Harry "Bud" Grant	1946-49	Bob Stein	1966-68
Sigmund Harris	1902-04	Sandy Stephens	1959-61
Bob Hobert	1954-56	Robert Tanner	1927-29
Mike Hohensee	1981-82	Darrell Thompson	1986-89
Julian Hook	1960-62	Clayton Tonnemaker	1946-49
Noel Jenke	1966-69	Francis Twedell	1936-39
Herb Joesting	1925-27	Rick Upchurch	1973-74
Ray King	1935-37	Andy Uram	1935-38
Doug Kingsriter	1970-72	Harold Van Every	1937-39
Frank "Butch" Larson	1932-34	Ed Widseth	1934-36
Vernal "Babe" LeVoir	1933-36	Dick Wildung	1940-42
Leonard "Butch" Levy	1939-41	Charles "Bud" Wilkinson	1934-36

least. With temperatures hovering in the mid-30's, the Gophers caught a break on the first play of the game when Ed Duren recovered a Badger fumble. Nine plays later, Dick Peterson punched it into the end zone to give Minnesota an early 7-0 lead. With the Gophers up 7-6 in the third, the Indiana vs. Purdue score was announced at Memorial Stadium. The Gopher players were obviously devastated. They kept it going though, putting together a 20-play, 77-yard drive that saw Quarterback Curtis Wilson score on the sneak from one yard out. Two plays into the ensuing Badger drive, junior Noel Jenke picked off his second pass of the game and eight plays later Wilson scored yet again from one yard out to give Minnesota a 21-6 lead. Wisconsin rallied though, behind a 51-yard touchdown by Stu Voigt, to make things interesting. Things got chippy down the stretch and eventually an all-out bench-clearing brawl ensued. Even the fans tried to get into the action, although unsuccessfully trying to make their way onto the field to join the fracas. Ironically, the only player ejected was Voigt, a future star tight end with the Minnesota Vikings. The game was put on ice late with just under a minute to go when Jenke grabbed his third interception of the game. The post-game report was described as such in the Min-

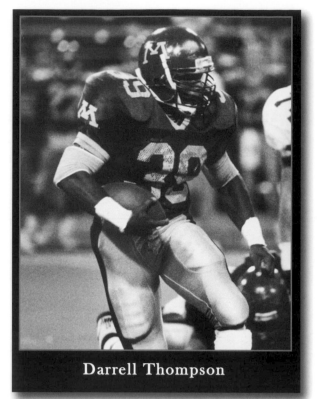

Darrell Thompson

neapolis Tribune: "There were no victory celebrations when the game ended and the Minnesota dressing room was cloaked in ironic stillness. Sixty-one Gopher players - 18 of them seniors - will not be making the trip they had figured to get. The champions will spend Christmas in Minneapolis."

Minnesota bounced back for a 6-4 overall record in 1968, finishing at 5-2 in the conference standings — good enough for a third place tie. After dropping the first two to USC and Nebraska, the U of M rallied to beat Wake Forest, 24-19, Illinois, 17-10, and Michigan State, 14-13. They then got beat by both Michigan and Iowa, 33-20, and, 35-28, respectively, only to come back with wins over Purdue, 27-13 (Running Back Jim Carter led the charge in upsetting the No. 1 ranked Boilermakers), Indiana, 20-6, and Wisconsin, 23-15. Leading the way for the Gophers that year was St. Louis Park's Bob Stein, who, for the second year in a row, received both All-American and Academic All-American honors. Stein would go on to play defensive end for the NFL's Kansas City Chiefs and Minnesota Vikings.

The next three years would also be the last three for Coach Warmath. That stretch included three losing seasons starting in 1969, when Minnesota

CHIP LOHMILLER

Chip Lohmiller made history for the Gophers from 1984-87 and emerged as one of the program's greatest all-time kickers. Lohmiller earned first team All-Big Ten and second team All-American honors in 1987. He finished his career ranked second on the U of M's individual records for scoring the most points in a career (268). He still holds the records for most PATs in a game (8); most career field goals (57) and highest percentage (.760). Lohmiller's longest field goal was 62 yarder, but his most important came in 1986, when he beat Michigan at Ann Arbor on a last second 30-yard prayer that gave the Gophers the Little Brown Jug. Lohmiller went on to play for nine years in the NFL, seven with the Washington Redskins (1988-1994), and one each with the New Orleans Saints (1995), and St. Louis Rams (1996). As a pro, the Woodbury, Minn., native made 71.8 percent of his field goals and even led the league in scoring in the 1991 regular season (149 points). That thrilling season culminated with the Redskins winning the Super Bowl back home in Minnesota at the Metrodome.

finished at 4-5-1, good for fourth in the Big Ten. In 1970 they wound up with a 3-6-1 record, while in 1971 they posted a 4-7 mark. One game of note in 1970, against Michigan State, saw Gopher Cornerback Walter Bowser run back 140 yards worth of interceptions, while Safety Jeff Wright picked off three of his own in the 23-13 victory. Fittingly, on the last drive of the last game of the 1971 season against Wisconsin, the boys of gold gave their coach a proper send-off by presenting him with a last-minute game-winning touchdown, courtesy of Craig Curry's pass to Mel Anderson, to eke out a 23-21 victory over the cheese-heads. It would be Warmath's 87th victory in 18 seasons.

One bright spot over those otherwise dismal last two seasons, however, was the outstanding play of Quarterback Craig Curry, who led the Big Ten in total offense over both of those years, including throwing a record nine touchdown passes in 1971. Another

A FEW WORDS WITH LOU HOLTZ

"When I came to the University of Minnesota I didn't know much about the state other than the fact that it was really cold!", quipped Holtz. "But really, it was a wonderful experience and I thoroughly enjoyed the people up there. Number one, it was such a great place to live. I mean you had culture, you had a tremendous business community, and it was just a beautiful place to live. I remember when my family went camping up in the Boundary Waters one Summer, that was something I will never forget. You also had such great people there too. I mean I became like brothers with Sid Hartman and Harvey Mackay, and then you had Paul Giel, who was such a legend up there too. When I got there, I quickly learned to appreciate the values that the people of Minnesota espouse. Then, as far as football went, it was actually easier to turn around the Gopher program than most people would think because of the character and integrity of the athletes who we had on our team. Being the only Division One program up there too, it gave you a real advantage when it came to recruiting. I mean the people really got behind us when I was there and that meant a lot to me. You know, the fans up there were just great, and really some of the best in the country. They supported us so much and were really a big part of our success during that time."

"Look, I went there to do everything I could to turn that program around. When I got there, I seriously planned on coaching there the rest of my life. I never went there thinking that it was going to be temporary or anything else. So, everything we tried to do, we tried to do it on a foundation that would last a lifetime. We never tried to cut corners, or play tricks, we just tried to build a good, solid program. You know, what people don't understand is that when I went to Minnesota, there were five other coaches who had already turned the job down. I mean they had lost 17 straight conference games by an average score of 47-13. So, I was hesitant to take the job at first, but finally decided to do it after praying on it. Then, I decided to put the Notre Dame clause in my contract. For me, being a Catholic, and following Notre Dame all my life, that was a very appealing job to me. What people do not understand about the clause, however, is that in it, it said that if we (Minnesota) had accepted a bowl bid, and Notre Dame had contacted me after that, then I was free to talk to them. I was not free to contact them, and I was not free to talk to them if we had not accepted a bowl bid. The logic was this. If we took a Minnesota program that was down and took it to a level where it was able to go to a bowl game, then I would be free to leave if I so desired. Because, by that time, the program would have gained respectability and wouldn't have any difficulty in recruiting and in bringing in a good, competent coach to take it to the next level.

"Now, Gene Corrigan was just hired as the new athletics director at Notre Dame at that time, and he had tried to hire me three different times when he was at the University of Virginia. So, I figured that if we were successful at Minnesota, then I would take the Notre Dame job if all of that played out. I wasn't sure if all of that would happen initially when I got to Minnesota, but I wanted to make sure that I had the chance to evaluate my options should it all play out. When it did, that is when I made my decision. I remember too that University of Minnesota President, Ken Keller, tried to get rid of that clause on several occasions. He came to me and wanted me to sign a lifetime contract. I initially agreed to what he had proposed, but he later withdrew the offer and said he couldn't do it. The two guys who can verify all of this are Sid Hartman and Harvey Mackay. That is what I want people to understand, is that I didn't go to Minnesota with the idea that I was going to leave. I came there thinking I was going to spend the rest of my life there. It didn't work out, but my time there was wonderful and I wouldn't trade it for anything."

emerging star was junior Doug Kingsriter, an All-American tight end from Richfield who became known for his spectacular one-handed grabs. Other great players from that era included: Walt Bowser, Jim Carter, Ernie Cook, Mo Forte, Phil Hagen, Kevin Hamm, Noel Jenke, Del Jessen, George Kemp, Wayne King, Bill Light, Chip Litten, Barry Mayer, Ray Parson, Doug Roalstad, Ray Stephens, John Wintermute and Jeff Wright, just to name a few.

By the early '70s times were tough in Gold Country and Warmath knew it. The numbers were down in the stands and it didn't take a rocket scientist to figure out that there was a direct correlation between the dwindling fan base at old Memorial and a very good "other" football team which was now tearing up the National Football League over at Bloomington's Metropolitan Stadium. With that, Warmath, after 18 seasons on campus, resigned. A man of dignity, toughness and pride, the Autumn Warrior took

a program in shambles and built it into a national champion, and for that he should be remembered as one of the great ones.

Re-Enter Paul Giel and a Man Named Cal

Times, they were a changin' in Minnesota during this tumultuous era. The war in Vietnam was raging and college kids had more important things to be worrying about than sports. Gopher football was hurting and needed a shot in the arm. Pressure was on from all sides to win. Bill Musselman, the Gophers new young basketball coach, came along in 1971 and led a rag-tag bunch of kids all the way to the school's first Big Ten championship since the 1930's. The football program now needed a new coach of their own to come in and turn it around 180 degrees, like Musselman had done at Williams Arena.

The answer came in the form of former Go-

pher All-American Paul Giel, who, after several years of pitching in the big-leagues, and a stint at WCCO Radio, came in to serve as the University's new athletics director. Giel came in and rounded up a lot of corporate support from local businesses, like Midwest Federal and Twin City Federal, to get the program off to a clean start. They were instrumental in helping the program to upgrade its facilities, which would include the future construction of the Bierman Building — complete with a training field, locker rooms and weight rooms. In addition, Giel decided to retrofit his new team with some classic golden colored uniforms, reminiscent of those dominant Gopher squads of the 1930s.

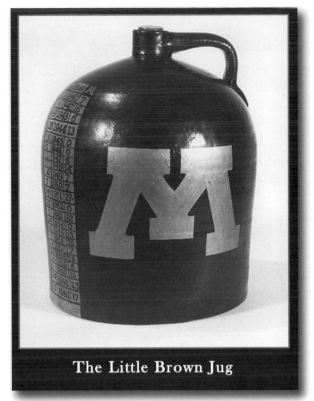

The Little Brown Jug

The next thing Giel did was to hire a new coach, and he did just that in landing former Gopher Defensive End, Cal Stoll, who had just led Wake Forest to back-to-back conference championships down in North Carolina. Stoll, who first learned the game playing six-man football up in tiny Tower City, North Dakota, was elated to come home to lead his alma mater. To his new post Stoll brought more than 20 years of coaching experience, and from the looks of his squad, he was going to need every bit of it. He had the support of the fans though. After all, he was the first "M" man since Bernie Bierman to come back as the school's head coach.

Stoll's Gophers got off to a rocky start in 1972, losing their first five games to Indiana, Colorado, Nebraska, Kansas and Purdue. They finally got in to the win column on October 21st, piling up more than 400 total yards of offense, including a 173 from Running Back John King, to beat Iowa, 43-14. After a 42-0 shut-out at the hands of Michigan, and a 27-19 loss to Ohio State, the Gophers rebounded to finish the season with three straight wins over Northwestern, 35-29 (a game which the team racked up nearly 500 yards of total offense), Michigan State, 14-10, and Wisconsin, 14-6. King led the charge for the Gophers that season as he pounded the opposition and set several rushing records along the way — including the single-season rushing mark with 1,164 yards on 237 carries. With a modest 4-7 record under their belts, the Gophers were poised to do even better that next year.

The Gophers, behind freshman Half Back

RAY CHRISTENSEN

One name that has become synonymous with Gopher sports over the years is that of broadcaster Ray Christensen, who, after more than a half century behind the microphone, decided to finally hang it up in 2001. Christensen attended school at the U of M during the 1940s and began his radio broadcast career in 1946 for the University radio station. In 1951, he began broadcasting Gopher football games, followed by Gopher basketball games in 1956. The rest, as they say, is history.

Christensen called more than 1,300 basketball games and 510 football games for the Maroon and Gold, entertaining and informing the Gopher faithful along the way. With his wonderful play-by-play and color-commentary, he became an icon both with the Gophers as well as with WCCO Radio. During his illustrious career, he has also broadcast games for the Minneapolis Lakers, St. Paul Saints, Minneapolis Millers, Minnesota Twins and Minnesota Vikings.

It was only fitting that in his last year before retiring that he finally get to witness the Gopher football team beat Ohio State, in Columbus. It was the first time that the team had beaten the Buckeyes on the road in over half a century, and for Ray it was worth the wait. Upon retiring, Christensen authored a book about his golden memories entitled appropriately enough, "Gopher Tales."

Larry Powell's running, did manage to improve their record to an impressive 7-4 that season, even finishing third in the Big Ten. Among their victims were Indiana, 24-3, Iowa, 31-23, Northwestern, 52-43, Purdue, 34-7, Illinois, 19-16, and Wisconsin, 19-17. The school's two conference losses came at the hands of Michigan, who won 34-7, and Ohio State, 56-7. During the 1970s, those two schools would absolutely dominate the world of college football. While King was the work-horse carrying the ball on the ground, and Receiver Mike Jones dominated through the air, the leader of the team was a kid by the name of Tony Dungy. Dungy, a speedy and crafty quarterback, would lead the Gophers for the next three years. (Dungy would go on to become a Super Bowl-winning NFL head coach years later with the Indianapolis Colts.)

One of the big stories of that 1973 season was the improbable saga of Powell, who tore it up that year only to nearly lose his life the next. Powell, the crown jewel of Stoll's recruiting class, came out of Michigan that year and made his presence felt with his blinding speed. However, Powell contracted French Polio during that off-season, dropping down to a mere 115 pounds, and nearly died. He did recover, but sadly he never played football again.

"I think if Larry Powell had stayed healthy, he would have won the Heisman Trophy," Stoll later said. "I know that sounds far-fetched, but that's how good he was. He was the best running back I ever recruited. Many scouts liked him better than Tony Dorsett, who was a contemporary. We might have gotten over the hump if Larry hadn't had such rotten luck. I'm serious. He was that good."

In 1974 Running Back Rick Upchurch hit the gridiron. He would go on to become one of the great ones in Gold Country, setting several

Brian Williams

rushing records over the next couple of years. The Gophers slipped to 2-6 in the Big Ten that season, beating only Iowa and Purdue, and ultimately finishing in just 7th place. One highlight though came on the last game of the season, when Upchurch returned a kick-off a record 100 yards against Wisconsin.

The 1975 season was more of the same for the Gophers, who managed just a 3-5 record that year. Dungy did throw 15 touchdowns though, en route to leading his team to wins over Iowa, 31-7, Northwestern, 33-9, and Wisconsin, 24-3. Minnesota then rebounded in 1976, behind the running of Jim Perkins and the passing of Dungy, to finish with a much improved 4-4 record in the Big Ten. The team got conference wins that year over Indiana, 21-13, Illinois, 29-14, Michigan State, 14-10, and Northwestern, 38-10.

Stoll's most exciting season was without question 1977. That was the year Minnesota finally turned the corner and gave the football faithful on campus a reason to once again get excited. After beating lowly Western Michigan, 10-7, in the season opener, the Gophers got waxed by Ohio State in Columbus, 38-7, with their only touchdown coming on an amazing Bobby Weber 100-yard kick-off return for a touchdown.

They mounted a nice pair of victories over their next two games at Memorial Stadium against UCLA and Washington though, beating them 27-13, and 19-17, respectively. Those two Western power-houses would later battle for the Pac-8 Rose Bowl berth, with the Huskies eventually getting the nod to go to Pasadena and beating the eventual Big Ten champs from Michigan. After suffering an 18-6 setback against Iowa, the Gophers rallied back to beat a respectable Northwestern team by the final score of 13-7.

Chris Gaiters

What followed that next Saturday, October 22nd, at old Memorial, was one of the most special moments in Gopher history. The No. 1-ranked Michigan Wolverines had come to town with an offense that had not been shut-out in 113 games as well as a stifling defense. Both of those things would change on that day though. The Gopher faithful hadn't forgotten about the thrashing they had received just a year earlier, when Michigan buried the Gophers, 45-0, in Ann Arbor, and they also remembered the last time they had won the Little Brown Jug, way back in 1967. All of these factors went into the making of one of the program's biggest upsets of all-time, which would ultimately foil Michigan's national championship hopes.

Thanks to sophomore Quarterback Mark Carlson and a pair of Michiganders, Paul Rogind, who tallied three field goals, and Freshman Running Back Marion Barber Jr., who scored the game's only touchdown, a four-yard run up the middle — the Gophers blanked the era's most dominant team by the final score of 16-0. The Minnesota defense was huge in this one, all but shutting down Michigan Quarterback Rick Leach, a player that Coach Bo Schembechler would, at the time, call his "best ever." Led by Linebacker Michael Hunt, who would be named as the

National Defensive Player of the Week, and Defensive End Mark Merrill, who forced an early fumble which led to a Gopher score, Minnesota never let Michigan into the game. They held the Wolverines to 80 net yards rushing and just 122 yards passing — most of which came late in the game against the Gopher's "prevent-zone" pass defense. "Unless you've been there, you can't know the feeling," Stoll said following the big win. "There is nothing like it."

The emotional win would get the best of them, however, as the Hoosiers ambushed the Gophers that very next week in Bloomington, 34-22, followed by a disappointing 29-10 loss at home to Michigan State. They would rebound though against a very good Illinois team in Week 10, thanks in large part to the running of Rochester's Kent Kitzmann, who carried the ball a record 57 times for 266 yards in the Gophers' 21-0 triumph over the Illini in Champaign. On one second half drive Kitzmann carried the ball 13 consecutive times, never once losing yardage. "The line was great," said Kitzmann. "My job was probably easier than theirs, considering the way they knocked people off the line of scrimmage."

Kitzmann took "only" 40 hand-offs against Wisconsin the following week, rushing this time for 154 yards in a 13-7 win. Marion Barber's 33-yard

MINNESOTA VS. WISCONSIN: COLLEGE FOOTBALL'S OLDEST RIVALRY

At 116 games and counting, the series between Minnesota and Wisconsin ranks as the longest, not to mention fiercest, in Division 1-A football. The Gophers won the first game in the series, 63-0, back in 1890. From there, the rivalry just grew and grew. The 1906 game was even canceled by President Theodore Roosevelt, who had "decided to cool off heated college football rivalries, because of injuries and deaths on the field."

In 1914, Minnesota invited the Badgers to be their first Homecoming opponent, with Wisconsin returning the favor as their first as well in 1919. The border battle has been epic over the years, and back then was no exception — from 1923 and 1925, the teams battled to three straight ties.

Wanting to "symbolically capture the amazing atmosphere of the annual match-up," in 1930 Dr. R.B. Fouch of Minneapolis fashioned a bacon slab out of black walnut to serve as a traveling trophy — similar to that of the "Little Brown Jug," which Minnesota and Michigan played for every year. The "Slab of Bacon" had a football carved on top inscribed with an "M" or "W," depending on which way it was held. The idea was that the winning team would "bring home the bacon."

Oddly, in the early '40s the slab went "missing." So, in 1948 "Paul Bunyan's Axe" was created to take its place, with the results of every game printed along its six-foot long handle in red ink. Meanwhile, the long-lost "Slab of Bacon" was "mysteriously" found in the summer of 1994 when a Camp Randall Stadium storage room was cleaned out. Despite the fact that the trophy had been missing for nearly a half century, somehow the scores of all the Wisconsin-Minnesota games had been printed on it. Hey, what's the deal with that, cheese-heads?

game-winning touchdown run was the big play though, as the Gophers clinched an invitation to play in the inaugural Hall of Fame Bowl. The 7-4 Gophers then headed south, to Birmingham, Alabama, where they would face the University of Maryland in the teams' first bowl appearance since the 1962 Rose Bowl win in Pasadena. With thousands of Gopher faithful on hand amidst the 47,000 fans at Legion Field, Minnesota took its opening drive 66 yards on 11 plays to take a 7-0 lead. Scoring for the Gophers was Barber, on a one-yard plunge, followed by Paul Rogind's extra point.

The Terrapins later connected on a 32-yard field goal, followed by a 69-yard touchdown drive midway through the second which was finished by Running Back George Scott's two-yard plunge over the middle. The Maroon & Gold, now down by three, let the wheels come off just two plays later by fumbling the ball on their own 14-yard line. Scott again made them pay, this time scoring his second touchdown of the day on a one-yard TD to make it 17-7 at the intermission. From there the Terrapin defense simply shut down the Gophers' offensive attack. Despite Kitzman's 76-yards rushing, Jeff Anhorn's 49-yards receiving, and Quarterback Wendell Avery's 130 yards through the air, Minnesota was held to just 268 total yards of offense for the game. Following a scoreless second half, which featured several valiant Gopher rallies that just came up short, the

Sean Lumpkin

game ended as a 17-7 loss.

Minnesota finished the 1977 season with a modest record of 7-5 and a fifth place Big Ten finish. They would go 5-6 in 1978, finishing fifth in the conference yet again that year. Quarterback Mark Carlson proved to be a solid performer in the pocket, while Receiver Elmer Bailey hauled in 27 balls for a modest 464 yards. In addition, Marion Barber lit it up on the ground, rushing for a school record 1,237 yards and eight touchdowns. Highlights included wins over Toledo, 38-12, Iowa, 22-20, Northwestern, 38-14, Indiana, 32-31, and Illinois, 24-6. The low-point of the year came on the season finale, when the lowly Badgers upset the Gophers, 48-10, at Wisconsin. Coming on the heels of Cal Stoll's best year, the crushing defeat left Minnesota no other choice but to start searching for a new head coach.

In his seven seasons on campus Cal Stoll's teams won 39 games and lost 39 games. His .500% record had its share of ups and downs, but was ultimately not impressive enough to earn him an eighth campaign behind the Gopher bench. Making matters even more difficult for Stoll was what was later referred to as the "Big Two" and the "Little Eight." The "Big Two" were Ohio State and Michigan, who won every football title in that 70s decade, while the "Little Eight" was simply everyone else — including Min-

nesota. With Woody Hayes at Ohio State and Bo Schembechler at Michigan, it gave teams little hope of ever getting over the hump. Incredibly, during the Stoll years, only Minnesota, Purdue, and Michigan State managed to win even one game from the "Big Two." To his credit though, Stoll outlasted all the other "Little Eight" coaches from the time he came into the conference back in 1972. Minnesota was 27-29 against Big Ten teams from 1972-78. However, if you were to exclude the Ohio State and Michigan games, they were a respectable 26-16. That translates to paltry 1-13 against the "Big Two," with the Michigan upset in 1977 being the only exception.

"Catching them was almost impossible," Stoll would later say of the "Big Two." "It's like running the mile, only they have a half-mile head start. And they aren't going to slow down."

Stoll's replacement in Gold Country would be none other than former Gopher Rose Bowl Quarterback, Joe Salem. "Smoky Joe," who had been an assistant with the Gophers in the mid-1960s, had moved on to coach at both South Dakota and Northern Arizona. Anxious to return to his alma mater, Salem opened his 1979 campaign with a 24-10 win over Ohio University, only to drop the next two to Ohio State and USC. They rebounded though, beating both Northwestern, 38-8, and Purdue, 31-14, before losing a tough one to Michigan, 31-21. They rallied to

CHARLES SCHULZ

"Good Grief!" Did you know that world famous cartoonist Charles Schulz was a die-hard Gopher Football fan? That's right. Schulz was born in Minneapolis on November 26, 1922, and grew up in St. Paul rooting for his beloved Gophers during the "Golden Era." After graduating from St. Paul Central High, Schulz went on to art school in Minneapolis. There, he created a comic strip about the adventures of a group of preschoolers (including a kid named Charlie Brown) called "Li'l Folks," which appeared in the St. Paul Pioneer Press in 1947. United Features Syndicate bought the strip in 1950 and renamed it "Peanuts" because 'Li'l Folks' sounded too much like another cartoon, "Li'l Abner." Seven newspapers carried the original "Peanuts" cartoon strip on October 2, 1950, and the numbers would just grow and grow from there.

Schulz later moved on to California, where he found fame and fortune. The multiple Emmy winner's cartoons would go on to be read daily by several hundred million people in nearly 75 countries, and in several dozen different languages. Schulz would go on to become one of the top 10 highest-paid entertainers in the U.S. and built an empire around that lovable pooch, Snoopy.

Today, the Minnesota Cartoonists League meets at O'Gara's piano bar in St. Paul under an original portrait of Snoopy drawn and signed by Charles himself. The reason they meet there is because that building was, from 1942 to 1952, Schulz's father's barber shop. An avid hockey fan, Schulz was inducted into the U.S. Hockey Hall of Fame in 1993. Sadly, he died in the year 2000.

beat Iowa, 24-7, and then tied Illinois at 17-apiece. From there the Gophers lost their final three games to Indiana, Michigan State and Wisconsin, to finish with a 4-6-1 record — good for sixth place in the Big Ten. Mark Carlson threw for 2,188 yards that year, while Running Back Garry White tallied 1,021 all-purpose yards.

The 1980 season would be another average year with the Gophers, finishing with a marginal 5-6 record and a fifth place finish in the Big Ten. Led by Tim Salem (Joe's son), the team did manage wins over Ohio, 38-14, Northwestern, 49-21, Iowa, 24-6, Illinois, 21-18, and Indiana, 31-7. Leading the way was Marion Barber, a three-time All-Big Ten honoree who set school rushing records for yards (3,094), touchdowns (34) and attempts (660), before going on to have a successful career with the NFL's New York Jets.

Salem's 1981 Gopher squad got off to its best start in years by winning their first three games over Ohio, 19-17, Purdue, 16-13, and Oregon State, 42-12. Against Oregon State, Gopher Quarterback Mike Hohensee threw a whopping five touchdowns. From there the Gophers suffered a pair of losses to Illinois and Indiana, sandwiched by a win over Northwestern in the middle. The highlight of the season was the 35-31 upset win over Ohio State at home that kept the Buckeyes out of the Rose Bowl. That game Hohensee set school records for completions (37), touchdowns (5) and yards (444) — of which 182 were caught by Receiver Chester Cooper.

"That was the highlight of my collegiate career, and the biggest thing that stood out to me was the look on the faces of the (Minnesota) players who had been there for four years, players who had never before come close to beating Ohio State," Hohensee would later say in a St. Paul Pioneer Press interview. "I was a JUCO transfer (from Mount San Antonio), and the

Jim Wacker

tradition hadn't really hit me yet. But for those guys who grew up in the state and had gotten those scholarships to Minnesota, what they had dreamed about for four years and couldn't beat (Ohio State), now they had tears in their eyes. These were tough men; all the bravado that goes along with being an athlete at that age ... and now the emotions were flying."

The Gophers closed out the remainder of their games with losses to Michigan, Michigan State and Wisconsin. Hohensee, who passed for 2,412 yards, also set a single-season record for touchdown passes that year, with 20. In addition, Running Back Frank Jacobs ran for 636 yards, while Wide Receiver Chester Cooper hauled in over 1,000 receiving yards and six TDs that year, en route to leading the team to a respectable 6-5 record, good for sixth place in the very tough Big Ten.

Incidentally, the 26-21 loss to Wisconsin, which took place on November 21, 1981, would prove to be one the saddest games in the history of Gopher football. That's because it proved to be the last game ever played at Memorial Stadium. The program would decide to take a big leap of faith by agreeing to move off-campus to the newly constructed Hubert H. Humphrey Metrodome in downtown Minneapolis, where they would be joined by the Vikings and Twins as fellow tenants. For the record, the last points ever scored by the Gophers at the Brick House came when Hohensee hooked up with Chester Cooper on a four-yard touchdown pass in the fourth quarter to give Minnesota a 21-20 lead. Unfortunately though, the Badgers rallied behind Quarterback Randy Wright, who connected with Michael Jones on a seven-yard touchdown pass with just under a minute to go in the game to

Pat Evans

give Wisconsin the victory. The fans showed their appreciation for the old stadium by tearing up everything that wasn't nailed down, as well as most things that were nailed down, and taking home as souvenirs to one day show to their grandchildren.

So Long Brick House, Hello Metrodome...

In the first game in the Metrodome, Sept. 11, 1982, the Gophers racked up a school record 742 yards of total offense in a 57-3 drubbing of Ohio. Quarterback Mike Hohensee threw for 332 yards

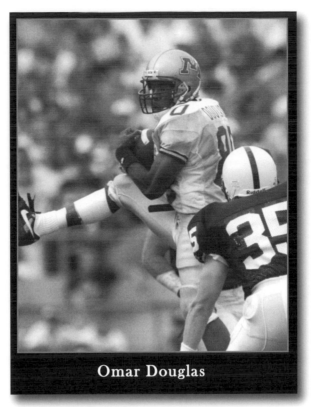
Omar Douglas

and two touchdowns to the delight of the 56,168 fans in attendance. They went on to beat Purdue and Washington State from there, outscoring their first three opponents by the insane margin of 134-24. The honeymoon ended pretty abruptly from there though, as the team lost the remainder of its final eight games and finished dead last in the Big Ten. One of the worst games of this awful stretch came in Evanston, where the Gophers got beat by lowly Northwestern, 31-21. The fans were so excited about their Wildcats winning their first Big Ten game in years that they tore down the goal posts and threw them into Lake Michigan.

It didn't get any better that next year either. In fact it got worse, as the team finished with a miserable 1-10 record and yet another spot in the Big Ten cellar. Hoards of injuries that season didn't help matters either. Minnesota, which was outscored by its opponents that season 518-181, gave up nearly 5,000 yards of total offense while fumbling 30 times and throwing 25 interceptions. In one particular game, an 84-13 blow-out courtesy of the top-ranked Nebraska Cornhuskers, the Gophers gave up nearly 800 yards of total offense. The blowout would later be referred to infamously as the "Nightmare on Chicago Avenue."

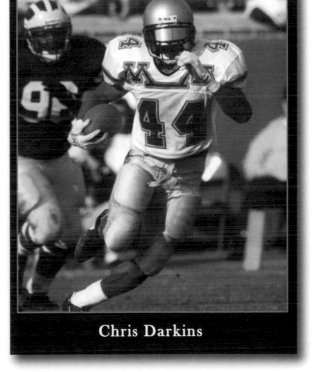
Chris Darkins

With that, Salem was canned. The Gophers needed to hire a new head coach, and quickly, before the recruiting season was awash. Paul Giel knew he had to right this ship, or his job would be on the line too. He needed to being in some heavy artillery to not only turn the program around, but to sell some tickets in the 65,000-seat Metrodome. Finally, after a whole bunch of persuading and lobbying, Giel was able to land Arkansas Head Coach, Lou Holtz. Holtz, who had just taken the Razorbacks to six consecutive bowl games, was considered by many to be one of college football's premier coaches. Full of confidence and charm, "Sweet Lou" would come to Minnesota amidst the hype and fanfare of a rock star. Holtz fever was everywhere and with it came a renewed sense of pride the Gopher football program hadn't seen in decades. Not only could Holtz coach, he was an amazing recruiter and salesman who could preach to the masses unlike anyone had ever seen before in Gold Country.

In 1984, his first year behind the Gopher bench, Holtz began one of the greatest turn-arounds the program would ever see. Fans would come out in droves to see the team — 60,000-plus strong — something that hadn't happened in many, many years. The last-place Gophers hit the field against Rice in their opener and behind the amazing play of freshman Quarterback Rickey Foggie, they beat the Owls, 31-24. The team hit a few bumps in the road from there, losing three straight to Nebraska, Purdue and Ohio State, before rebounding to beat Indiana and Wisconsin, 33-24 and 17-14, respectively. Believe it or not, the victory over the Hoosiers was the team's first Big Ten win in the Dome!

Then, after losing their next four to Northwestern,

Michigan State, Illinois and Michigan, the team rallied to beat rival Iowa by the final score of 23-17 at the Metrodome. The game saw Adam Kelly boot a school record 83-yard punt, only to watch Iowa's Bill Happel return it for a touchdown. Happel returned the favor late in the fourth quarter, however, when he fumbled a Gopher punt at Iowa's 14 yard line. Gary Couch's ensuing 14-yard touchdown run with 4:17 to play would prove to be the game-winner. With the team excitedly hoisting Floyd of Rosedale proudly above their heads down on the Metrodome turf, the 63,479 fans just knew that this was going to be the beginning of something special.

That next season the Gophers greatly improved to finish with a 7-5 record, which included the program's first post-season bowl appearance since '77. Leading the charge once again was Rickey Foggie, who tore up the Big Ten that year. There have been quite a few memorable T-formation quarterbacks at the University of Minnesota, but none of them was as versatile a performer as was Foggie — who could run, pass, scramble, and simply wreak havoc on opposing defenses.

Led by Foggie, who scored three touchdowns on 140 yards rushing while throwing for another 157, the Maroon and Gold kicked off the season with a 28-14 win over Wichita State. From there, they crushed Montana, 62-17, as the Gophers piled up over 500 yards of offense. Foggie rushed for three touchdowns and passed for another to Mel Anderson, while tailback Valdez Baylor added two touchdowns of his own.

In Week Three Minnesota, despite Foggie's TD pass to Kevin Starks late in the game, lost a heartbreaker to the top-ranked Oklahoma Sooners, 13-7. The team rebounded though by pouncing

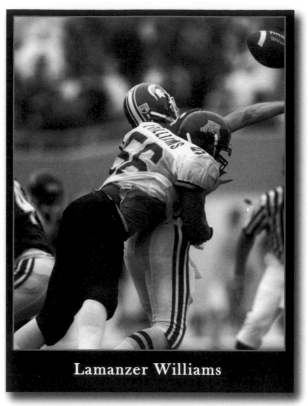

Lamanzer Williams

all over Purdue, 45-15, as Foggie threw for 212 yards and a TD, while rushing for 47 yards and another touchdown. The Gophers went on to beat Northwestern in Week Five, 21-10, behind nearly 300 yards of total offense from Foggie, in addition to 102 yards receiving and a TD from Tight End Kevin Starks. In Week Seven they beat Indiana, 22-7, in a game that featured Valdez Baylor rushing for a career high 141 yards and a TD, along with three Chip Lohmiller field goals.

Minnesota then lost a pair of nail-biters, one to Ohio State on Homecoming, 23-19, and the other to Michigan State, 31-26. Foggie scored the only two touchdowns in the Buckeye game, and then sat out the Spartan game with a pulled groin, as backup QB Alan Holt came up just short in leading the team back from a huge deficit. In Week Nine, the Gophers beat Wisconsin, 27-18, in a game that was highlighted by an 89-yard record-setting TD bomb from Foggie to Mel Anderson. The Gophers finished out the season on a huge downer though, getting pummeled by both Michigan, 48-7, who was led by Quarterback Jim Harbaugh, and Big Ten champion Iowa, 31-9.

Despite finishing only fifth in the Big Ten with a 4-4 record, Minnesota was invited to play the Clemson Tigers in the 10th annual Independence Bowl. Nearly 43,000 fans, many of whom made the trip from the Land of 10,000 Lakes, crowded into Independence Stadium in Shreveport, La., to watch the big game. Now, in a bit of off-the-field drama, Coach Holtz controversially opted to exercise a little-known secret clause (which would later become known affectionately as the "Notre Dame Clause") in his contract which entitled him to step down to take the head coaching position at Notre Dame, should it become avail-

Glen Mason

able. It did, and he went, leaving his Defensive Co-ordinator, John Gutekunst, to take over as head coach of the team. "Gutie," who had served as an assistant at both Duke and Virginia Tech before joining Holtz at Arkansas and then Minnesota, was eager and excited to make the most of his "golden" opportunity.

"Lou's got to be one of the top five greatest college coaches of all time, without question," said Foggie regarding the coach's decision to leave. "Everywhere Holtz has been, he's won. He turned our 'U' football program around and got people in the stands. He was able to recruit good athletes to come in and make us competitive again. His greatest asset was to be able to recruit and to motivate his players to go out and win at all costs. I just wish he would've stayed at Minnesota longer, because there's no telling where the program would be today if he had."

"This was a big change for us, but, because Gutie was already on the staff, we were familiar with him, and we kind of knew what to expect," Foggie added. "But, going from Lou Holtz, who was a fiery, up-tempo guy, to Gutie, who was a more laid-back kind of coach, was a big change. Gutie wasn't the motivator that Coach Holtz was, but he knew the X's and O's of the game, and he was a good guy."

With Gutekunst at the helm, the Gophers took to the field and made a statement on the game's first play from scrimmage. That's when Clemson QB Rodney Williams hit wide Receiver Ray Williams on a screen pass. Williams, upon being leveled by Gopher defender Doug Mueller, then proceeded to cough up the ball at the Tiger 39-yard line. Minnesota took over and began to drive downfield behind Ed Penn's 25-yard run, which got the Gophers down to the Clemson five-yard line. But after a holding penalty, they could only muster a field goal attempt. Kicker Chip Lohmiller came in, but was wide-right on a 22-yarder, keeping the score at 0-0. But two plays later, Clemson again fumbled on their own 26-yard-line. After a failed attempt to get the ball into the end-zone yet again, Lohmiller

came in and this time drilled a 22-yarder through the uprights to put the Gophers up 3-0.

In the second quarter, after forcing the Tigers to punt, the Gophers put together an impressive drive that started with two David Puk nine-yard scampers up the middle. Foggie then hit Tight End Craig Otto on another nine-yarder to get to their own 43, followed by 15 and 20-yard runs by Baylor. Finally, on third-and-four, at the Tiger nine, Foggie hit Anderson on a nine-yard scoring strike and the Gophers went up 10-0. Clemson rallied back in the third though, thanks to a pair of Jeff Treadwell field goals to make it 10-6. Then, behind the running of Clemson tailback Kenny Flowers, the Tigers drove and scored on a Jennings touchdown catch to take a three-point lead, 13-10.

The valiant Gophers came back in the fourth quarter behind their leader, Foggie, whose running and passing sparked an 85-yard drive that was capped by another Lohmiller "Chip-shot" to tie the game at 13 apiece. After the Gopher defense forced the Tigers to punt, Foggie came out and lined up in the shotgun formation. He started out the drive on a 10-yard pass to Anderson, followed by a 16-yard Baylor run to the Clemson 36. Foggie then hit flanker Gary Couch on a 14-yarder, quickly followed by a Baylor run that gave him 12 more of his team-high 98 yards. Baylor then launched himself into the end-zone two plays later as the Gophers took a seven-point lead.

But the Gophers weren't out of the hot water yet. Faced with a fourth-and-six at their own 39, Clemson pulled off a fake punt to stay alive. Williams then completed a 21-yarder to Jennings on another critical fourth down to reach the Gopher 31-yard line. So, with 90 seconds left in the game, the Tigers tried a trick play. Williams tossed a long, backward pass to wide Receiver Ray Williams, who then turned around and lofted a pass of his own to Tight End Jim Riggs near the goal line. That's when Cornerback Donovan Small dove, and just barely got enough of his finger on the ball to deflect it out of

TYRONE CARTER

Tyrone Carter, a two-time All-American safety for the Gophers, won the Jim Thorpe Award as the best defensive back in college football in 1999. Carter would go on to play in the NFL with the Minnesota Vikings, New York and Pittsburgh Steelers.

bounds and preserve the Gopher victory.

"When they first threw that ball out wide," said Small, who was named as the Defensive Player of the Game, "I was going to come up to try to tackle the guy. I thought it was a screen pass. But just out of the corner of my eye I saw this Clemson guy running really hard downfield. I wondered why that guy was running so hard, so I decided I'd better try to catch up to him."

"I have fond memories of that game because I always wanted to attend Clemson," added Foggie, who threw for 123 yards and a touchdown in the game. "But the Clemson coach told my high school coach that I was too slow to run their offense. So there was a definite revenge factor there for me personally. I knew a lot of the guys that played for Clemson, so to go out and play well and to beat those guys was just really satisfying for me. Minnesota hadn't been to a bowl game for a while, so to win it was a really special experience for everyone."

For the season Foggie accounted for 1,821 yards in total offense and was named to the All-Big Ten team. Baylor led the team in rushing with 680 yards, while Lohmiller led the team in scoring with 75 points. In addition, Linebacker Peter Najarian, who described the win as the "greatest feeling I've ever had," was the Golden Gophers' top tackler (for the third straight season) with 133 total hits.

The beginning of the 1986 season brought more hype and hoopla to campus than perhaps every before. That season a kid from Rochester hit campus by the name of Darrell Thompson, and by the time he was done four years later, he would own most every rushing record in the books. "Darrell and Rickey" became quite the dynamic duo that year, as the upstart Gophers were anxious to show the football world that

Thomas Hamner

their Independence Bowl victory the year before was no fluke.

The season got underway against Bowling Green as Thompson made an immediate impact by rushing for 205 yards and scoring four touchdowns en route to a 31-7 victory. Next up were the top ranked University of Oklahoma Sooners, however, who crushed the Gophers by the ugly score of 63-0. The men of gold followed that up with a 24-20 loss to tiny Pacific University, despite two more touchdowns by Thompson. From there the team went on a roll, beating Purdue, 36-9 (as Foggie scored three rushing touchdowns and passed to Mel Anderson for another), Northwestern, 44-23 (led by Thompson's 176 yards rushing and two touchdowns, as well as Mel Anderson's 90-yard kickoff return for another), and Indiana in a squeaker, 19-17 (where Thompson ran wild for another 191 yards to set up Chip Lohmiller's 21-yard game-wining field goal with two seconds to go in the game).

Minnesota ran into some more trouble in Weeks Seven and Eight, when they got shut-out by Ohio State, 33-0, and then lost to Michigan State that next Saturday by the final of 52-23. The Gophers rebounded as they had done all season long in Week Nine, this time defeating Wisconsin, 27-20, to retain Paul Bunyan's Axe. In that game Foggie threw a 27-yard strike to Dennis Carter for the go-ahead touchdown, while Thompson rushed for 117 yards to become the first Gopher freshman to rush for 1,000 yards.

Next up were the No. 2 ranked Michigan Wolverines, who had beaten the Gophers the past eight seasons. The Michigan game, in all of its pomp and circumstance, would prove to be one of the greatest ever for the University of Minnesota. After back and forth scoring the entire afternoon, it all came down to the

Ryan Thelwell

wire in this one. Down 17-16 with just over two minutes to go in the game, Michigan Coach Bo Schembechler opted to go for the tie instead of a two-pointer to win. He succeeded, and with the game now all tied-up, Minnesota drove the ball downfield. Then with 47 seconds left, Foggie took off from the Michigan 48 and ran for 31 yards to the Michigan 17. The stage was now set for Woodbury Kicker Chip Lohmiller, who came in and nailed a 30-yarder as time ran out to give the Gophers a dramatic 20-17 victory, as well as the rights to the coveted Little Brown Jug.

Famed Gopher radio announcer Ray Christensen would later refer to that moment, right after Lohmiller's kick sailed through the uprights, in his book "Gopher Tales," as his all-time favorite in his more than 50 years of covering the team. "Over 100,000 Michigan fans sat in stunned silence," he wrote, "the most thrilling lack of sound I can ever remember."

The momentum ended the next week, however, as the Gophers, despite Lohmiller's school record 62-yard field goal, finished out their season by losing to Iowa, 30-27. It didn't matter though as the team still earned a berth in the Liberty Bowl down in Memphis, where they would face the University of Tennessee. The game got underway with the Volunteers jumping ahead 14-0 on two Jeff Francis touchdown passes. The first came to Joey Clinkscales in the left flat as he beat both Cornerback Matt Martinez and Safety Steve Franklin to scoot into the end zone for an 18-yard touchdown. Then, after a second quarter Foggie fumble at midfield, Francis hit Fullback William Howard a screen pass to make it 14-0. The Gophers came close twice in the half — once to the Vols' six-yard line, where Foggie came up short on a sneak — and then again when to the Vols' 33-yard line, where Thompson fumbled. Min-

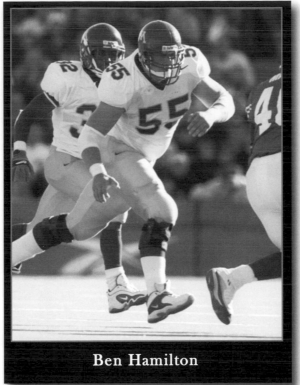
Ben Hamilton

nesota's only points came on a Lohmiller 27-yard field goal that ended a 70-yard drive at the end of the half.

When the third quarter opened Foggie appeared to be a man on a mission. The junior quarterback led Minnesota on a 10-play, 88-yard drive that was capped by an 11-yard quarterback-keeper for a touchdown. Thompson then added a two-point conversion to make the score 14-11. Still in the third, behind 38 of Thompson's game-high 136 yards, the Gophers started a long march down to the Tennessee 14. But, a holding call nullified their touchdown hopes, Minnesota had to settle for another field goal.

Tied at 14-apiece in the fourth, the Vols cruised upfield on a 67-yard drive that was capped by Clinkscales' second TD catch of the game less than two minutes later. With Tennessee up, 21-14, the Gophers tried to rally. Their next drive got stalled on their own 49-yard line, but after an exchange of punts Minnesota got the ball back at midfield largely because of two great plays by freshman linebacker Jon Leverenz — who forced a two-yard loss on a first-down play, and then broke up a key third-down pass on another. So, with Foggie and Thompson poised for the upset, they tried one last drive to win it all. The final

Willie Middlebrooks

rally, a seven-play drive, started out well but unfortunately ended near midfield when Foggie's fourth-down pass to Waconia's Ron Goetz fell incomplete. Tennessee took over with 16 seconds left and simply ran out the clock to win it. Minnesota outgained Tennessee in the game 374-324, but in the end the final score read 21-14 in favor of the Vols.

For the season the Gophers finished at 6-6 and tied for third in the Big Ten with a 5-3 record. Thompson, who led the conference in rushing that year, also set a new Gopher single-season rushing mark with 1,240 yards.

"It was a big deal because you grow up watching the bowl games on TV, and when you finally get to play in one, it is a very special event," said Thompson, who was named to the All-Big Ten team. "I mean, only the year before I was playing for Rochester John Marshall High School, and now here I was starting at running back in the Liberty Bowl, it was an exciting time."

Furthermore, Foggie set a new University of Minnesota career total yardage record by reaching the 5,118 mark. Lohmiller, who set a new team record by nailing a 62-yard field goal against Iowa, was named to the All-Big Ten team. Bruce Holmes, a senior linebacker, who led the team with 118 tackles also made the All-Big Ten team. In addition, there were a lot of players on that team who deserve credit for the team's outstanding season, including Ray Hitchcock, Jim Hobbins and Norries Wilson who anchored a veteran offensive line, as well as defenders Donovan Small, Anthony Burke, Larry Joyner, Don Pollard, Matt Martinez, Steve Thompson, and Duane Dutrieuille.

The Slide to Mediocrity

The Gophers were feeling pretty good about their prospects in 1987 and won their first three games out of the box against Northern Iowa, Cal and Central Michigan. Then, when they beat Purdue, 21-19, in Week Four to go 4-0, people started to sense that this group might be once again flirting with the post-season. That's where the good news stops and the bad news starts. The Gophers would win just two more games during that entire season, against Northwestern, 45-33, and Wisconsin, 22-19. One loss in particular, a 27-17 come-from-behind killer in Week Eight, was orchestrated by a

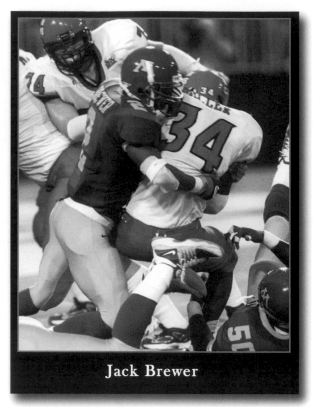
Jack Brewer

young Illini Quarterback by the name of Jeff George, who came in and rallied the team back from three scores down in the fourth to beat the Gophers.

Minnesota did finish the season with a 6-5 record but were not in consideration for any bowl games due to their relatively easy non-conference schedule. One highlight of mention from that year came against Michigan, in Week Nine, when Darrell Thompson set a Big Ten record with a 98-yard touchdown run. With the ball at their own two-yard line and holding a slim 10-7 lead, Thompson took the handoff, cut to the right sideline and was off to the races. (The run broke Rick Upchurch's school record of 84 yards set in 1974 and established a new Big Ten record, which was previously held by Iowa's Eddie Vincent, with 94 yards.) Incredibly, Thompson's 200 yards rushing that day were the most ever surrendered by a Wolverine team. For the season Thompson ran for 1,229 yards and tallied 13 touchdowns. Foggie, meanwhile, threw for 1,232 yards and eight TDs, while adding six more touchdowns on the ground as well.

In 1988 the bottom fell out as the Gophers finished ninth in the Big Ten with an awful 0-6-2 conference record. With Foggie gone to the pro ranks the team struggled. Thompson did manage to rush for 910 yards and post nine touchdowns that year, while his new quarterback, Scott Schaffner, threw for 1,234 yards and seven TDs. You knew it was going to be bad when the team started off the season with a pair of ugly losses to Washington State, 41-9, and Miami of Ohio, 35-3. They did rebound to beat Northern Illinois in non-conference action, but lost to everyone else except Northwestern and Illinois, who they managed to tie at 28-28 and 27-27, respec-

Michael Lehan

tively.

The 1989 and 1990 Gopher teams made a solid recovery to get back to respectability. Both clubs finished with identical 6-5 overall records, good for fifth and sixth in the conference, respectively. One of the most disappointing losses in program history, however, came on October 28, 1989, when the Gophers lost to Ohio State 41–37. The Buckeyes scored with under a minute to go to take the lead and the Gophers had one shot at the end zone on the final play of the game, only to see Scott Schaffner's pass fall incomplete. The 1989 team did manage to beat Purdue, 35-15, Northwestern, 20-18, Wisconsin, 24-20, and Iowa, 43-7.

Darrell Thompson rounded out his glorious career in Gold Country at the end of the 1989 campaign, literally rewriting the record book on the way out. Thompson now owned nearly every rushing record on campus, including Total Rushing Yards (4,654), Rushing Touchdowns (40), All Purpose Yards (5,109) while ranking second in Career Points Scored (262). Meanwhile, the 1990 club wound up finishing 6-5. The season opened on a real downer when they lost a heart-breaker to Utah, 35-29. The Utes built up a 19-0 first quarter lead, only to see the Gophers rally to tie it up at 29-29. Late in the fourth quarter the Gophers blocked a punt at drove it down to the Utah 11 yard line, where they called time out with enough time left for just one play. They then lined up for the game-winning 28-yard field goal attempt, but the snap was low, the kick was blocked, and Utah picked the ball up and returned it the other way for what proved to be the game-winning touchdown.

The Gophers would go on to garner wins over Purdue, 19-7, Northwestern, 35-25, Indiana, 12-0, Wisconsin, 21-3, and Iowa, 31-24 — which was particularly sweet. In fact, beat-

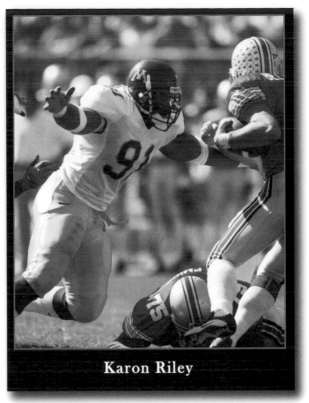
Karon Riley

ing the Rose Bowl bound Hawkeyes in front of nearly 65,000 fans at the Dome and keeping Floyd around the Bierman Complex for the second year in a row would have to rate as one of the highlights of the Gutekunst era. Keswic Joiner was the hero in this one as he recovered a punt blocked by Omar Douglas in the Iowa end zone for one touchdown and then added another score in the fourth quarter on a 28-yard pass from Marquel Fleetwood. With the win, Minnesota finished the season with a winning record for the fourth time in the previous five seasons.

In 1991 the Gophers sunk to last place in the Big Ten with a paltry 2-9 overall record. Their only Big Ten win came against Purdue, a team they edged out by the whopping final of 6-3, thanks to a nine-yard touchdown run by Quarterback Marquel Fleetwood. Highlights from this year included a 58-0 beating on national television by Quarterback Kordell Stewart and the defending national champs from Colorado, and a 52-6 drubbing by Quarterback Elvis Grbac and the Michigan Wolverines at the Dome. Let's not forget about the 34-8 loss to Indiana or the 35-6 pasting by Ohio State either. All in all it was not a good year to be a Gopher Football fan, but there were some great performances from Fleetwood, who passed for 1,642 yards and six TDs, and Running Backs Chuck Rios and Antonio Carter, who combined for more than 1,000 yards on the ground. In addition, Sean Lumpkin was a star in the defensive backfield that year, as he would later go on to play with the NFL's New Orleans Saints.

After the 1991 season, Gutie was let go and Texas Christian University Head Coach Jim Wacker was brought in to right the ship. A winner of two national coach of the year wards, Wacker was known for his ability to rebuild

Tellis Redmon

and run clean programs. Coming in like a Texas twister, full of energy and a sharp wit to boot, Wacker was an instant fan-favorite. In his first year on campus he succeeded in unseating two of Minnesota's biggest rivals, the Rose Bowl bound Wisconsin Badgers and the Iowa Hawkeyes, 28-13, in the season finale.

Wacker's teams struggled though, finishing 10th in 1992, eighth in 1993, 11th in 1994, 10th in 1995 and ninth in 1996. One of the highlights of the '92 season was the fact that the Gophers kept Iowa home for the Holidays following their 28-13 victory, which denied the Hawks a trip to the Copper Bowl. Trailing 13-10, Minnesota scored 18 unanswered points in the fourth quarter. Following a fake field goal in the fourth quarter, Quarterback Rob St. Sauver connected with Steve Cambrice to give Minnesota a 16-13 lead. St. Sauver then hit Aaron Osterman on a 59-yard touchdown pass on the next possession to seal the deal.

Wacker's best season was 1993, when his team went on a three game Big Ten winning streak, beating Purdue, 59-56, Northwestern, 28-26, and Wisconsin, 28-21. Against Wisconsin, Minnesota capitalized on five interceptions, including Jeff Rosga's 55-yard TD return off of Darrell Bevell. Minnesota would build a 21-0 first-half lead behind a pair of Scott Eckers touchdowns passes and never look back. The turning point in the game came late when Wisconsin drove to the Gopher eight yard line and then went for it on a key 4th and 1. Jerome Davis busted through the line and threw Brett Moss for a three yard loss, thus giving the Gophers the ball back. The Gophers then scored on their next possession when Rishon Early caught an 84 yard pass from Scott Eckers, setting up a two yard Chris Darkins touchdown run that gave the Gophers a 28-14 lead. Minnesota's defense held from there, handing Barry

Thomas Tapeh

Jermaine Mays

Alvarez's 15th-ranked Badgers their only loss of the season. Wisconsin went on to beat UCLA in the Rose Bowl, but the Gopher loss likely cost them a national championship.

Meanwhile, the Purdue game on October 9th was epic. The Gophers broke eight school records, including combined points (115), combined yards (1,184), TD passes (six by Scott Eckers) and TD receptions (five by Omar Douglas). The Gophers racked up 625 total yards of offense: 402 through the air and 223 on the ground. Minnesota trailed for most of the game until Justin Conzemius returned an interception 55 yards to give the Gophers a 49-42 lead. This wild one went back and forth until Kicker Mike Chalberg nailed the game-winner with just eight seconds left on the clock. Purdue's bruising Fullback Mike Alstott had a huge game as well, rushing for 171 yards and scoring five touchdowns.

Then, just two weeks later, the Gophers picked off five balls en route to upsetting the 15th-ranked and unbeaten Badgers in front of the fourth-largest crowd (64,798 fans) at the Metrodome. Another big win of the Wacker era came versus Purdue on October 7, 1995, when trailing 38-31 late in the fourth quarter, Cory Sauter capped a 66-yard drive on a quarterback sneak with just over a minute to go to make it 38-37. The Gophers then went for it and won the game, 39-38, on a thrilling two-point conversion from Sauter to Ryan Thelwell. Purdue then advanced down the field and missed a game-winning field goal attempt as time expired, giving the Gophers the thrilling victory. Chris Darkins rushed for a school record 294 yards and three touchdowns in this one, including a 45-yarder in which he lost his shoe while leaping a defender.

One of the most exciting

players of this era was Safety Tyrone Carter, who, on Sept. 21, 1996, returned an NCAA record two fumbles for touchdowns in a span of just 56 seconds in a 35-33 upset of No. 23 ranked Syracuse at the Metrodome. The Donovan McNabb-led Orangemen were leading the game 12-0, when shortly before halftime, Cory Sauter hit Tutu Atwell on a 50 yard touchdown to get the Gophers back in the game. Then, early into the third quarter, Carter scooped up a Syracuse fumble and returned it 63 yards for touchdown. Less than a minute later the true freshman picked up another Syracuse fumble and returned it 20 yards for yet another score. Minnesota would emerge victorious following Adam Bailey's game-winning 26 yard field goal with just 42 seconds remaining on the clock. This was probably Jim Wacker's biggest non-conference win as Gopher coach.

Indeed, there would be many ups and downs during Wacker's tenure in Gold Country, but after five seasons behind the Gopher bench his record stood at just 16-39. The numbers didn't lie and in the end he would be let go. Despite his poor record, however, Wacker would be remembered as a coach who demanded excellence both on the field and in the classroom, where his teams finished at the top of the Academic All-Big Ten selections for three straight years.

There were some great football players to pass through during that era though, including Running Back Chris Darkins, who ran for 3,235 career yards from 1992-95, good for second all-time in team history. Others would include Quarterbacks Cory Sauter and Tim Schade. Sauter would hold the record for all-time career passing yards with 6,834, and career touchdowns with 40, while Schade ranked fifth in that category with 22 TDs. Receivers Tutu Atwell and Ryan Thelwell

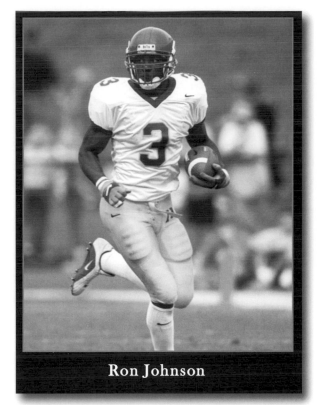
Ron Johnson

ranked No. 1 and No. 2 respectively for career receptions with 171 and 136, while Chuck Rios, Omar Douglas and Aaron Osterman ranked No.'s 3, 4 and 5 in that same category as well. (Thelwell even set a record in 1996 when he caught eight balls for 228 yards in a 26-23 win over Ball State.) In addition, all but Rios, who was a running back, also ranked in the top-five all-time for career receiving yards, with Atwell leading the list at 2,640 yards. There was also All-American Lamanzer Williams, who, from 1994-97 became the team's career leader in sacks, with 132. Furthermore, Linebacker Craig Sauer went on to play with the Atlanta Falcons, while Tackle Mike Giovinette suited up for the Tampa Bay Bucs.

Enter Coach Mason

In 1997 Glen Mason took over the reigns as the University's newest head coach. Mason, who spent nine seasons turning around the fortunes of the University of Kansas' football program, had led the Jayhawks to a top-10 national ranking in 1995. A former linebacker on Ohio State's 1970 Big Ten championship team, Mason knew what it was going to take to right the ship.

Mason's immediate impact was felt during his inaugural campaign in Gold Country, when the Gophers finished fifth in total defense in the Big Ten, the program's best effort in more than a dozen years. Minnesota broke or tied a total of 28 school records during that season, which, at 3-9, was slowly showing signs of life. Led by Quarterback Corey Sauter and Running Back Thomas Hamner, the Gophers kicked off the season with a 17-3 loss at Hawaii, followed by Mason's first win as a Gopher, a 53-29 shellacking of Iowa State. Against the Cy-

Asad Abdul-Khaliq

clones, it was all about receiver/return guru Tutu Atwell, who accounted for a school record 349 all-purpose yards. He also set an NCAA record with a pair of kickoff returns for touchdowns as well — one for 89 yards and the other for 93. Atwell, who also had one carry for 33 yards as well as four catches for 36 yards, even had a 90 yard punt return called back in the first quarter due to a penalty. It was an amazing performance to say the least.

The Gophers followed that up with a 20-17 win over Memphis but then lost a heartbreaker to Houston that next Saturday by the final of 45-43, as Sauter threw for 368 yards and three touchdowns in the defeat. The team struggled from there on in, losing to Michigan State, 31-10, Purdue, 59-43, Penn State, 16-15, Wisconsin, 22-21, Michigan, 24-3, and Ohio State, 31-3. Many of those game were closer than they looked on paper, particularly the one-point Penn State contest, which could've been one of the biggest upsets of the year. They rebounded that next week against Indiana, beating the Hoosiers, 24-12, only to get shut-out by Iowa in the season finale, 31-0.

In 1998 the Gophers began to turn the corner, finishing with an improved 5-6 record, good for seventh in the Big Ten. Quarterback Billy Cockerham, Receiver Tutu Atwell and Running Back Thomas Hamner provided one of the most solid 1-2-3 punches in the conference that season, and all would eventually go on to play professionally. The team won its first three games that year against Arkansas State, 17-14, Houston, 14-7, and Memphis, 41-14. Against Arkansas State, Safety Tyrone Carter returned the opening kick-off 86-yards for a touchdown. Then, after a Hamner score late in the second, Gopher Kicker Adam Bailey came in to boot the game-winner with no time left on the clock. Cockerham's two touchdown passes to Luke

Ukee Dozier

Leverson and Ron Johnson were enough to seal the deal against Houston, while Hamner, Cockerham and Byron Evans each ran for touchdowns to lead the Gophers past Memphis.

After suffering set-backs to Purdue, 56-21, Penn State, 37-27, and Ohio State, 45-15, Minnesota rallied to beat Michigan State, 19-18, finally ending their 17-game losing streak to the Spartans. After a back and forth first half, MSU recorded a safety with 9:54 remaining in the game to put them up 18-10. Cockerham then threw a 24 yard TD pass to Luke Leverson (his second of the day) with 1:47 to play, pulling the Gophers to within two points. The Gophers missed the ensuing two-point conversion but managed to recover the onside kick instead. Minnesota then drove down the field and went ahead when Adam Bailey made a 37 yard field goal with just 13 seconds remaining. Parc Williams' interception on the final play of the game secured the victory.

Minnesota then lost a couple of very close games starting with Michigan, 15-10, Wisconsin, 26-7, and Indiana, 20-19. The Gophers, who got an early fumble recovery for a touchdown from Trevis Graham, hung tough with Michigan only to get beat on a late safety and field goal in the fourth quarter. Leverson's 53-yard TD was the only offense Minnesota could muster with Wisconsin, while Ron Johnson tallied twice in the narrow defeat against Indiana.

The team did finish on a high note, however, beating Iowa on the last game of the season, 49-7, at the Dome. It was the final game for legendary Hawkeye coach Hayden Fry and the Gophers sent him out in style. Minnesota had 501 yards of total offense, which included 348 yards rushing. Cockerham and Leverson each scored a pair of touchdowns in this one, while

Darrell Reid

Hamner added 148 yards and a touchdown. Byron Evans pitched in with 108 yards, while Antoine Henderson scored on a 34-yard touchdown run in the fourth quarter as Minnesota rolled to its biggest win over the Hawkeyes since 1955.

The 1999 Gophers surpassed everyone's expectations, finishing the season with a greatly improved 8-4 record. Fans were coming out in droves to see their Maroon and Gold that season, something that hadn't been happening in years past. In addition, the Gophers made their first post-season appearance since 1986 by being selected to play in the Sun Bowl. The team was led by a cast of future pros including: Running Back Thomas Hamner, Quarterback Billy Cockerham, Safety Tyrone Carter, Receiver Luke Leverson, Linebacker Parc Williams, Center Ben Hamilton and Defensive End Karon Riley.

The Gophers, behind Cockerham's two rushing touchdowns and 89-yard TD pass to Antoine Henderson, pummeled Ohio University, 33-7, in their opening non-conference game. From there the team beat Louisiana-Monroe, 35-0, thanks in large part to Hamner's three touchdown runs along with Willie Middlebrooks' 26-yard TD interception return. The Gophers were gaining confidence and it showed big-time in their 55-7 pounding of Illinois State. Cockerham again led the charge in this one with a pair of rushing touchdowns along with two more through the air to both Ron Johnson and Henderson.

The team continued to roll when the Big 10 season got underway by manhandling Northwestern, 33-14, at Evanston. Cockerham, continuing his amazing offensive output, ran in a two-yarder and also hit Hamner on a 64-yard touchdown pass, while Hamner and Leverson each added scores on the ground as well.

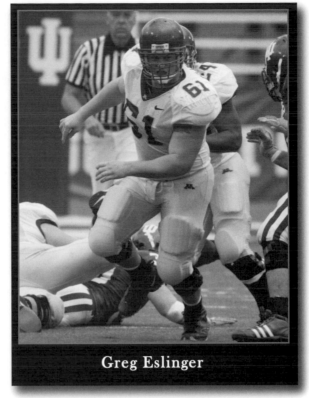

Greg Eslinger

Against Wisconsin the Gophers got a dose of reality, losing a heart-breaker, 20-17, at the Dome. Arland Bruce opened the scoring in the first on a nice 24-yard TD pass from Cockerham, only to see Heisman winner Ron Dayne get the equalizer midway through the second on a three-yard plunge. Hamner then put Minnesota back on top when he caught a 49-yard touchdown pass from Cockerham. Wisconsin tied it up again late in the third on an 81-yard bomb from Brooks Bollinger to Nick Davis, only to see the Gophers take the lead once again on Dan Nystrom's field goal. But, after a pair of Vital Pisetsky field goals in the fourth, the final one coming as time ran off the clock, Wisconsin was able to leave town with Paul Bunyan's Axe.

The Gophers rebounded that next Saturday against Illinois though, beating the Illini in Champaign, 37-7. Leverson's 74-yard punt return for a touchdown late in the first got things going. Cockerham then hit Jermaine Mays on a six-yard TD strike, followed by Nystrom's first of three field goals on the day to put Minnesota up 17-0. Hamner and Evans each scored in the second half as well, as the Gophers cruised to the easy win.

Minnesota then suffered another gut-wrenching loss at the Dome that next week, this time to Ohio State, 17-20. Down 7-0 in the first, Cockerham scored on a nine-yard run around the end to even it up. After a Nystrom field goal to go ahead, 10-7, OSU answered on Michael Wiley's second touchdown run of the day midway through the third. Hamner answered with a seven-yarder of his own, only to see Buckeye Kicker Dan Stultz nail a pair of field goals late in the fourth to ice it for Ohio State.

Mason's squad came up short that next week too, this

Ben Utecht

time to losing to Purdue on homecoming. Down 10-0, Hamner scored on a nine-yard run up the middle late in the second. The Boilers then went up 19-7 in the third, only to see Minnesota rally. Cockerham capped a long Gopher drive by scoring on a one-yard dive in the fourth, only to see Purdue's Montrell Lowe answer with a one-yarder of his own just three minutes later. Hamner then scored on a brilliant 60-yard run through a maze of Boiler defenders to get the Gophers to within five at 26-21. Purdue Quarterback Drew Brees then hit Randall Lane for a touchdown with just five minutes to go make it 33-21. The Gophers, down but not out, drove 80 yards on 12 plays and scored at 2:39 of the fourth when Cockerham found Johnson on a 12-yard touchdown pass. They tried to rally late, but came up just short in the 33-28 loss.

From there, the Gophers took on No. 2 ranked Penn State, in what would prove to be one of the greatest games in program history. The Penn State crowd was ecstatic. Not only were they were just three wins away from a trip to the national championship game in the Sugar Bowl, but their legendary coach, Joe Paterno, was coaching in his 400th game in Happy Valley. It was also their homecoming, which meant that the partying had started early on that morning and their fans were ready to party. The Nittany Lions got on the board first in this one when Mike Cerimele busted through the Minnesota line on a five-yard plunge early in the opening quarter. Nystrom answered for the Gophers at 4:59 of the first with a 27-yard field goal. They then took the lead early in the second when Johnson caught a 25-yard touchdown pass from Cockerham to go up 10-7.

MARION BARBER III

Marion Barber III ran for over 4,500 all-purpose yards and 30+ TDs at the U of M before going on to stardom in the NFL with the Dallas Cowboys. Barber's father, Marion Jr., and brother, Dom, also played for the Gophers.

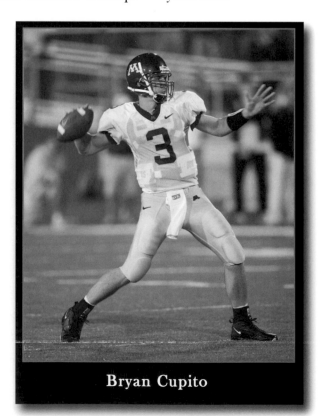

Bryan Cupito

Penn State answered though, as QB Kevin Thompson found Bryant Johnson in the back of the end-zone with a 17-yard TD pass, followed by a Travis Forney 44-yard field goal to take the lead back early in the fourth. Hamner then put the Gophers back on top when he capped off a seven-play, 71-yard drive by hauling in a beautiful 49-yard touchdown pass from Cockerham.

The Lions roared back though, and despite being held out of the end-zone, did manage to take the lead back with a 44-yard field goal midway through the final quarter. Then, after both teams exchanged punts, Minnesota got the ball with just under two minutes remaining in the game. Cockerham drove the team down the field and with 1:22 on the clock he found himself faced with a fourth-and-16 from Penn State's 40-yard-line. Cockerham dropped back and heaved a prayer which somehow bounced off Ron Johnson's hands and right over to Arland Bruce, who grabbed the ball out of the air for a 27-yard gain and a first down on Penn State's 13-yard line.

After a few plays to run down the clock, freshman Kicker Dan Nystrom came out and made history, kicking a 32-yarder straight through the uprights as time expired to give Minnesota the unbelievable 24-23 upset victory. The shocked crowd stood in silence as the Gophers mobbed Nystrom at midfield. For the first time in Gopher history, the team would return home with the Liberty Bell traveling trophy.

"When Ron tipped it, I just saw the ball hanging in the air saying, like 'Come get me, come get me!' ", Bruce excitedly explained after the game.

"I just grabbed it. It just hung there, in slow motion, like it was meant to be."

"This program went from a losing program to a winning program today," added Thomas Hamner. "We knocked off the No. 2 team, a great Penn State team, at home. It doesn't get any better than that."

After doing the improbable, the Gophers came back that next week and crushed Indiana, 44-20, in Minneapolis. Cockerham scored a pair of short rushing touchdowns in this one while also throwing a 39-yard TD to Ron Johnson. Cornerback Jimmy Wyrick tallied on a 61-yard interception return as well.

Next up were the Iowa Hawkeyes, at Iowa City, in a game which had post-season implications written all over it. But, thanks to some more fourth quarter heroics by Arland Bruce, who scored what proved to be the 73-yard game-winning touchdown run at the 9:15 mark of the fourth quarter, the Gophers rallied to win, 25-21. Nystrom kicked his third field goal of the day with just over three minutes to go to ice it for Minnesota. With the win, the Gophers found themselves ranked in the top-20 of every college poll in the nation. Coach Mason had officially turned the program around.

From there the Gophers were invited to play the Oregon Ducks in the Sun Bowl, on Dec. 31, 1999, in El Paso, Texas. It would be the team's first bowl appearance since the Liberty Bowl back in 1986. Droves of Gopher fans made the trek south to see the game, giving the program a much needed boost. The Gophers got on the board first in this one, when Cockerham, after hitting Leverson on a 36-yarder, capped a seven-play, 62-yard drive by finding Ron Johnson in the back of the end-zone for a

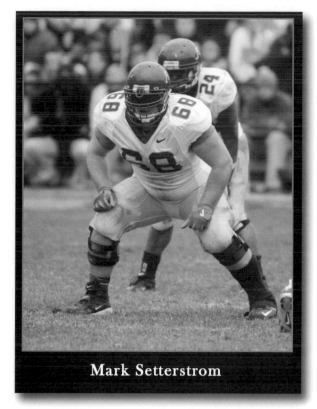

Mark Setterstrom

LAURENCE MARONEY

Laurence Maroney ran for over 4,500 all-purpose yards and 30+ TDs at the U of M before going on to stardom in the NFL with the New England Patriots.

one-yard touchdown. Oregon's Quarterback Joey Harrington answered by scoring on a five-yard keeper, only to see Cockerham strike again early in the third — this time to Bruce with a 38-yard TD pass on the final play of an 80-yard drive (Nystrom's kick failed).

Harrington then added his second score of the game just a few minutes later, on another one-yard keeper, followed by a Villegas field goal at the 3:11 mark of the third to put Oregon up 17-13. The drive was kept alive when the Gophers were stung with a key pass interference penalty on a fourth down. Then, after a 10-play, 72-yard drive, Cockerham, after hitting Leverson on a key third down strike for 34-yards, threw his second touchdown of the afternoon to Johnson — this one measuring just seven yards to put the Gophers up 20-17. The Ducks rallied back though, behind Running Backs Reuben Droughns and Herman Ho Ching, who led the team down-field 87-yards on 12 long and methodical plays.

Then, with just over three minutes to go in the game, the Gophers were poised to win it. All they had to do was hold Oregon in a do-or-die fourth-down and 11 situation on the Gopher 44-yard line. Harrington came up huge though, connecting first with Tony Hartley on a 23-yard pass, and then again three plays later to Receiver Keenan Howery, on a 10-yard touchdown strike with a minute and a half to go in the game. The Gophers got the ball back twice after that but were unable to gain any momentum. The first of the two late drives ended when Cockerham fumbled after being sacked at the Oregon 45-yard line, while the second came with just 12 seconds to go with Minnesota trying to start a last-second rally from their own eight-yard line. The Ducks hung on to win by the final score of 24-20.

Incredibly, after the game Billy Cockerham, Dyron Russ and Ryan Rindels were named as the game's Most Valuable Player, Most Valuable Lineman and Most Valuable Special Teams Player, respectively. Did anyone mention to the awards people that these guys were all members of the losing team? That's just how the game went that afternoon, it was a game that the Gophers should've won, and could've won, had they just caught a few breaks along the way. "We won all three awards, but I'd trade all three of them in for the team trophy," said Mason after the game.

It was a bitter loss, but a tremendous shot in the arm for a program that had completed a 180-degree turn in the right direction. For his efforts, Mason was named as the Football News "Coach of the Year." After the season two-time All-American Safety Tyrone Carter, who finished as the NCAA's all-time leading tackler (529) was named as the country's top defensive back. He would go on to sign with the Minnesota Vikings and later win a Super Bowl as a member of the Pittsburgh Steelers. Thomas Hamner, meanwhile, who became the team's second all-time leading rusher, signed with the Philadelphia Eagles. Other players who had great seasons included Defensive End Karon Riley, who led the Big Ten in sacks, Center Ben Hamilton and Punter Preston Gruening, who both earned All-America honors, and Wide Receiver Ron Johnson, who led the team in receptions (43), receiving yards (574), and receiving touchdowns (7).

After going 8-4 in Mason's breakout season of 1999, expectations were high in 2000 and there was even talk of the team advancing on to a major bowl game that year. After winning their first pre-season game against Louisiana-

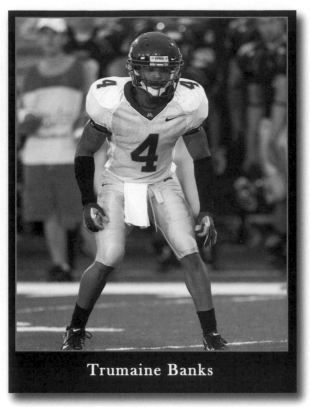
Trumaine Banks

Monroe, 47-10, the Gophers came home the next week and laid an egg against Ohio University. The Gophers were three touchdown favorites over the Bobcats but wound up getting embarrassed, 23-17. They rebounded behind Thomas Tapeh's 183 yards rushing and two touchdowns that next week, however, to beat Baylor, 34-9.

After losing to Purdue in the Big 10 opener, Minnesota got hot and rattled off three big wins over Illinois, Penn State and Ohio State — perhaps the biggest trio of wins over such marquis teams for the program in decades. Running Backs Tellis Redmon and Travis Cole led the way in this one as each tallied a pair of touchdowns and rushed for 183 and 82 yards, respectively, in the 44-10 drubbing. The Gophers 25-16 upset win over Penn State was due in large part to the foot of Kicker Dan Nystrom, who booted four field goals. Ron Johnson caught five balls for 114 yards and a pair of touchdowns from Quarterback Travis Cole, while Tellis Redmon rushed for 150 yards in this one as well. The Lions rallied late but the Gopher defense hung in there to preserve the win and secure the Liberty Bell.

That next week the Gophers headed east to take on the No. 6 ranked Ohio State Buckeyes. This one would prove to be a classic as the Gophers beat up on the Big Ten's top ranked defense and the won the game, 29-17, giving them their first victory in Columbus since 1949. Travis Cole threw for 243 yards, Ron Johnson caught eight balls for 163 yards and a touchdown — his school record 18th, Tellis Redmon ran for 118 yards and a score, and Kicker Dan Nystrom nailed three field goals. The win left the nearly 100,000 Buckeye faithful speechless that afternoon to say the least. It was an amazing win for the program and with it they found themselves sitting atop

Amir Pinnix

the conference leader board.

The honeymoon wore off pretty quickly after that, however, as the team took a nosedive from there and lost three straight to Indiana, Northwestern and Wisconsin. In the loss to the Wildcats, the Gophers managed to blow a 35-14 lead late into the 3rd quarter. Northwestern rallied to tie the game on a touchdown with just 1:24 to go and were then able to pooch their ensuing kickoff deep in Minnesota's end following a Gopher personal foul penalty. Minnesota ran on their first play but then threw a pass on second down, which was dropped, and thus stopped the clock stopped with 57 seconds left. The Gophers ran on third down, at which point Northwestern then called their final timeout with 51 seconds to go, forcing the Gophers to punt. The Wildcats then got the ball back and on fourth down managed to score the game-winner on a miraculous 45-yard Hail Mary pass on the final play of the game to win, 41-35. Needless to say, all the Metrodome homecoming crowd could do was to sit in silence and horror.

The Gophers got it together in the season finale against Iowa at the Dome, however, beating the Hawkeyes, 27-24. Trailing 24-12 in the fourth quarter, the Gophers rallied. On fourth and 13 with 7:43 to go, Ron Johnson out-leaped Iowa cornerback Benny Sapp in the back of the end zone for the touchdown. Then, following a defensive stop, Travis Cole connected with Jermaine Mays for an 81-yard touchdown strike to give Minnesota the lead for good. The Gopher defense, which tied a school record with eight sacks, then prevented the Hawkeyes from crossing midfield for the final six minutes of the game to preserve the victory.

With that, Minnesota had earned itself a trip to Miami, where they would face North Carolina State in the MicronPC.com Bowl. Tellis Red-

Matt Spaeth

Rhys Lloyd

mon rushed for a pair of touchdowns on a record 246 yards that day, only to see his team surrender a 24-0 lead and lose a heart-breaker, 38-30. Led by future NFL stars Quarterback Philip Rivers and Wide Receiver Koren Robinson, the Wolfpack rallied to win the game in the final minutes.

Minnesota got off to a rough start in 2001, losing to Toledo right out of the gates. Following a win over Louisiana-Lafayette, which was highlighted by 173 yards of rushing by Marion Barber III, the son of former Gopher Halfback Marion Barber Jr., the Gophers lost in overtime to Purdue in Week Three, 35-28. The Boilers tied it up on a field goal with no time left on the clock and then won it in sudden-death after scoring a touchdown on their opening possession. It appeared that Gophers tied it up on Antoine Henderson's touchdown reception, but the official apparently got confused by the end zone paint and controversially called him out of bounds. This was before instant-replay in college football, so, sadly Minnesota was out of luck.

With nine new defensive starters and a revamped offensive line, the Gophers took some time to find their groove that season. They finished with a disappointing 4-7 mark but did manage to beat Wisconsin in the season finale at the Dome, 42-31, to reclaim Paul Bunyan's Axe. Tellis Redmon ran for 128 yards in this one, while Quarterback Asad Abdul-Khaliq connected with Tight End Ben Utecht for 104 yards and a pair of touchdowns in the big win. Further, Ron Johnson had four catches for 74 yards and a touchdown, thus ending his illustrious career in Gold Country as the program's all-time leading receiver. Johnson also tied an NCAA record by catching a pass in his 46th consecutive game that day as well.

Minnesota made it back to the post-season in 2002 after posting a much improved 8-5 record. The team won all five of its non-conference games and then, after losing to Purdue, rattled off wins over Illinois, Northwestern and Michigan State to go 8-1. With that, they were ranked No. 23 in the nation and there was already buzz about going to Pasadena to make a run for the roses. Sadly, however, the team came back to earth that next week when they got crushed by Ohio State, 34-3, and then went into a free-fall from there, losing their finals three games to Michigan, Iowa and Wisconsin.

They did manage to secure a post-season invitation, however, this time to the Music City Bowl in Nashville, where they would face the No. 25 ranked Arkansas Razorbacks. Arkansas took a 7-0 lead in this one, only to see Minnesota rally back behind five Dan Nystrom field goals to take the lead. Abdul-Khaliq found Utecht on a 19 yard touchdown pass in the third, while Tapeh scored from 33 yards out midway through the fourth to ice it for the Gophers. The 29-14 victory was a sweet ending to an otherwise bitter season that had started out oh so promising.

The 2003 Gophers came storming out of the gates for the second straight season, this time going 6-0, which included wins over Penn State and Northwestern, even outscoring their opponents during this stretch 249-82 en route to a No. 17 national ranking. With buzz of Pasadena yet again starting to permeate Gold Country, the No. 20 ranked Michigan Wolverines came to town where they were greeted by more than 62,000 Gopher faithful for a nationally televised Friday night contest on ESPN. Minnesota stormed out of the gates in this one and were up 28-7 heading into the fourth quarter. Behind Marion Barber III, Thomas Tapeh, Laurence Maroney

Ernie Wheelright

Gary Russell

and Asad Abul-Khaliq, Minnesota literally ran all over the Wolverines, finishing the game with 424 rushing yards. The fans were beside themselves, seemingly ready to drink champagne from the Little Brown Jug at any moment. That's when the bubble burst, and no, it wasn't pretty. Michigan, somehow, rattled off 31 points in the final quarter and rallied to beat the Gophers, 38-35. After Michigan pulled to within 14, Abdul-Khaliq threw an ill-advised pass while under pressure, which was intercepted and run back for a touchdown. Abdul-Khaliq redeemed himself a short while later though, scoring on a 52-yard touchdown run to put the Gophers back up 35-21. Michigan was not to be denied that night though, as they scored the final 17 points of the game to pull off one of the biggest comebacks in their program's history.

After losing yet another heart-breaker that next week at Michigan State, 44-38, Minnesota got back on track and rattled off three big wins over Illinois, Indiana and Wisconsin. Against the Hoosiers at the Metrodome, the Gophers exploded for 55 points while surrendering just one touchdown. The 48-point margin was the Gophers' biggest Big Ten victory since 1949. Led by Maroney's 164 yards and Barber's 108, Minnesota rushed for 435 yards. Seven different Gophers found the end zone on that afternoon.

The 37-34 win over the Badgers, meanwhile, was a thriller as Kicker Rhys Lloyd nailed a 35 yard field goal as time expired. What transpired next would prove to be one of the most memorable scenes in Gopher football history: Lloyd leading the entire squad across the field to the Wisconsin sideline and leaping over their bench to rightfully claim Paul Bunyan's Axe. It was truly surreal. Meanwhile, backup Quarterback Benji Kamrath set up the game-winning field goal thanks to a 22-yard toss to Aaron Hosack on third down and nine from the team's 33 yard line. Barber and Maroney combined for 274 rushing yards and two touchdowns to boot.

After losing to Iowa in the season finale, the Gophers were invited to play Oregon in the Sun Bowl, in El Paso, Texas. It wasn't the Rose Bowl, but Gopher fans were thrilled to be playing football in late December, nevertheless. The two teams, which previously met four years earlier in the Sun Bowl, would score early and often in this one. After back and forth scoring all day, however, the Gophers came out on top, 31-30. Trailing by two points, Rhys Lloyd then calmly came in and kicked the 42 yard game-winning field goal with just 23 seconds to go on the clock. Leading the charge for the Maroon and Gold was Lawrence Maroney, who rushed for 131 yards and a touchdown. Thomas Tapeh added 40 of his own, as well as three short yardage touchdowns to boot. Aaron Hosack, meanwhile, caught six balls for 107 yards.

The Gophers, who set a Big 10 record for total offense with 6,430 yards, finished the season with a 10-3 record — the first time they had reached the 10-win plateau since 1905. As such, expectations were running high in Gold Country in 2004. And, just like in the past few seasons, the team jumped out to a quick start — going 5-0 right out of the gates. Among those early victories were wins over Northwestern and Penn State, which set up a dramatic rematch with Michigan in Ann Arbor. It would be one of the biggest games in recent memory, with the Gophers coming in ranked No. 13 and the Wolverines at No. 14. Maroney, Barber and Ellerson all tallied for Minnesota in this one, but Michigan rallied late to score 10 fourth quarter points and retain the Little Brown Jug, 27-24. The Gophers struggled

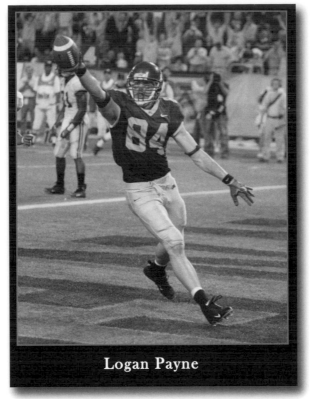
Logan Payne

from there, beating only Illinois down the stretch to finish with a 6-5 record. In the 29-27 loss to Iowa, the Hawkeye fans were so excited about winning the Big 10 title that they tore down the Metrodome goal posts and paraded them around the field — adding insult to injury.

Luckily, with their better than .500 record, Minnesota was still able to accept an invitation to play Alabama in the Music City Bowl in Nashville, Tenn. The Tide got on the board first in this one, with the Gophers evening it up at 7-7 on Keith Lipka's fumble recovery in the end zone. Minnesota then took the lead on Barber's five yard touchdown run, followed by a Lloyd 27-yard field goal. Alabama answered to get to within three at 17-14, but the Gophers iced it on another Lloyd field goal, followed by a safety with just over three minutes to go. The Gophers would go on to beat Bama by the final score of 20-16, salvaging an otherwise mediocre season.

Barber, playing in his last game as a Gopher, and Maroney were the keys in the win, with Barber going for 187 yards and Maroney adding 105. Not bad, considering Alabama hadn't allowed a single back to rush for 100 yards that season. That dynamic duo was simply amazing that season, rushing for a combined 2,617 yards, 23 rushing touchdowns and 13 100-yard games. In fact, when it was all said and done, they would become the first tandem in NCAA history to both rush for 1,000 yards in consecutive seasons. Blazing their trail, by the way, were offensive linemen Greg Eslinger and Mark Setterstrom, who both earned All-America honors that year as well. (Barber racked up over 4,500 all-purpose yards and 30+ TDs during his tenure in Gold Country before going on to become a Pro Bowler in the NFL with the

Mike Sherels

Dallas Cowboys.)

The 2005 Gophers went 3-0 in the pre-season and then met up with No. 11 ranked Purdue in the conference opener. This one would prove to be a wild one as the Gophers came from behind to finally put a halt to their seven-game losing streak against the Boilers. Trailing 28-20, Gopher Quarterback Bryan Cupito connected with Tight End Matt Spaeth on an eight yard touchdown pass with just 1:34 remaining in the game to pull within two at 28-26. Cupito, who was not known for his scrambling ability, then scored on an unlikely option play for the two point conversion to tie it up. Cupito connected with Logan Payne on fourth and goal in the first overtime, while Gary Russell scored on a three yard run up the gut to seal the deal in overtime No. 2. The Gopher defense held from there as they pulled out the dramatic 42-35 victory. Laurence Maroney, meanwhile, finished the game with 333 all-purpose yards.

The No. 18 Gophers next headed to Happy Valley, where they had hopes of extending their five game winning streak over Penn State. The Nittany Lions saw otherwise though and crushed the Maroon and Gold by the ugly score of 44-14. Minnesota rebounded that next week, however, to upset Michigan, once again in Ann Arbor. Wide Receiver Ernie Wheelwright hauled in a 20 yard touchdown pass from Cupito, while the new dynamic duo of Maroney and Russell combined for 257 yards rushing. This one came down to the wire with Cupito, suffering from a concussion, hitting Matt Spaeth on a 61-yarder which got the ball down to the 13 yard line. Gopher Kicker Jason Giannini then nailed his third of three field goals on the afternoon with just one second on the clock to break the 20-20 tie and give Minnesota the rights to the Lit-

Willie VanDeSteeg

tle Brown Jug – something Minnesota fans hadn't seen since 1986. The 112,000 Wolverine fans at the "Big House" sat speechless as the Gophers celebrated at the 50 yard line.

The No. 22 ranked Gophers then faced off against the No. 23 ranked Badgers the following week at the Dome. Minnesota built a 20-10 lead midway through the third quarter behind Laurence Maroney's spectacular 93 yard touchdown run. (He would rush for 258 yards on the day!) Then, after trading touchdowns, Gary Russell tallied on a one yard run with just over three minutes to go to give the Gophers a seemingly insurmountable 34-24 lead. Wisconsin rallied to score, however, to pull to within 34-31. The Badgers then attempted on on-side kick, which gave the Gophers the ball back at their own eight yard line. Three straight Maroney rushes could not get the Gophers the game-clinching first down, however, and they were forced to punt. Freshman Punter Justin Kucek fumbled the snap though and instead of trying to just fall on it, or kick the ball out of the back of the end zone for a safety, he attempted to pick it up and kick it. Bad idea. Wisconsin blocked it and recovered the ball in the end zone for what proved to be game-winning touchdown. The 65,089 Gopher fans in attendance, the second largest crowd in Metrodome history, sat stunned, wondering what could have been.

After losing to Ohio State, 45-31, Minnesota rebounded to beat Indiana and Michigan State, before getting clobbered by Iowa in the season finale, 52-28. With that, the 6-5 Gophers accepted an invitation to play Virginia in the Music City Bowl down in Nashville, Tenn. Minnesota got on the board first in this one when Cupito connected with Justin Valentine on a seven yard touchdown strike

Dominique Barber

midway through the first quarter. They then made it 14-0 just a few minutes later when Cupito hooked up with Ernie Wheelwright on a 44-yard bomb. Virginia answered, only to see the Gophers go up 21-7 on Cupito's third TD of the afternoon, this one being a 57 yarder to Jared Ellerson. The Cavs rallied from there, however, and tied it up at 24-24 late in the third. Cupito tallied his fourth TD early in the fourth quarter when he connected with Ellerson again, this time on a 23-yarder to make it 31-24. Virginia came back though and wound up winning the game in the final minute, 34-

Eric Decker

31, on a 39-yard Connor Hughes field goal. It was a bitter pill to swallow for the thousands of fans who made the trek. Maroney finished with 111 yards rushing, in what would prove to be his final game in Gold Country. (Maroney, who ran for over 4,500 all-purpose yards and 30+ touchdowns as a Gopher, would go on to stardom in the NFL that next year with the New England Patriots.) Russell, meanwhile, who ran for 87 yards in the loss, set a team record with 19 rushing touchdowns that season.

Minnesota opened the 2006 non-conference schedule with a pair of wins over Kent State and Temple, outscoring their opposition 106-0, but then suffered a crushing loss to Cal, 42-17. The Big Ten season got underway from there and it wasn't pretty as the team dropped four straight to Purdue, Michigan, Penn State and Wisconsin. Against the Nittany Lions the Gophers lost a 28-27 overtime heart-breaker in front of 45,227 fans at the Metrodome. The team rallied from a 21-14 deficit to score with 1:02 remaining, forcing the extra session. Minnesota scored on its first possession of overtime on an Eric Decker 25-yard touchdown reception from Cupito, only to see Giannini miss the extra point. PSU then scored on a 2-yard touch-

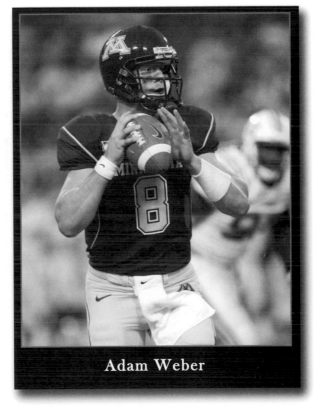

Adam Weber

down run by Tony Hunt and won it on the PAT. Cupito led the attack, passing for 347 yards and two touchdowns — one of which went to All-American Matt Spaeth, who moved past Ben Utecht for the all-time lead for career receptions by a tight end with 87. Amir Pinnix, meanwhile, ran for 76 yards and a pair of touchdowns in the loss.

The Gophers broke their losing streak in Week Eight when they snuck past North Dakota State, 10-9, in front of nearly 63,000 fans — most of whom were wearing green jerseys. The game marked the first time the two teams had played one another since 1937. The Division I-AA Bison gave the Gophers trouble all day and nearly won the game in the final seconds, only to have Shawn Bibeau's field goal blocked with no time remaining on the clock. Pinnix led the Gophers with 97 yards and a touchdown, while the Gopher defense held the Bison to just three field goals in the win.

"It was one of those games," said Coach Mason afterwards. "I say it like that, because I've been on the other side before. This is the kind of game that puts a smile on your face. When you're out-coached and outplayed, and still win. I credit NDSU, they have a good team, they have good players, they play hard, are well-coached and did a great job. I'm not happy with the way we played, but I'm happy with the end result."

From there, Minnesota got crushed by top-ranked Ohio State, 44-0, in Columbus. They rebounded though and rallied to win their next three games against Indiana, 63-26, at Michigan State, 31-18, and Iowa, 34-24, to reclaim Floyd of Rosedale. Against the Hoosiers on homecoming, Cupito tossed four touchdowns on 378 yards — 137 of which went to Logan Payne. In the 100th anniversary game vs. Iowa, meanwhile, the Maroon and Gold scored 21 points off of five Hawkeye turnovers — including two interceptions by Safety Kevin Mannion. Amir Pinnix had 119 yards and two touchdowns, surpassing the 1,000-yard mark for the season, while Jay Thomas added a career-high 79 yards and one touchdown as well.

With that, the 6-6 Gophers had earned a trip to a bowl game for the fifth straight season. This time they would

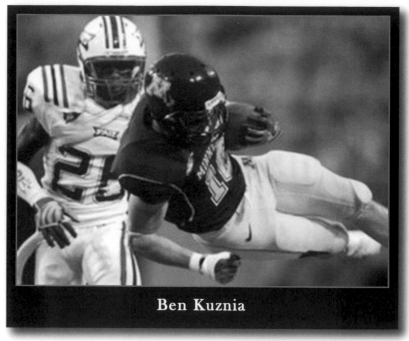
Ben Kuznia

be traveling to Tempe, Ariz., where they would be facing Texas Tech in the 2006 Insight Bowl. There, the Gophers played a wild one and ultimately came up short in a 44-41 overtime heart-breaker. Minnesota jumped out to a 38-7 lead in this one and then watched the Red Raiders do the unthinkable — rally to score 31 straight points. Texas Tech tied the game on a 52-yard field goal with no time on the clock to send it to overtime. The Gophers then scored on a Joel Monroe 32-yard field goal, only to watch the Red Raiders win it on Shannon Woods' three yard touchdown run just moments later. It would go down as the largest comeback to win a bowl game in NCAA Football history. Needless to say, it would also go down as, arguably, the worst defeat in Gopher history. For the record, Cupito threw for 263 yards and a trio of touchdowns, one of which went to Jack Simmons,

who caught seven passes for 134 yards on the day. In addition, Amir Pinnix rushed for 179 yards and a touchdown as well.

Two days later, Gopher Athletics Director Joel Maturi announced that Coach Mason's decade-long tenure behind the Gopher bench would sadly be coming to an end. The Texas Tech fiasco would prove to be the straw that broke the camel's back. Overall, Mason would finish with a 64-57 record in Gold Country, but his true legacy with lie in the fact that seven of his teams made it to post-season bowl games.

"I want this program to be successful like any other Minnesotan and not just in the short term, not just during my tenure, but forever," Mason would later say. "Hopefully we have made a lot of progress that will continue to build on that foundation. That way Gopher Football will be successful for a long, long time — even when I am just sitting up there in the stands as a supporter."

The Tim Brewster Era Officially Begins
With a new stadium finally being built back on campus, across from Mariucci Arena, the Gophers wanted

HAYDEN FOX: HEAD COACH OF THE *"MINNESOTA STATE SCREAMING EAGLES..."*

Did you know that actor Craig T. Nelson was sort of a Gopher? Nelson, A.K.A. "Hayden Fox," was the fictitious head coach of the late '80s and early '90s ABC show "Coach," which chronicled the life and times of a bumbling college football coach, his bone-head assistants, "Luther" and "Dauber," and their mythical team — the *"Minnesota State Screaming Eagles."* Oddly enough, the show used old Gopher football video footage from the late '80s in the Metrodome that was color enhanced to make the maroon jerseys appear as purple. How's that for a bit of good ol' fashioned *"Cliff Claven"* Gopher trivia!

to bring in some new blood to rally the troops. With that, on Jan. 17, 2007, Tim Brewster was named as Minnesota's 26th head football coach. A former two-time All-Big Ten tight end at the University of Illinois, Brewster had spent the previous five seasons as an assistant coach in the NFL, most recently as the tight ends coach of the Denver Broncos. Well known in football circles as a top-notch recruiter, Brewster wasted little time in making himself known throughout the "Gopher Nation." In fact, he would go out and meet with every single high school coach in the state, determined to improve the University's image and reputation amongst the areas best prep players. He was also committed to changing the team's offense — even if that meant taking a few lumps along the way. Needless to say, Coach Brew would be taking his fair share of lumps during his first season in Gold Country.

The Brewster era officially began on September 1, 2007, as the Gophers lost to Bowling Green in overtime, 32-31. The team came back that next week though, behind Amir Pinnix's two-yard touchdown run in the third overtime period of Minnesota's emotional 41-35 victory over Miami of Ohio at the Metrodome. The victory was short-lived, however, as the Gophers struggled mightily from there and went winless in their next 10 games. There were some close contests along the way, including the 49-48 double-overtime heart-breaker to Northwestern — which Minnesota lost despite 580 yards of total offense — its eighth-highest total offensive output in school-history. Freshman Adam Weber threw for a career-high 341 yards and five touchdowns while also running for 89 yards and another touchdown in the loss. Ernie Wheelwright had seven receptions for 116 yards and a career-high three touchdowns as well.

Things didn't get much better that next week either, when the formerly Division 1-AA North Dakota State Bison came back to town and upset the Gophers, 27–21. NDSU amassed 585 total yards, including 394 yards rushing. Bison junior Running Back Tyler Roehl was the star of the game, rushing for a school-record 263 yards on 22 carries. The Metrodome turned from Maroon and Gold to green that day, as the NDSU fans celebrated their program's biggest win of all time. From there the team suffered losses to Michigan, Illinois, Iowa and Wisconsin, to finish with their worst record of all-time, 1-11. The Gophers came close against Wisconsin but the Badgers kept the Axe with a 41-34 victory. Adam Weber finished with 352 yards passing, giving him 2,895 for the season and putting him atop the Gopher single-season passing list. Weber also threw for three touchdowns, giving him a school-record 24 on the season. His 3,512 yards of total offense was also a Gopher single-season team record as well.

The Gophers came out more determined than ever for the 2008 season and wasted little time in letting the college football world know that the 2007 season was nothing more than a fluke. Minnesota went 4-0 in its non-conference schedule and then fell to No. 14 ranked Ohio State in Columbus to open the Big Ten season. They rebounded from there, however, winning their next three games over Indiana, Illinois and at No. 25 Purdue. Against the Hoosiers, junior Wide Receiver Eric Decker caught a program-record 13 passes for a career-high 190 receiving yards en route to leading Brewster to his first Big Ten win.

"Eric puts the team on his back and says 'throw me the ball,' ", said Adam Weber after the game. "He'll find a way to get open. Every single week you ask the question, how are we going to get Eric the ball? He just stays open. It's just one of those things that is a testament to a good player, a good wide receiver, and a competitor."

In the Illini game DeLeon Eskridge ran for a season-high 123 yards and two touchdowns, while Decker caught nine passes for 87 yards and a touchdown as the Gophers beat Brewster's alma mater, 27-20, in Champaign. Meanwhile, Defensive End Willie VanDeSteeg, who finished with three sacks, five tackles, and a pass breakup, also forced a Juice Williams fumble early in the fourth quarter that teammate Simoni Lawrence returned nine yards for a touchdown to put the Gophers up 27-13. VanDeSteeg's pressure on Williams later in the fourth quarter also led to a Ryan Collado interception that helped Minnesota ice the victory.

Minnesota then defeated

Tim Brewster

Purdue, 17-6, in a classic Big Ten defensive battle in West Lafayette. Weber was once again the hero, this time accounting for 276 total yards and two scores as Minnesota improved to 7-1 for the first time since 2002. By the end of October the Gophers were ranked No. 17 in the BCS, and believe it or not, there was even talk of the Gopher Nation going to Pasadena. Sadly, that's when the wheels came off. The team nose-dived from there, losing their next four in a row — starting with Northwestern, 24-17, on homecoming. With the game tied at 17-17 late in the third quarter, the Gophers drove 92 yards down the field, only to see Joel Monroe miss a 20 yard field goal. Then, with less than a minute remaining on the clock and the game still tied, the Gophers drove down the field for a game winning score. That's when Northwestern picked off a pass that somehow bounced off Eric Decker and returned it 54 yards through a maze of Gophers for what turned out to be the game-winning touchdown. The 54,000 Gopher fans in attendance could only sit and wonder what could have been.

After losing to Michigan, 29-6, Minnesota lost a heart-breaker at Camp Randall Stadium in Wisconsin, 35-32. Minnesota led 21-7 at halftime and 24-17 after three quarters but couldn't hold on for the final 15 minutes as Wisconsin rallied behind a pair of safeties and a touchdown off a Gopher turnover late

in the game. Weber threw for two touchdowns and ran for another in the loss. From there, the Gophers returned home and prepared to face Iowa for the team's final game ever in the Metrodome. With a bowl berth still in their grasp, the players took to the field in what most assumed would be an emotional send-off. What they got, however, was one of the worst butt-kickings in the program's history. The Hawkeyes destroyed the Gophers that night, 55-0, holding them to 134 yards of total offense and just one rushing first down the entire game. It was an ugly end to one of the ugliest stadiums ever built.

Despite the crushing defeat to the Hawkeyes, the 7-5 Gophers gladly accepted an invitation to play Kansas in the 2008 Insight Bowl in Tempe, Ariz. With the bowl bid, Brewster had successfully led the Gophers to one of the biggest single-season turnarounds in NCAA history. And, considering the fact that the team had gone 1-11 the year before, the boosters were thrilled to be playing in the post-season that new year's eve. The Gophers got off to a quick start in this one and thanks to Jon Hoese's two first quarter touchdowns, Minnesota jumped out to a 14-7 lead. The Jayhawks rallied from there though and rattled off 28 unanswered points before the Gophers got back on the board with an Eric Decker six yard touchdown pass from Adam Weber early in the fourth quarter. KU added another touchdown late, however,

THE "ALL-METRODOME" TEAM...

(According to GopherHole.com)

Offense

QB	Rickey Foggie	(1984-87)
RB	Darrell Thompson	(1986-89)
RB	Laurence Maroney	(2003-05)
WR	Ron Johnson	(1998-01)
WR	Tutu Atwell	(1994-97)
TE	Matt Spaeth	(2003-07)
OL	Greg Eslinger	(2002-05)
OL	Mark Setterstrom	(2002-05)
OL	Ben Hamilton	(1997-00)
OL	Troy Wolkow	(1984-87)
OL	Rian Melander	(2001-04)

Defense

DE	Karon Riley	(1999-00)
DT	Jon Schlect	(1998-00)
DT	Darrell Reid	(2001-04)
DE	Lamanzer Williams	(1994-97)
LB	Ben Mezera	(1997-00)
LB	Peter Najarian	(1982-85)
LB	Bruce Holmes	(1983-86)
DB	Tyrone Carter	(1996-99)
DB	Jack Brewer	(1999-01)
DB	Willie Middlebrooks	(1998-00)
DB	Sean Lumpkin	(1988-91)

Special Teams

K	Chip Lohmiller	(1984-87)
P	Adam Kelly	(1983-85)
Ret.	Chris Gaiters	(1987-89)

and never looked back, winning easily, 42-21. For the record, Weber threw for 176 yards on the day, with 149 of them going to Decker.

When it was all said and done, Decker and VanDeSteeg both earned first-team All-Big Ten honors. Decker set a school record for receptions in a season for the second consecutive year and became just the third Gopher wideout to record a 1,000-yard receiving season. VanDeSteeg, meanwhile, finished his career as the school's all-time leader in tackles-for-loss and finished No. 4 all-time in sacks. In addition, Weber earned second-team All-Big Ten honors, just as Safety Dominique Barber (Marion's brother) had done in 2007 before going on to be drafted in the sixth round by the NFL's Houston Texans that off-season. All in all it was a solid season, considering how far the team had come from the year before.

Here's To The Next 125 Years...
The future for our beloved Gophers looks very bright indeed. On Saturday night, September 12, 2009, the Gophers will make history when they line up against Air Force and christen their new home, TCF Bank Stadium. After 27 years as tenants of the Metrodome, the Maroon and Gold will finally have a home of their own — and Gopher Nation couldn't be more excited about being back outside in a true college football atmosphere. With it will come a new sense of pride and excitement that has been long overdue in Gold Country. Gone are the days of teams being able to recruit "against" the Gophers for their lack of an on-campus stadium.

Leading the charge for the U is Coach Brewster, the man with the plan. In his two seasons as head coach he has taken some big steps towards getting the football program back on top of the college football world and he seems poised for even bigger and better things in the years to come. In 2008 the Gophers returned to postseason play and even cracked the top-20 in the national rankings for part of the season. It was a huge turn-around that showed a lot of guts and character. Brewster's positive outlook and charisma have helped bring in a pair of highly-regarded consensus top-25 recruiting classes and the sky is the limit with regards to just how far this program can go in the next decade and beyond.

The University of Minnesota's Golden Gopher football program is one of the most storied and successful in American sports history. What began in the 1870s is now in its third century and is without a doubt looking better than ever. From Nagurski to Giel, and from Bierman to Barber, the tradition and ora of this storied program will only continue to grow and prosper. Surely, the ghosts of Gopher past are looking on proudly. So here's to the next 125 years of Gopher football and beyond... may they be filled with not only plenty of jugs, pigs, sxes and bells... but many, many Rose Bowls, Big Ten titles and National Championships.

— Go Gophers! —

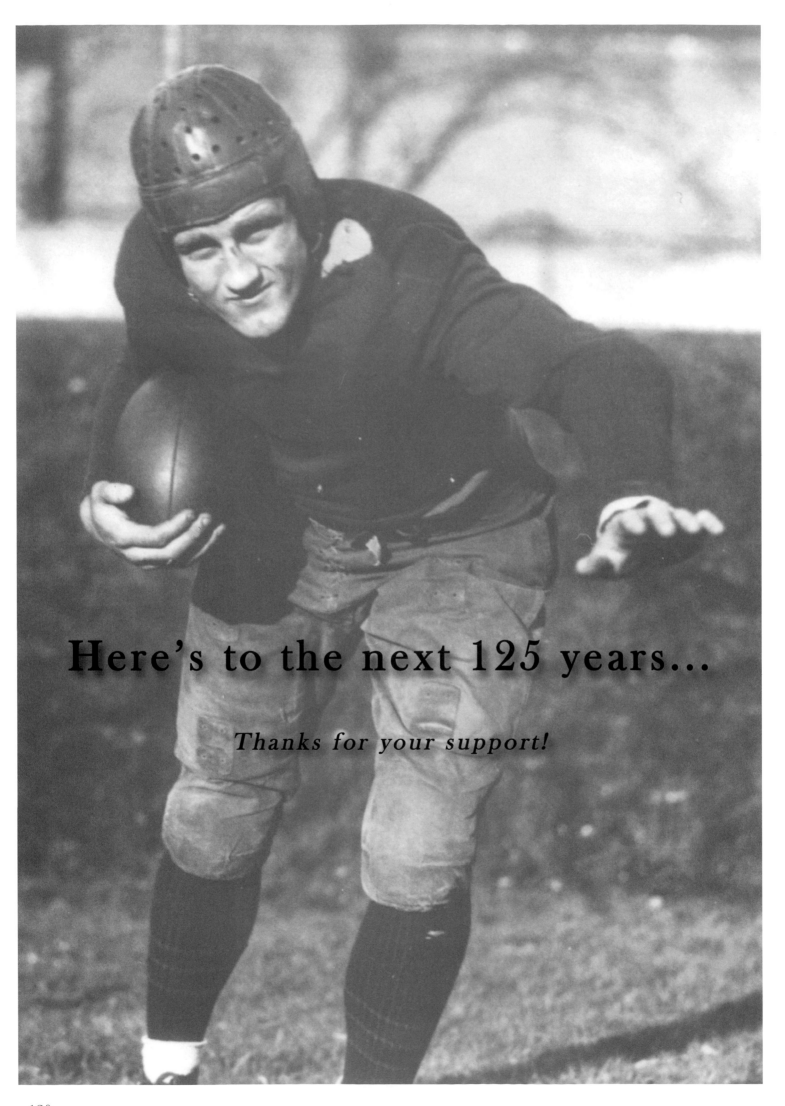

Here's to the next 125 years...

Thanks for your support!

120